Dangerous Economies

EARLY AMERICAN STUDIES

Series editors: Daniel K. Richter, Kathleen M. Brown, and David
Waldstreicher

Exploring neglected aspects of our colonial, revolutionary, and early
national history and culture, Early American Studies reinterprets
familiar themes and events in fresh ways. Interdisciplinary in character,
and with a special emphasis on the period from about 1600 to 1850, the
series is published in partnership with the McNeil Center for Early
American Studies.

A complete list of books in the series is available from the publisher.

Dangerous Economies

Status and Commerce in Imperial New York

SERENA R. ZABIN

PENN

University of Pennsylvania Press

Philadelphia

Published by
University of Pennsylvania Press
Philadelphia, Pennsylvania 19104-4112

Printed in the United States of America on acid-free paper

10 9 8 7 6 5 4 3 2 1

Library of Congress Cataloging-in-Publication Data

Zabin, Serena R.
    Dangerous economies : status and commerce in imperial New York / Serena R. Zabin.
        p.   cm. — (Early American studies)
    Includes bibliographical references and index.
    ISBN 978-0-8122-4160-0 (alk. paper)
    1. New York (N.Y.)—Economic conditions.   2. New York (N.Y.)—Economic conditions
—18th century.   3. New York (N.Y.)—Commerce.   I. Title.
HC108.N7Z33   2009
381.09747′1—dc22
                                                                                    2008047140

For Chris

Contents

Introduction: Imperial New York City   1

1. Where Credit Is Due   10

2. Webs of Dependence   32

3. The Informal Economy   57

4. Masters of Distinction   81

5. Black Cargo or Crew   106

6. Status, Commerce, and Conspiracy   132

Notes   159

Bibliography   193

Index   197

Acknowledgments   203

Imperial New York City

First, a picture. Looking north into Manhattan from the East River, one sees a panorama of boats: dinghies, sloops, and three-masted schooners. The mass of ships, many with sails billowing, nearly obscures the modest collection of buildings in the background. A more careful inspection of the ships reveals that each one is flying an outsize Union Jack. Upon even closer inspection, one sees tiny figures on the dock in the foreground. Individuals on the Manhattan shore are too distant to distinguish. Hidden from view behind the big sugar warehouses are other landmarks of the city. A telescope might allow us to see the city's gallows on the northeastern shore.[1] (See Figure 1.)

At those gallows one man jumped off the hangman's cart "with a halter around his neck." Another "behaved decently, prayed in Spanish, kissed a crucifix, and declared his innocence." A woman "stood like a lifeless trunk." Yet another man removed his wig and helped fit the noose around his own neck. Another seemed to hope that even at the scaffold he would receive a pardon. Still more terrible were the deaths of thirteen men burned at the stake. One man laid his leg onto the burning wood and then accused two others with his dying breath. In all, thirty-four people were sentenced to horrible deaths in New York City in 1741. Seventeen men and two women were publicly hanged; some of their corpses were displayed in iron cages on the shores of the East River until they decomposed and burst open. Some ninety people were banished from the colony, and many of them were exiled outside the British Empire. Nearly all of the ninety were black slaves.

These deaths make sense only within the larger picture of a city nearly veiled by British flags fluttering in the wind. The executions ended a series of events that began with the burglary of a small shop but grew to become an enormous cause célèbre, generating publicity throughout the British Empire: a conspiracy, some said, of slaves and Catholics to burn down the city of New York and hand it over to Britain's Catholic foes.[2] This vivid illusion of New York in flames has gripped the imaginations of all who studied the events, from contemporaries to modern-day scholars.

Figure 1. William Burgis's engraving *A South Prospect of ye Flourishing City of New York in the Province of New York in America*. This 1746 update of a 1717 view shows Fort George in the upper left corner with an enormous flag flying and a bristling battery of guns pointed out to the harbor. Although the church and the secretary's office in the fort burned in the 1741 fires, the artist has left them in this image. I. N. Phelps Stokes Collection, New York Public Library.

At one level, the events of 1741 look like a typical colonial panic over a slave conspiracy, in which the specter of race in the New World determined the colonies' legal, social, economic, and political interactions. Yet the story of those events is simply one small part of a larger and equally captivating tale of an imperial port culture defined by war, migration, markets, and social status. These seemingly disparate aspects of the city's culture were paradoxically bound together by New Yorkers' anxious fascination with hierarchy. Residents of the city never questioned the ideal of order and a society organized by social rank, but they continually wrestled with the definition of those ranks. The kinetic nature of this port city undermined hard and fast taxonomies of social distinction. It is this larger story of New York's imperial nature that deserves our attention.

We are much more accustomed to thinking of eighteenth-century New York as a colonial rather than an imperial city. Before the American Revolution, however, those who lived in British North America were not just colonists but also subjects of the British Empire. The British Empire in its turn has usually connoted more or less competent government officials, a bewigged and distant Board of Trade, and an enormous British military humming the chorus of *Rule Britannia*: "Britons never shall be slaves." Yet all empires, regardless of their modes of administration or control, consist at heart of individuals living their daily lives and often unconscious of what it might mean to live in an empire. Far removed from the administrative center of London, port cities such as New York nonetheless shaped the commercial empire on whose edges they rested. (See Figure 2.)

The hustle and bustle of New York's wharves and streets came from the city's full incorporation into the commerce that lay at the heart of the British Empire. The networks of trade, war, and family that tied together these vast overseas holdings intersected in ports such as New York. People and goods traveled along these networks. The frequency and rapidity with which individuals and their property traveled into and out of port also created a social world in motion, a world in which social status might be able to shift with the tides.

To think, then, of eighteenth-century New Yorkers as Britons living on the edge of empire rather than incipient American citizens allows us fresh investigations into their world. How did the British Empire appear to those who lived at its margins? How much of it could they consciously grasp? How did the seemingly minor transactions between those who were members of the city's elite and those who were not shape the larger networks of the early modern Atlantic world, and how were they shaped by them? How, in short, did the mundane affairs of ordinary people coalesce into an enormous commercial empire?

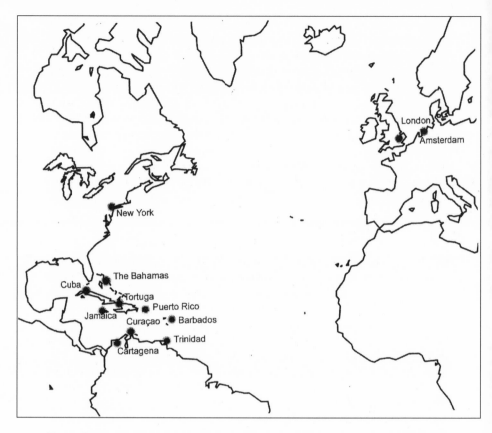

Figure 2. Partial map of the Atlantic world, mid-eighteenth century. Although New York was on the rim of Great Britain's Atlantic empire in the first two-thirds of the eighteenth century, networks of trade and travel integrated the city into the empire.

This study is primarily concerned with the first two-thirds of the eighteenth century, when the so-called "first British Empire," which included settlements in North America and the Caribbean, came to an end. The Seven Years' War (1756–63) marked a noticeable turning point in the empire: France and Spain were no longer serious threats to the North American colonies, and British fears of Catholic infiltrators in the American colonies dropped accordingly. Although British victories in the Seven Years' War boosted British patriotism among British Americans, the economic and military realities of the war also precipitated the first of the revolutionary conflicts; in 1765, only two years after the signing of the peace treaty, Americans took part in widespread protests against the Stamp Act, which had been intended to raise revenues for the British army in North America. Yet while the Seven Years' War was still under way, few living in North America—including Native American allies and African slaves—could have imagined that British colonists would oppose any part of the British Empire. *Dangerous Economies* focuses on the New York City of this earlier era, in which British provincials, far from desiring colonial independence, clung to their powerful empire in the face of near-constant threats from the rival French, Spanish, and Native American empires that surrounded them.

In the early eighteenth century, Britain was just starting to catch up with its imperial rivals, France and Spain. Britain possessed nothing equal to the huge colonies of Spanish America or France's small but extremely profitable sugar colonies of the Caribbean. Instead, Britons set themselves off from their competitors by defining themselves as free and rational merchants, spreading Protestantism and the rule of law. The twin pillars of British imperial identity were far-flung commerce and their naval and moral superiority over their Catholic rivals.

For much of the century Britain was preparing, waging, or recovering from war with France and Spain. Since its earlier rivalry with the Dutch had been quelled by its alliance with the Netherlands and Sweden in 1688, England could afford to focus on its Catholic foes. This new military focus resulted in three protracted conflicts: Queen Anne's War in 1702–13; King George's War in 1739–48; and the French and Indian War in 1754–63. During all of these violent conflicts New York experienced notable economic and demographic volatility. Twenty-nine years between 1700 and 1763 were spent in open warfare, and many more years were spent preparing for or recovering from war. New York's own multifaceted development was closely tied to these struggles for empire.[3]

New Yorkers also linked themselves to the British Empire through trade. The city depended heavily on its trading networks around the Atlantic, in particular the export of foodstuffs from the Hudson Valley to the West Indies and the export of furs to Europe. Although the city eagerly measured its exports of fur at the beginning of the century and wheat in the middle and end, New York's primary function as a port was as a central warehouse, not a major exporter of raw goods. Its strength lay in its ability to handle the complicated banking functions that became an increasingly important aspect of international trade. Moreover, the range of individuals who took part in trade was surprisingly wide. Although a small number of elite merchants dominated the market for some commodities, traders also extended far down New York's social scale.[4] Widows and slaves found ways to participate in both local and international trading networks. Some of these exchanges involved the newest fashions, while others were in secondhand goods. All of them, however, brought people of all ranks into a common marketplace.

Remarkably, the early eighteenth-century Atlantic world had some space and opportunities for socially marginal people to participate economically, thereby holding out the potential for those who were not members of the elite to alter their social status. However, there were costs, to both big players and small. It was a perilous, if forced, choice to participate in the New York marketplace. The hazards arose from the very personal culture of this place of exchange. For all of these New Yorkers, personal interactions defined economic transactions.

Throughout the eighteenth century, North Americans from merchants to slaves engaged in a "consumer revolution," importing an ever larger amount and variety of goods (china, tea, sugar, and cloth in particular) from the rest of the British Empire and around the Atlantic. The nature of these items also shifted dramatically from those imported earlier. Seventeenth-century imports had focused on comfort: glass provided more and better light in a house, and bedclothes offered warmth and a durability that ensured they could be passed on to the next generation. Eighteenth-century imports, however, often had cultural meaning far beyond their practical value. Tea warmed the body, but the china in which it was served also proclaimed those who drank it to be persons of taste and refinement. The truly revolutionary part of this consumer revolution was not so much the simple expansion of imported items as the cultural relevance that was attached to these items. Goods were not just imported; they also became important.[5]

The ships that carried goods to New York also carried people, and the city's growth in trade went hand in hand with a growth in population. Many of those newcomers did not become permanent residents; the city also served as a point of entry for Europeans to move quickly up the Hudson River or across to New Jersey. New York was full but not full of New Yorkers. When Alexander Hamilton visited New York City in 1744, he misjudged its population to be greater than Philadelphia's. Both cities, in fact, had about eleven thousand residents at the time; what deceived Hamilton was the quantity of visitors passing through the city. The sailors in the harbor and the soldiers at Fort George were all transients as well.[6] New York was thus a city of itinerants, and their mobility created a world that offered certain possibilities to the more marginal members of the resident society: poor white women, slaves, and sailors.

Despite New York's location in the Middle Colonies, far from the region traditionally associated with slavery, a significant proportion of the city's population was made up of enslaved Africans, African Americans, and African Caribbeans. Throughout the eighteenth century, New York's black population (most of them slaves) hovered between 11 and

15 percent, making it the largest black community north of the Chesapeake.[7] Urban slavery tended to distribute blacks widely across the city; both women and men performed a large variety of jobs, including domestic, artisanal, and marine work.[8] This large slave population created a vibrant society whose most basic human rites of companionship, family, and burial were continually hindered by the city's white officials.

New York's culture emerged from these larger and volatile forces of politics, commerce, and race. The city's individual residents and visitors, in turn, defined their own and each others' identities within this ever-changing imperial context. The transience of the city's people, its goods, and its fortunes created a notably fluid social hierarchy, a structure that did not do away with distinctions of status but made it difficult to establish one's own status or verify another's. New Yorkers shared the human desire to succeed in making a better life and a name for themselves; their city's shifting imperial identity created new avenues for success but also undermined the clarity of whatever success they might achieve.

As befits a study that examines the ways in which the actions of individuals come together to create an immense commercial empire, this book is studded with the stories of a diverse array of New Yorkers, from slaves to royal officials. Many of these characters were quite conscious of their social status, or of the markers that would indicate their status to others. All of them were engaged, in some way, in the commercial marketplace. Their worlds reveal the relationship between the eighteenth-century obsession with status and the commercial focus of the British Empire.

New York's commercial culture was a particularly appealing place for confidence artists and tricksters looking for a smart swindle. The complex interplay between credit and credibility offered these men, and occasionally women, their chances. Through cleverly deploying a particularly gendered idea of respectable financial and social status, these con artists often managed to swindle others into giving them some financial credit. Merchants looking to make some easy money sometimes ended up holding the bag.

Tricksters were not the only ones trying to make the most of limited opportunities and fluid credit networks. New York was justly famous for its female merchants, despite the handicaps put on married women in the marketplace. Relatively well-connected women turned these constraints to their advantage by using the financial credit of their family relationships to trade successfully in the British Atlantic world. Often the same relationships that limited their abilities to act as independent agents, such as coverture, were the routes to their success. At the same time, however, their fiscal credibility was often thrown into jeopardy by these gendered financial practices.

While social status may have structured the ways that women participated in the market, it did not exclude the poorer women from New York's economy. Without the overseas connections of their wealthier fellow residents, laboring women had to operate under the radar of the legitimate economy. Women often found lucrative opportunities, especially in secondhand markets, by going into partnership with black men. Yet because their business practices seemed to threaten the city's social hierarchies of class and race, these women also found the New York economy a dangerous place.

The elite of New York feared that this market in secondhand goods would not only encourage racial mixing but also, even more terrifying, undermine the status implications of those luxury goods that passed through it. They therefore developed other ways to cultivate social distinction and reassert their status, including bodily deportment. The usage of fashionable goods and clothing, rather than the mere possession of them, could separate the elite from those bounders who only aspired to that status. Elite society thus turned to manners, corporeal and otherwise, to shore up their claims. Given their location on the edge of empire, these New Yorkers needed experts with knowledge of the latest trends in metropolitan polite behavior. They thus turned to so-called "dancing masters," who, for a price, taught them the intricacies of performed gentility in order to assert their elite imperial status. This segment of the city's society resented its dependence on paid itinerant experts but possessed few other connections to metropolitan cultural knowledge. Both dancing masters and their students discovered the perils of buying and selling social status.

Elite bodies were not the only ones who proclaimed status. Black sailors captured on Spanish ships by British privateers found that the color of their bodies often determined their initial fate. Looked upon as part of the proceeds of war for commercial supremacy, these sailors refused to let their skin color have the final word. They lobbied in New York's courts to change their legal and social status from enslaved spoils of war to one that mirrored that of their white shipmates: prisoners of war with political standing. New York's booming profits in privateering could not continue to depend on enslaving Afro-Spanish sailors for British gain.

In 1741 this volatile world momentarily ignited. In a desperate response to the city's unpredictable social hierarchies, government officials instituted a series of slave conspiracy trials. Thirty-four people were executed, almost half suffering gruesome agonies as they were burned alive at the stake. Nearly ninety more were banished from the colonies. For their families, their friends, and presumably many of the blacks and whites who lived in the colony, their deaths were meaningful and terrifying. Yet these trials had almost no noticeable impact in any other measurable way. There was no new slave code passed in the wake of the trials, as there had been two years earlier in South Carolina. There were no new crackdowns on any of the economic or social practices in which many of the suspected conspirators had participated. Perhaps most striking of all, the trials' primary prosecutor and chronicler, Justice Daniel Horsmanden, found his account of the trials remaindered just four years after publication for lack of purchasers. These trials could not permanently inscribe a fixed social world, because the fluid social world of the imperial marketplace was the foundation of the port city's culture. The New York slave conspiracy trials and their aftermath make sense only in a world in which commerce, status, and empire were inextricably bound.

Dangerous Economies examines how issues of status were continually contested in the context of an imperial port city. It uncovers the ways the city's location at the edge of empire and its commercial character combined to weaken strict social hierarchies. The fluidity of status that this concoction of empire and commerce allowed created opportunities for elite and nonelite New Yorkers alike. However, with those opportunities came risks, often with devastating consequences. A look at New York in the eighteenth century thus reveals the cultural power of the commercial foundation upon which the early British Empire was based.

Chapter One
Where Credit Is Due

In the winter of 1737 a New York City shopkeeper named Nathaniel Hazard hauled Thomas Harris, a Connecticut laborer, into court. The shopkeeper claimed that Harris had forged a letter, purportedly written by a minister living seventy miles away, that asked Hazard to give the bearer more than four pounds in cash. Confronted by a court consisting of the city's mayor and aldermen, Harris gave a full confession of his forgery. The court sentenced Harris to the harshest possible corporal punishment—thirty-nine lashes on his naked back—and then banned him from the city forever.

The Connecticut man's attempt to swindle the New York shopkeeper illustrates the potentials and pitfalls of commercial credit in eighteenth-century New York City. Harris used his personal and local knowledge of the Reverend Isaac Chalker, a Yale graduate and Connecticut native whose family still lived in the colony, to give credence to his request for money. He may even have known that Chalker had done business with Hazard when the minister lived on Long Island before he became a pastor in a Presbyterian church in Orange County, New York. A world of commerce in which financial transactions were regularly performed impersonally and at a distance made it possible for Harris to bring in a false written instrument—a piece of fiction—to the shopkeeper and hope that he would be believed. At the same time, a man whose appearance did not reassure the object of his confidence trick was most unlikely to succeed. If Harris could not disguise his status as a "laborer," it may not be a surprise that Hazard saw through the trick immediately.[1]

The story of Harris and Hazard reveals the close and unstable ties between commercial activity and status. Private credit referred to trust in an individual's personal and commercial worth, a trust that was often based on imperfect or secondhand knowledge. An examination of confidence tricks and counterfeiting points up the ways in which commercial culture was a product of social practice as well as structured by it.[2] At the same time, however, these social practices were not simply the exercise of neighborly and local relationships; they were also imperial and intercontinental. These commercial transactions were certainly not anonymous. Both in practice and in imagination, the local continued to matter, but it was not the only context for business deals. Instead, the tentacles of the local stretched into an increasingly wide-ranging and impersonal commercial culture. Yet the promise of local knowledge as a reliable foundation for granting credit was often misleading, unstable, or simply false. Commercial actors depended on practices of local interaction, such as letters of introduction, that played on personal connections, but such dependence often led New Yorkers astray.

These con artists exposed the mutability of commercial status in eighteenth-century commerce by manipulating two aspects of the city's commercial and imperial culture. First, they exploited an early capitalist system that created personal credibility and financial credit, a system with analogs in the local and the international. Second, they took advantage of the instability of the markers of status and trust that characterized eighteenth-century New York City.

The commercial economy as it developed in colonial New York City and throughout the eighteenth-century British Empire became increasingly dependent on circulating systems of exchange. These circulating systems included specie, state-financed bills of credit, and privately backed bills of exchange. The instability and mobility of fiscal circulation carried with them attendant dangers, particularly confidence artists and counterfeiters. As Craig Muldrew and others have noted, "credit in social terms—the reputation for fair and honest dealing of a household and its members—became the currency of lending and borrowing."[3] The city's fluidity of class, gender, and trust allowed confidence artists to counterfeit both money and self.

The Emergence of Credit

When the Duke of York ordered the capture of New Amsterdam in 1664, he had already imagined the commercial advantages of English control of North America from Maine to the Carolinas. It is unlikely, however, that he envisioned New York's remarkable physical and commercial growth over the next 150 years. The city's population increased almost tenfold in under a century, from around fifteen hundred people in 1664 to nearly five thousand in 1698 and over thirteen thousand in 1749. As the city grew, it competed with Philadelphia and Boston for commercial supremacy, and after 1700 its harbor often saw more and bigger ships than Boston's. Unlike Boston, moreover, whose commerce was irreparably harmed by imperial conflicts such as the War of Jenkins' Ear in 1739, New York turned those wars to its commercial advantage. Not until the middle of the eighteenth century did Philadelphia, with its superior access to productive farms, become the larger port.[4] Yet, New York did not acquire its commercial strength simply through its volume of trade, and it was never dependent on its hinterlands for goods to export.[5] Rather, it became a colonial mercantile capital through its unique ability to handle the complex business of imperial trade. As a result of the city's entrepôt functions such as banking and brokerage, New York alone of all the colonies was able to achieve a favorable balance of trade with Great Britain.[6]

As the British Empire expanded in size and complexity, so did the economy of New York. Both coin and paper money were fundamental to this growth.[7] The more that New Yorkers involved themselves in the business of empire, the more fluid they needed their currency to be. Throughout the seventeenth century, specie had been sufficient to fuel the city's trade. Coins were "real money," made of precious metals and with value theoretically equal to their weight. Because coins were so scarce in New York, however, their market value increased.[8] Beginning in 1709, New York began to experiment with "imaginary money"[9] by printing its first paper money. Queen Anne's War (1702–14) had already lasted seven years, and New York's coffers continued to be drained of the hard currency that flowed out of the colony to pay for the imperial conflict. The governor was worried that New Yorkers would be unable to repay their war debts without additional currency. So, to stem the loss of currency and the threat of insolvency, the colonial government printed its first paper money, known as bills of credit.[10]

The value of a coin did not depend on the trustworthiness of its user, but bills of credit required faith in the government that issued them. These bills were neither insured nor tied to any standard, so those who used them had to trust that the paper would not depreciate. Colonial governments did not even trust each other; the New York government did not accept the bills issued by other colonies as legal tender, claiming that unlike other colonies, "the bills of New York keep up their credit."[11]

The shift from "real money" to "imaginary money" paved the way not only for a nimbler economy but also for more extensive and creative financial frauds. The trust inherent in paper money raised the stakes considerably for the colonial government's financial transactions; as a result, the original legislation enacting bills of credit also made the counterfeiting of those bills a capital felony without benefit of clergy (that is, unlike other "clergyable" capital offenses, defendants found guilty of counterfeiting could not be given a lesser penalty than death). The government's public credit would be at risk if merchants and others refused to accept bills of credit for fear that they were counterfeit. For the first time counterfeiting became a capital offense.[12]

Paper currency in eighteenth-century New York was not limited to government-issued bills of credit. The expanding economy also relied on an equally "imaginary" but qualitatively different form of currency known as a bill of exchange. Unlike a bill of credit, issued by a government, a bill of exchange was more like a modern-day check. In the absence of banks, however, those who used bills of exchange had to depend on personal accounts that they held with their overseas partners. Like the government's bills of credit, these privately issued bills of exchange acquired their own value as a circulating medium throughout the century.[13]

A bill of exchange required the involvement and the trust of at least three and usually four persons in order to function.[14] In the modern world, a person writing a check (a debtor, or, in legal terms, a "drawer") asks his or her bank to pay the value of the check to the recipient (the creditor, or, in legal terms, the "payee"). In an eighteenth-century world without banks, an individual (known legally as the "drawee") had to act as the bank. A person writing a bill of exchange would ask the drawee to pay the value of the bill to the payee. Once presented with the bill, the drawee was obligated to pay out the money to the payee.

For example, when young James Beekman began trading in dry goods from England in 1753, one of his suppliers wrote him, "We have yours [that is, your letter] . . . with a bill drawn by Taylor and Wilson on Messrs. Coleman and Co. for £100 which was duly honoured and your account credited for the same."[15] In this scenario Beekman had approached Taylor and Wilson, who kept an account with William Coleman and his business, and bought a bill of exchange, perhaps paying a bit more than one hundred pounds British sterling for the convenience of using their reliable London contact. He then signed the bill over to his agents, Pomeroy and Streatfeild, so that when they went to Coleman, he paid them out the one hundred pounds. They, in turn, credited the bill to Beekman's account.

This was not the only possible scenario for a bill of exchange. The payee could also sign the bill over to someone else to receive the payment. The worth of the bill was not static; it depended on the fluctuating rate of exchange between London and the colonies as well as the reputations of the local merchant (the drawer) and his or her overseas agent (the drawee).[16] The person acting as the bank—the drawee—might refuse to accept the bill when the payee presented it. There might be legitimate problems, such as the drawer not having enough credit in his or her account or the drawee not having the cash for which to exchange the bill. If the drawee trusted the drawer, he might accept the bill. If he doubted the debtor's credit, however, he might reject or "protest" the bill, with expensive legal ramifications; a payee of a protested bill might have to wait months or years to get his money. Thus the signature of a reputable drawer or drawee added to the worth of the bill. Likewise, a reputable drawer might be able to negotiate a better rate of exchange. In short, a bill of exchange was an impersonal mode of exchange that nonetheless depended on personal credit.

Cadwallader Colden, the future lieutenant governor of New York, understood that the reputation of the people who backed a bill directly affected that bill's worth. In 1714 he wrote to a fellow merchant, "We desire you would take special care if you deal for Bills that the Drawer or Endorser be of good repute or Credit. . . . Trouble me with as few bills as possible unless they be the very best."[17] Almost forty years later the merchant Henry Cruger wrote to his agent en route to Jamaica that he wanted the profits from his shipment remitted in either "Cash or Bill [of] Exchange on England, preferring the Latter if the Drawees are to be Depended on."[18] Bills of exchange were more fluid, easier to transport, and sometimes more profitable than specie, but only if all the parties who signed the bill were credible. Merchants and agents had to inquire carefully into the reputations of those who tried to sell bills of exchange; otherwise they might find themselves saddled with discounted or even bad bills.

Bills of exchange were not unknown in the commercial world of seventeenth-century New York, but it is their proliferation in the eighteenth century that makes them a particularly apt symbol of the colony's hybrid economy.[19] During this period the "culture of credit" in New York City was characterized by the uneven integration of international business, which relied on circulating credit, and local business, based on debts recorded in shopkeepers' ledgers. The shift from a local, face-to-face economy to an international, impersonal economy did not happen overnight. Throughout the first half of the eighteenth century many traders participated in both sorts of exchanges, often in the same or related transactions. In addition, the trust that energized international trade was also at work in local transactions, since face-to-face dealings were not necessarily between people who knew each other; New Yorkers could not always verify each other's family status or financial position. Traders therefore expected that they would have to gamble on some of their international transactions, but they also assumed that they could tell whether a business associate whom they met in person was worth the risk. Thus local trade and international trade were not two entirely different ways of doing business. Middling New Yorkers all engaged in trading practices that struggled to integrate both modes of exchange. The bill of exchange, a financial instrument that depended on both local and international credit, perfectly encapsulated this transitional economic practice.

Another example of this uneasy integration of local and long-distance trading practices is found in the eighteenth-century grants of powers of attorney to collect debt. Like the bill of exchange, an eighteenth-century power of attorney was an impersonal document that depended on personal relationships in order to function. Recovering debts from a distance was a perennial challenge, one that some traders did not bother to pursue. Other merchants asked their foreign correspondents to draw upon their own connections to collect from the merchants' debtors. That foreign correspondent, in order to collect on behalf of the original merchant, needed to obtain a formally notarized power of attorney.[20]

The New York merchant Gerard Beekman was particularly fond of authorizing his colleagues in other colonial ports to collect his debts, but his lack of success shows the limits of this part of the financial system. Early in his career Beekman used a scattershot approach to empowering his correspondents to arrest his debtors. On April 22, 1754, for example, Beekman distributed his power of attorney north and south. He asked Gamaliel Wallice, a Boston merchant, if he would "Accept a power against" John Codman. Codman had been Beekman's correspondent in Halifax, but their relationship had soured when two years later Codman still owed Beekman over one hundred pounds for goods consigned to him. Codman apparently was only visiting Boston, but Beekman hoped that Wallice might track him down and arrest him for the debt.[21] On the same day, Beekman also wrote to Peter Rutgers, a correspondent in North Carolina, hoping to track down a New York ship captain named William Dobbs. Following up a rumor that the captain might have stopped in New Berne on his way to Jamaica, Beekman pleaded desperately, "I beg You Will Enquire after him and If you Can meet with or here [hear] of him any Where in North Carolina you will have him arrested." Eager to collect from Dobbs any of the debt that he could, Beekman added, "Inclosed You have my geniral power of attorney which may Serve at any time on Some Other Occaision and must beg youl accept the trouble of it."[22]

Neither Wallice nor Rutgers was successful in getting back Beekman's money. The next year Beekman was still hoping that another correspondent in Boston would retrieve some of the debt from Codman.[23] Beekman finally collected his debt from Captain Dobbs the next year, after the mariner had returned to New York and Beekman himself was able to have him arrested as a debtor.[24] This distribution of the power of attorney clearly was successful only when the correspondent had a personal relationship with the debtor. This impersonal legal document had little success without a more intimate connection between the middleman and the debtor. Beekman's wide web of correspondents around North America was not enough to make the dissemination of his power of attorney effective. It required a more personal touch.

Yet even when one's distant correspondents did have a personal relationship with the debtor in question, there was a hitch in asking them to collect on one's behalf. As Beekman wrote in 1763 to his half brother William in Liverpool, "it is a very unthankfull office and often offends the persons Sued or their friends, whome we have Some Connections with and by that Means proves a damage to our own Interests."[25] Calling in debts from one's business associates might well upset the web of indebtedness in which both the middleman and the debtor were entangled. One merchant's lack of trust in another's ability to pay back debt might be another trader's way of doing business. Forcing the issue by acting as an attorney could engender distrust in a relationship that had previously functioned smoothly.

Counterfeit Money

Bills of exchange, book debt, and powers of attorney were all understood to be predicated on relationships of trust. Currency, however, was usually assumed to be a priori trustworthy. Even so, in the fluid fiscal world of an imperial market, money was as likely a medium for tricks and counterfeiting as were more personal forms of financial exchange.

Neither fraud nor counterfeiting was unique to eighteenth-century New York City. The forms that these crimes took, however, and their implications for the colony's residents are unique to this time and place. There is little need simply to reiterate the historical details, since the answers to these questions—who created false money, which bills were counterfeited, what sorts of changes were counterfeiters likely to make, and how legislators dealt with the growing problem—have all been well documented. Rather, these schemes also reveal the instability of the cultural world of commerce. The city's emphasis on money rather than goods made it a particularly attractive place for counterfeiters, and as the confidence artists in the following stories will demonstrate, the gaps in a still-emerging culture of credit, one that looked to both local and international connections in order to give and to assess credibility, allowed tricksters of all stripes to succeed in New York.[26]

As early as the city's commercial origins in the seventeenth century, New Yorkers engaged in one of the oldest known forms of financial fraud: clipping coins. The practice of shaving the precious metals off the edges of coins highlights the ways in which later financial frauds were inextricably tied to social markers of gender and status. The high proportion of women accused of clipping coins relative to their accusations in credit-based frauds indicates both that women were as likely to defraud the market as men were and that they were less able to do so in credit-based transactions.

Although there were plenty of clipped coins in circulation, it was difficult for prosecutors to find evidence to convict the accused. The first five years of the eighteenth century saw a rash of clipping accusations. Of the seven cases that came before the court of general sessions, four were against women. Women such as Susannah Elliot and Anna Vanderspregel, both of whom a grand jury found guilty of "uttering newly clipt and hammered money," were found not guilty by juries. In May 1705 both John Kingston, a baker, and Mary Barnes, a tavern keeper, were accused of "clipping Royalls and double Royalls." Both were found not guilty.[27] Clipping coins appears to have been a gender-neutral activity, and the courts were no more likely to suspect men of doing so than women.

Others pushed the blame onto strangers from outside New York. William Fowler was accused of passing a large number of clipped royals along with good money. Fowler managed to convince the court that the 135 underweight coins had gotten mixed into his "large sum" of money without his knowledge. All the coins, he claimed, came from somewhere in Rhode Island. Clearly, the court shared Fowler's suspicion of the New England colony; Fowler was acquitted, although the court insisted on melting down the clipped coins.[28]

Fowler's acquittal was no doubt aided by the "several persons of note" who attested to his "good fame and Reputation." Even so, unwittingly passing clipped or counterfeit coins was not a serious crime in the early eighteenth century. Although to counterfeit the coin of the realm or foreign coins that passed as legal tender was high treason in England, in New York it was treated merely as a "cheat," which classed it as only a misdemeanor. In a time and place where small change was scarce, perhaps most people winked at a little coin clipping.[29]

The counterfeiting of coins was less prevalent than the mere passing of them, but it was equally free of serious legal consequences. In 1702 the silversmith Gerrett Onclebagg was found guilty of "coining and uttering false money of base and mixt metals." Onclebagg's profession made it possible for him to counterfeit coins, and the prosecution found evidence against him; he was fined twenty pounds. This was, to be sure, a hefty fine but far less onerous than the charge of treason he might have faced in England. Onclebagg was unluckier than most; the person whom he tried to pay with the false coins was willing to bring him to court. When Peter Watson was accused of coining "false dollars," no witnesses appeared for the prosecution, so the case was dismissed.[30]

In early cases, moreover, where the accused were found guilty, their punishments were public, to emphasize the public trust that these counterfeiters had undermined. Thomas Copley, convicted of "having false dollars with intent to utter or pass them in payment," was sentenced to the public pillory. When Patrick Macarty was sentenced in 1735 for committing both a theft and a "cheat," the court ordered twenty lashes for the theft and fifteen minutes in the pillory for the cheat. Margaret Haynne was convicted simply of passing rather than making false coins; she was sentenced to be "publicly whipped at the Public Whipping Post on the naked back" and confined to three months of hard labor.[31] The conviction of Bartholomew Vank and Thomas Roberts for counterfeiting coins in 1706 resulted in the most public punishment: a flogging tour of the city. After they were tied to a cart, the public whipper gave them three lashes each at eight of the most visible areas of the city, including the "Well in the Broadway . . . the most publick part of the market Place . . . and the City Hall." They then stood in the pillory for an hour with "an inscription in Capital letters fixt over each of their heads on the Pillory with these words 'for Counterfeiting Dollars.' "[32] Unlike the fines for keeping a disorderly house or even the whippings at the public post for theft or prostitution, being whipped around the town was an attempt to make as many residents as possible cognizant of the crime and its perpetrators. Such public punishments destroyed the credibility of counterfeiters, and credibility was the confidence trickster's true coin.

For some tricksters, counterfeiting coins was only one of several potential swindles. Patrick Butler, for example, counterfeited coins among other frauds. Using names such as Samuel Gall and Oliver Lovewell to disguise his Irish background, Butler committed a number of crimes, including horse stealing and bigamy. Like many runaway slaves and servants, Butler had skills as well as stories. He was, according to the court, a wandering tinkerer, a practitioner of a trade that provided him with the tools for counterfeiting and with a reason to travel. Butler's frauds were those of a man trying to cheat other poor New Yorkers, not wealthy shopkeepers. Thus, Butler swindled an elderly widow out of her husband's old clothes. Rather than counterfeiting letters of credit, he made false money. The court ordered Butler to stand in the stocks the same day it found him guilty. The next day the court ordered him whipped all around the city, tied to a cart's tail, and given the maximum possible physical punishment, thirty-nine lashes. He was then ordered to be passed from constable to constable until he reached his last known place of residence in Westchester County.[33]

The redefinition of counterfeiting, at least for state-issued bills of credit, from a misdemeanor to a capital offense in the year 1709 demonstrates clearly legislators' understanding that the possibilities for fraud had now increased exponentially with the introduction of paper money into circulation. Following England's lead, New York emphasized the importance of state-funded credit, although neither extended the death penalty to issues involving private bills of exchange. In an execution sermon for a counterfeiter, one minister fulminated that a counterfeiter, unlike those who commit only crimes of violence or against property, chose to "take a more expeditious method . . . to become rich, by ruining whole Provinces and Colonies; aiming by one fatal stab, to let out the very Heart's Blood of Communities. . . . Of this kind are our money-Makers, a Brood of Vipers, that are eating out the Bowels of Provinces and Colonies . . . [by] their devilish Craft and Cunning." Counterfeiting was not an individual, personal offense; it was now a public crime closely tied to the colony's credit within the commercial empire.[34]

State-backed paper money was an easy mark for counterfeiters. Rather than simply devaluing the currency, passing counterfeit bills of credit usually meant convincing people to take paper that they did not quite recognize and assuring them that it was legal tender. Since each colony printed its own bills, the lack of consistency permitted counterfeiters to make mistakes at little cost.

As those who had been convicted of clipping coins suffered public humiliation, so the presence of counterfeit bills of credit required publicly visible remedies. In 1726 the legislature put into law the already common practice of publicly destroying counterfeit money. Such bills were to be "delivered from time to time to the court or Courts of the Quarter Sessions to be held for the City and County of New York who thereupon are either to destroy the same in the Said Court or to Proceed thereon as in their Discretion Shall Seem meet."[35] The court held frequent public burnings of counterfeit bills in the courtroom. As early as 1720 the court minutes had recorded that "false and counterfeit bills were burnt and destroyed in open court."[36] The few cases of false coinage were also settled by "breaking" or melting the counterfeit coins in open court. Subsequent courts were even more thorough, burning the false bills to ashes at least once a year and frequently every session.[37] With these public bonfires, courts dramatized how dangerous and how worthless (and how prevalent) false money was. By openly ridding the system of false bills, the courts could symbolically cleanse the money supply.

Before counterfeiters were caught, New York officials had to depend on newspapers to warn the public against false money. In 1731 an article in the *New-York Gazette* reported that there had "been a Suspicion of some counterfeit dollars being made here in this City." Although one of the suspected counterfeiters had disappeared and the other was acquitted, the paper nonetheless hoped that the report "may caution People to take care what Dollars they receive."[38] Other articles that reported the presence of counterfeit bills gave explicit instructions on how to tell the difference between false and genuine bills. In 1754 the *New-York Gazette* listed five ways to distinguish legal three-pound bills from the counterfeit kind.[39] These careful descriptions aided in the removal of the false bills from the system.

The greatest challenge for counterfeiters was to put the bad money into circulation without being caught. At times counterfeiters used enormous rings of people through the North American colonies. Over the course of the first three-quarters of the eighteenth century, ninety-nine people in New York were accused of counterfeiting or passing bad money.[40] The number of people actually caught can have been only a small fraction of those who printed or coined false money; eighteenth-century estimates put the number of counterfeiters working "in a clan" from New Hampshire to North Carolina at five hundred. The New York courts destroyed more than £707 of bills between 1720 and 1766 from small hauls or individually passed bills. This figure does not include the enormous amounts found on some counterfeiters, ranging from £90 to £3,500. Others confessed that they had passed £1,600 of counterfeit bills in a single day. Given that one could live "Like a Gentleman" in New York on an income of £300 in year, it is difficult to imagine how anyone could pass more than five times that amount in one day.[41]

With its high volume of travelers and commerce, any port city was a natural place to try to pass bad money, even if some attempts were unsuccessful. The increasing presence of money from other colonies and countries decreased suspicion of unfamiliar bills and coins.[42] Garrit Van Voorhees, a sailor, had just completed a run to Ireland when he tried to pass New York bills of credit in Philadelphia. He admitted to the court that he had gotten the bills from a passenger on the vessel, who had taken the rest of these counterfeit bills in a roll "as big as the small of his Leg" up the river to Albany. Van Voorhees escaped from jail before his sentencing, so he escaped a penalty of a death sentence without hope of a commutation.[43] In another instance the next year, local officials received a tip that a sailor would try to bring false Delaware bills of credit into the city. When a suspicious vessel landed, they searched all the crew's sail chests until they found one with a false bottom concealing nearly one thousand pounds of counterfeit bills. As the signatures of Delaware's officials were missing from the bills, the sailor was unlikely to have had much luck in passing them.[44] Although neither of these sailors was successful in his attempt to pass forged bills of credit, their efforts reveal the close relationships between transient New Yorkers, unfamiliar money, and counterfeiting.

The confession of one itinerant demonstrates the extent to which paper money, counterfeit as well as legitimate, circulated freely across the Atlantic. Two men were arrested in New York in 1727 for a scheme to put counterfeit bills into circulation throughout nearly all of the North American colonies. David Wallace, one of the ringleaders, admitted that he had brought into Philadelphia nearly a thousand pounds in counterfeit money, made in Ireland. The money was designed by a Maryland man then living in Dublin who had firsthand familiarity with several colonies' bills of credit. The two detainees were carrying bills from Pennsylvania, New Jersey, and New York, and they were planning to move on to New England. Fortunately for them, the two men were found guilty only of passing false New Jersey money and not of counterfeiting New York bills. As a result, they escaped the death penalty, but their punishment was as public and exemplary as the counterfeit coiners' had been twenty years earlier; they were pilloried, carted around the town with a halter around their necks, and flogged at the public whipping post in four separate counties, including New York City.[45] In its wide-ranging geography, their punishment matched their attempted crime.

There were other dangers in looking for accomplices outside one's local networks. In February 1739 Samuel Flood and Joseph Steel came from Massachusetts to New York to find a smith who would engrave the plates for printing New Hampshire and Rhode Island bills. The two men found a goldsmith quickly enough, and they asked to speak with him privately. However, their research was flawed; they had picked an honest goldsmith. After agreeing to engrave a plate for them, the smith immediately went to the magistrates. When the men returned for the plate, the constables were waiting for them. As a good New Englander, Flood pleaded guilty to the charges of attempting to convince a goldsmith to make false plates, acknowledging that "he was now senseible of his error and hoped God would give him more grace for the future."[46] Pleading God's grace might have worked in New England, but Flood had no such luck in New York.[47] The court sentenced him to the maximum thirty-nine lashes, to be administered as he was dragged behind a cart through "the Principal Streets of this City." His accomplice was wiser; he continued to plead his innocence, and the court reluctantly decided that there was no evidence by which to convict him.[48] Despite their failure, Flood and Steel's premise was good; to find a counterfeiter in another colony who would forge bills from other colonies would have allowed them both to exploit the unfamiliarity of nonlocal bills and to take advantage of New York's fluid population.

New Yorkers who tried to counterfeit their own local currency were no safer. Joseph Johnson was a bookbinder and printer who printed up illegal tender as well as pamphlets and books. One evening in 1734 a New Yorker who had received the forged bills from Joseph brought them back. Joseph did not deny that he had given the man the counterfeit bills, and he offered to exchange them for legal tender. As he did so, however, he was "in an Agony and Trembled"; an hour later he packed up his bags and absconded to Philadelphia in the middle of the night, leaving his wife Catherine and their six-year-old son. The authorities never found Joseph, but they arrested Catherine for trying to put "a great number" of bills into circulation. She was convicted of a misdemeanor (the court assumed that she had not been a part of their manufacture) and sentenced to receive twenty-one lashes.[49] Successful counterfeiting at the local level required, at the very least, a successful escape route.

On one hand, state-sponsored bills of credit unquestionably created more opportunities for much more lucrative counterfeiting than did mere coin. On the other hand, the scope that such bills of credit gave to con artists was very limited in comparison with that of private bills of exchange. Because bills of credit were printed rather than handwritten, and because their value was negotiated only at the time of exchange (since the state had set the value when it printed the bills), the fraudulent ends to which they could be put were relatively restricted. Bills of exchange, on the other hand, offered many more possibilities for the confidence artist. Not least among their possibilities was the chance to counterfeit oneself.

Counterfeit Credibility

Recent work on the early modern "culture of credit" offers useful insights into the cultural meaning of the marketplace in this period. Working from the eighteenth-century belief that "*Confidence . . .* is the soul and essence of credit," historians have begun to examine the ways that reputation, trading across increased distances, and the expansion of credit as a means of transacting business were inextricably connected.[50] Thus the market was at the same time a place of exchange both for material goods and for social trust. As one scholar explains, "Credit as a currency of reputation was the means by which such trust was communicated beyond local face-to-face dealings between people who knew each other." In other words, people granted credibility to strangers by doing business with them.[51] This expansion in credibility as well as credit could have impressive payoffs for merchants, but it could also go badly wrong. Confidence artists could use the inherent instability of a long-distance credit-based system to foster creative financial frauds. To their regret, some New Yorkers found that financial actors at times could be precisely that: very good actors.[52]

Forgers and other tricksters were successful for two reasons: the potential anonymity of long-distance trade; and the plethora of financial transactions based on trust and correspondence rather than on face-to-face interactions. Yet the personal interactions were essential as well. Confidence tricksters who wanted to exploit the possibilities in bills of exchange had to present themselves (or an accomplice) in person to send their false bills on their way. These and other forgers could not depend only on long-distance communication; they had to find a merchant who did not know them but who would trust them. They sought to gain confidence through casual reference to people, places, or exchanges that the merchant would recognize and trust. These appeals to local knowledge, often combined with a display of genteel clothing or a purported connection to known elite families, allowed the confidence artist to bring off a swindle within the merchant's nonlocal and international networks.

The swindling of Henry Row is a case in point. Row was a New York ship captain who made regular trading voyages to the West Indies beginning in the 1720s. In 1736 a man brought him a letter instructing Row to give the bearer nearly four pounds' worth of goods, to be paid for from the account of the New York merchant Charles Arding. Unfortunately, the letter had been written not by Arding but by a con man named Miles Peartree Weeks, who then asked the unsuspecting courier to deliver the letter and return with the goods. Once the deception was discovered, it did not take long to track down the courier, who insisted that he had been "imposed upon" by Weeks and was an unwitting partner in the scheme. Perhaps sympathetic to the plight of a man caught between an older mode of personal interaction and a newer world of credit fraud, the court dismissed the charges against the letter carrier. Weeks, however, having confessed to his crime, was given the maximum thirty-nine lashes at the public whipping post.[53] The striking feature of the case is that although Row may or may not have recognized the handwriting, he seems to have accepted the letter as a normal way of doing business, and he gave the man the goods.[54] For a captain such as Row, the authorization to draw from another person's account was routinely made in writing rather than in person.

The story of Weeks illustrates that a fluid urban culture could not guarantee the financial honesty of its face-to-face transactions. Swindlers used this fact to their advantage. Like other Atlantic port cities, New York had a much more transient population than did the small towns in which most British colonists lived, and small-town habits of personal interactions could not be sustained in such a changing city. London likewise suffered a similar but much more enormous fraud only a few years earlier, when a well-known merchant forged bills of exchange and used a young man newly arrived in London to cash them at unsuspecting financial institutions. The merchant was caught because an alert clerk found the handwriting suspiciously familiar, though the bill had been brought in by a stranger. Both the London and New York frauds speak to the dual nature of British commercial culture. On the one hand, as one historian of financial fraud has pointed out, "It remained remarkably personal: people recognized names as well as particular ways of conducting business." On the other hand, despite the aspects of the "intimate quality of commercial life," the use of these anonymous go-betweens reveals "the increasing impersonality of exchange."[55]

Even men who were not professional swindlers found ways to exploit the uneven integration of credible appearance and long-distance trade. In May 1750 Gerard Beekman consigned some goods to a man named John Lord, who was sailing to Nova Scotia. Before a month had passed, Beekman wrote to a Rhode Island correspondent (a hogshead of whose rum he had likewise consigned to Lord) in June of that year, "I am afraid that the hhds. [hogshead] Rum John Lord had of yours will prove a bad Debt with the addition of £21 of my Own." Yet, Beekman protested that Lord's appearance when he was in New York had completely captured his confidence as well as that of other New Yorkers, lamenting that Lord "has Considerable of goods Which he got on Credit in this town for he always apeared like a very honist man and of good Caracter I Should have Trusted him for £100 if he had askt it."[56] Lord was able to obtain credit through personal meetings with New York merchants, and then he successfully exploited Beekman's desire to expand his trade networks into British Canada.[57]

Commercial exchange was becoming less personal because traders' social environment was following the same trend. The extensive and continual movement of people through the port city meant that New Yorkers often had never before seen the people whom they passed on the street. All the swindlers who have left traces in the historical record used travel as part of their schemes; the relative anonymity of these men allowed them to exploit systems of trust that had been established for more sedentary communities.[58] Social anonymity fostered violent crime too. When Robert Livingston, Jr., and his friends pulled Abigail Cottrell off the street and tried to rape her in a public park known as the Spring Gardens, she screamed until a crowd of people came. Cottrell could not identify any of her rescuers, however, because she was "a stranger" who had only recently moved to the city.[59] Thus the personal mobility and social fluidity that created possibilities for clever tricksters had a far more violent underside. As the attempted rape of Abigail Cottrell shows, men could also exploit the city's anonymity—in this case a woman with relatively few friends or acquaintances—for noncommercial purposes such as rape. Thus rakes and tricksters shared the same methods and made use of the same contradictions that New York's culture of commerce had created.

Yet despite the dangers of the eighteenth-century economy, most New Yorkers did not in fact give up their commitment to personal contact as a means of doing business. A personal introduction or invocation of the name of a mutual acquaintance often smoothed initial encounters. Gerard Beekman wrote to William Snell, his correspondent in London, that he had recommended the London merchant to John Provoost, another New Yorker on his way to London. Beekman brokered their meeting, assuring Snell that "I know hel Seek you[r] acquaintance if he does he is worth your notice for he is a gentleman of fortune and good understanding."[60] When Provoost did meet Snell, he could be assured that Beekman had already told the Londoner that he was a man of reputation and credit.

As with financial swindles, more social frauds also depended on claims to shared personal contacts. When James Mayne first came to Elizabeth Wright's house, he told her "not to be alarmed for that he was her country man and came to see her and knew her relations." Even though his appearance at her door with a drawn sword aroused her suspicions, she nonetheless let him in. A few days later he came back "with one Captain Blair, a relation" of Wright's, in order to assuage her concerns. Wright's suspicions turned out to be well founded: over the next three weeks Mayne attempted to rape Wright, her twelve-year-old servant, and another woman who worked for her. Although Mayne's drawn sword clearly signified his intentions, Wright nonetheless allowed him into her house because she interpreted his claim that he "knew her relations" to mean that he was credible.[61] As a confidence man, Mayne exploited the other links that people used to substitute for the knowledge of someone's face, such as letters of credit or the invocation of a friend's name. Indeed it was the very split between the expectation of a local interaction and the fluid society that prohibited it that permitted rakes and tricksters to pursue their schemes.

Attempts to put strangers into the context of social trust were fundamental to the combined social and commercial worlds of New York's port. The "currency of reputation" by which New Yorkers made social and financial decisions was part of a larger trend toward wide-flung personal and business networks that still depended on individual reputations. Manipulating the system—whether for violent or financial gain—meant exploiting the nature of credibility itself.

Mobility, Gentility, and Trust

Because financial credit depended so closely on personal credibility, markers of status—particularly of class, gender, and age—played a central role in determining credibility. By the second half of the eighteenth century, both established male merchants and fathers who were trying to prepare their sons for careers as traders gave particular thought to the ways in which they considered themselves and other competitors as "men of credit." Men's concern with their reputation in the marketplace reveals some of the ways that this culture of credit became weighted toward a particular sort of genteel masculinity.[62] Mercantile credit came to be seen as the exclusive provenance of men; women's credibility was solely sexual. As the *New-York Weekly Journal* explained, the "Credit of a Merchant . . . is the same Thing in its Nature as the Virtue of a Lady."[63] Knowing this, many confidence men tried to use the most obvious signs of genteel masculinity to swindle New Yorkers out of their money. At the same time, falsely appropriating polite behavior and clothing worked only in an environment in which the actor was a stranger.

Moreover, the appearance of a refined upbringing was useless without a useful medium for fraud. Undoubtedly, the most effective way of turning movement into large amounts of cash was to forge bills of exchange. The complexity of that transaction and the number of times that these bills had to change hands made them ripe for exploitation by forgers and other scam artists. Bills of exchange relied on a close relationship between overseas commerce and personal credibility, and it was precisely this reliance that allowed serial imposters who could claim a genteel credibility to take advantage of them.

Some con artists honed their role-playing skills on the stage. Thomas Allman, also known as Thomas Vernon, had clerked for a business partnership in Jamaica. From there he had gone to South Carolina, where he forged three different bills of exchange, worth a total of £1,283, in the names of the business partnership for which he had been a clerk. A Carolina merchant had accepted them and sent them on to London. The men he had swindled in Jamaica took out an unusual front-page advertisement in the *New-York Weekly Journal.* Jacob and Moses Franks, merchants of New York, had a large stake in the Jamaica firm and were just as eager as the island merchants to apprehend the confidence man who had embroiled the merchants of four different cities in his scheme. The New York advertisement for his capture described him as "well-spoken [and] courteous in his behavior," clearly able to pass himself off as a reputable man of business. At the same time, he obviously had the requisite background for a confidence trickster: besides his experience as a clerk, he had "acted as a comedian with applause." The aptly named Allman had some experience slipping into other roles.[64]

An even bolder trickster was Moses Rainey, an attorney and legal clerk who spent a year working for Daniel Dulany in Maryland. Under the pretext of setting off on a short business trip, Rainey absconded to Philadelphia and New York. There, far enough from Annapolis that no one knew him but close enough for people to recognize the Dulany name, Rainey successfully convinced several people to advance him money on Dulany's account. This scheme was aided by the fact that Rainey had spent a great deal of time with Dulany's papers and was thus able to forge his signature. His experience in the legal trade had provided him with an education in the broader habits of gentility and the narrower details of his master's finances. Dulany, fearing the loss of his money and reputation, advertised in the *Pennsylvania Gazette* and begged its readers not to accept any bills, notes, or letters in his name.[65]

The danger of forged handwriting was also known to London factors. In 1757 the banking firm David Barclay and Sons wrote to one of its biggest New York clients, Mary Alexander, that a letter of credit drawn from her account had missed its intended recipient, a young military officer, before he left for New York. Thus, "in Case [the letter of credit] should by accident fall into any dishonest hands," the Barclays enclosed a copy of the young man's handwriting for her to compare before she advanced him any money or credit. In such a complex fiscal system, however, no safeguards could entirely eliminate the chance of fraud.[66]

Even publicly backed bills of exchange offered some scope for a bold swindler. In 1747 the governor of Massachusetts advertised the theft or loss of four blank bills of exchange signed by him and Charles Knowles and drawn on "the Paymaster General of his Majesty's forces." As a sign of how local and individual the marketplace seemed at the middle of the century, Governor Shirley added a description of the bills: "wrote upon single half sheets of demy paper, in a small round hand." Yet the chance that the bills had slipped far beyond the borders of Massachusetts Bay evidently worried the governor, since he advertised their disappearance also in the Philadelphia newspaper. A merchant in New York who read the papers diligently and promptly might know not to accept any of these bills; anyone who missed the advertisement might find the bills rejected and his pocket considerably poorer.[67]

Given the fluidity and vibrancy of New York's population and markets, it is no surprise that the most famous trickster of colonial North America found his way there on several occasions. Tom Bell's travels through the other British colonies allowed him the opportunity to try different sorts of scams: stealing a borrowed horse, robbing a host's house, and more than once passing himself off as a minister. His frauds in New York, however, were all financial. On his first trip in 1738 he employed the same ruse that Moses Rainey had used in 1736: appropriating the name of an elite family from a colony near enough for it to be recognizable but too far to be easily confirmed. Bell borrowed the Connecticut name Wentworth to forge a letter of credit from the Bostonian William Bowdoin. The fraud was discovered, and Bell was sentenced to be whipped and sent out of the colony; yet he somehow managed to procure a pardon from the governor.[68] Bell later admitted to the fraud but shrugged it off as a youthful indiscretion. New Yorkers, however, did not take it so lightly; for more than a decade after the original crime, the local papers continued to print "sightings" of Tom Bell, with warnings to guard against his next potential swindle.[69]

The newspapers were right to warn New Yorkers to be suspicious of Bell. His next New York swindle occurred in 1743, and like its predecessor, it relied on the facade of gentility and the flaws of financial credit. When Bell reappeared in New York after a five-year absence, his first move—and the one that caught the eye of suspicious New Yorkers—was to obtain a new set of clothes, one of the most obvious and persuasive signs of gentility. His story, however, was commercial: he claimed that he needed to inform the city's merchants of his considerable loss at sea and could do so only in the proper attire.[70]

Status and commerce play supporting roles in Tom Bell's story. Like many young men, Bell knew that his credibility depended on his fashionable appearance; dressed in a suit of clothes appropriate to his pretended status, a swindler was far more likely to persuade potential investors to pay out more money. Con artists could exploit the fact that many people did not look beyond a first appearance of gentility. However, Bell's attempted scam reveals more than a flaw in the practices of politeness. By looking for new clothes to create his persona as a failed merchant, Bell harnessed the overseas element of his story to the genteel impression that he sought to make in a face-to-face encounter. His goal was twofold: one, to convince merchants that they could trust the well-dressed man who stood before them with a tale of woe; and two, to spin a story whose overseas nature made it difficult to verify. With this swindle, Bell neatly pegged the flaws in New Yorkers' systems of local and long-distance credit. Only his fame spoiled his scheme.

The interrelated effects of gentility and commerce are at the heart of a final display of fraud. Gerard G. Beekman must have seemed a perfect target for a confidence man who wanted to exploit bills of exchange. Beekman's wide and varied commercial contacts had accustomed him to dealing with many different clients and correspondents, and his great success as a merchant was the result of his willingness to take risks in the hope of turning a profit. In August 1754 a young man named William Ashburner arrived in New York from Jamaica. He introduced himself to Beekman and asked him to honor £1,100 worth of bills of exchange that had been drawn and dated in Jamaica against credit in London firms. Ashburner had no letters of credit or introduction, and Beekman was at first wary of accepting bills from a man whom he had never met. He wrote to William Lloyd, his agent in Jamaica, and asked him to check Ashburner's reputation with a man whose name the young man had given him. He also asked Lloyd to check up on the signers of the bills of exchange to ensure that they had in fact authorized withdrawals on their London accounts.

Despite his suspicions, Beekman nonetheless saw opportunities in Ashburner. The young man claimed an interest in exporting grain to the West Indies, and Beekman thought it worth his while to join the project. He bankrolled half of the cargo and persuaded Ashburner to send his vessel to Lloyd for distribution in Jamaica. Beekman wrote to Lloyd, "tho it is a small Cargo it may Interduce more business for the future."[71]

Before Beekman heard back from Jamaica, Ashburner returned to him with a number of New Yorkers who vouched that the man he claimed as his father was a "Gentleman of Good fortune, family, and Credit at Lancaster." Ashburner was indeed the name of a Lancaster family, but they apparently gave William little financial backing, even though he actually belonged to this family. Beekman, however, was not the only New Yorker to be duped by William's talent for donning the mask of gentility. Perhaps thinking that he still needed to convince his creditor of his credibility, Ashburner bought himself a suit of black clothes a few days later and told Beekman that he was in mourning for an uncle who had "Left him an Estate of five Thousand a year and a place in Particular Called ashburners Hall." He showed Beekman a letter, purportedly from his sister, that announced the news.[72]

Not wanting to raise Beekman's suspicions any higher, Ashburner suggested that Beekman advance him only four hundred pounds of the bills, leaving the rest until the first set had passed muster in London. He also assured the older man that he would not skip town but would wait in New York until his sloop was ready to go back to Jamaica. At the time Beekman thought that "this all appeared very honist in him" and lent him the four hundred pounds against the bills of exchange, which Beekman immediately sent off to London. The merchant also sent some of his goods to Jamaica by Ashburner's sloop.

Beekman was in the habit of extending small loans to less wealthy gentlemen or merchants at interest, so his willingness to lend money to Ashburner is not a simple example of misplaced credulity. As a merchant who believed it was a waste of capital to allow it to "lay dead," he was looking for any pecuniary opportunity,[73] and the hope of making nearly fifty pounds as commission for endorsing the bills of exchange would have tempted any merchant.

Only a few days after the sloop lifted anchor for Jamaica, Beekman stumbled across the first hint that Ashburner was "Guilty of so much Villainy that none but the Greatest Rogues would Venture to Commit." The young man had forged a receipt and a note from a local ship captain, who threatened to press charges. Beekman, "out of regard to [Ashburner's] Youth and family," paid the twenty-eight pounds in question to Captain Price. Now very suspicious, Beekman worried that the bills of exchange were forged. He wanted his four hundred pounds back from Ashburner. Knowing that the young man did not have the cash, he began to arrange to have Ashburner's sloop and the cargo made over to his name for security. Before he could do so, however, Ashburner slipped away to Philadelphia.

Beekman had been right: all the bills of exchange from Ashburner that he had sent to London were forged. Beekman was livid, and not only because he had to pay 20 percent in penalties on the forged bills when they were refused in London.[74] By his account, he had lost an additional £230 in damages because of this encounter.[75] Beekman told his fellow merchants in Philadelphia, Jamaica, and London to apprehend Ashburner. Although one friend managed to track the young man down in Philadelphia, Ashburner soon slipped off to Jamaica. The forged bills were publicized in the Jamaica newspapers, and the London merchants offered a reward for finding the forger, but Ashburner disappeared for good. Ten years later Beekman was still trying to track down this confidence man.[76]

A plausible story, a set of fashionable clothes, a doctored letter, a facility in handwriting: exploiting the fundamental contradiction of bills of exchange did not require many props. In a scam developed for long-distance trade, the presence of these bills in the hands of strangers was both necessary and problematic. Doing what he could to hedge his bets, Beekman had tried to determine Ashburner's creditworthiness and reputation, but the distances were too far and the possibilities of gain were too great. Ashburner's story fit the pattern of much of Beekman's business: local trade with international implications. Beekman gambled on both his personal impressions of Ashburner and the credit networks that underlay bills of exchange, and he lost on both counts.

Justice Daniel Horsmanden himself found charges of itinerancy and poverty could overthrow even an established political elite. In September of 1747, the governor removed Horsmanden from his council. Although the governor was clear that he ejected Horsmanden because he felt the man was the leader of a cabal against him, in his explanation of the dismissal, Governor Clinton gave financial instability as the leading reason. The governor accused the justice of having "no visible Estate in this Province, or anywhere else that is known; he left England deeply in Debt; has since contracted considerable Debts in this Province. . . ." Equally suspicious was his marriage to a rich widow.

Ashburner is rare in being one of the few successful con artists whose swindles are preserved in the historical records. Newspapers and court documents tend to record only the failures. He succeeded because he was able to flee New York City before his bills of exchange bounced and he could be exposed as a thief and a fraud. His credibility, in other words, was only temporary, but his victory was permanent.

Credit in eighteenth-century New York City meant both fiscal solvency and personal reputation. In a world with few consumer protections, all commercial transactions depended on the appearance of probity in one's trading partner. Those with access to credit-based forms of currency never imagined refusing to use them, but there were risks inherent in their expanded use. New Yorkers did their best to reduce risk by using cultural assumptions of trustworthiness, especially class status and masculinity. This system offered abundant opportunities for abuse, however, and many entrepreneurial confidence artists took advantage of the offer. They used commercial markers of gentlemanly status, such as fashionable clothes and letters of introduction, in order to exploit the modes of commercial exchange that depended on both personal interactions and long-distance exchange.

These colorful confidence artists embodied the eighteenth-century relationship between commerce, status, and trust. The broker between the three was the British Empire, and particularly the way that a port city on the edge of empire was forced to maintain its long-distance commercial ties. In New York, commerce based on "the currency of reputation" was fundamental to its economic functioning. One of the unexpected results of this culture of credit was that ideas about status were themselves altered by the practices of imperial commerce. Though status was essential to commercial enterprise in imperial New York, because the markers of status were so fluid and uncertain, they had less value and authority than some merchants hoped. The nature of status made it both powerful and uncertain. Was a gentleman truly a gentleman? Was he credible? On what grounds should one take him as trustworthy and extend him credit?

Counterfeiters and con artists could exploit the mercurial nature of status because financial trust ultimately rested on personal relationships. However, credit under such circumstances was not always fraud. Legitimate traders also used their claims to status and their personal relationships to extend their credit networks. One set of traders created claims to credit based on a particular nexus of gender and personal connections, and the fluidity of status at the margins of empire made those claims both viable and dangerous.

Chapter Two
Webs of Dependence

In 1724 Cadwallader Colden, a member of the New York Council and the colony's surveyor general, asked his London agent for help setting up a game for his young children. In exchange for a small bag of specie, Colden hoped his correspondent would be willing to send over a few goods as a "small Adventure." He wanted them, he explained, "to please a litle boy & Girl who want to be merchants as soon as they can speak like their play fellows the Dutch Children here." Colden's offhand comment reveals the pervasiveness of trade in the lives of men and women, British as well as Dutch. Even a conservative British official found it easy to imagine that his young son and daughter would both want to become merchants, and Colden's kind thought may well have shown them how to harness the market to their advantage. Yet, despite an equal start, the little boy and girl whom Colden set up as merchants were unlikely to have the same experience. Webs of family and empire would have shaped the two children's interactions in the market quite differently.[1]

The markets that were emerging in the early modern Atlantic world allowed all sorts of people to participate: women, slaves, servants, and sailors, in addition to con artists, forgers, and elite men such as Colden. Nonetheless, these markets were bound by the powerful fictions of their time. This was not a world of limitless possibilities but one structured by Anglo-Americans' deeply held beliefs about the nature of social status. In imperial New York, ideologies of markets and gender came together in complex and contradictory ways to construct the Anglo-American marketplace.

Because the eighteenth-century marketplace was created out of the personal transactions between participants, their relationships, both actual and idealized, are central to understanding the nature of imperial commerce. Women's legal and economic practices both overrode and were constrained by the common-law fiction of coverture, the idea that women had no legal standing in commerce. Under coverture, married women could not take their trade partners to court, but neither could they be sued for debt, since the debts that they had in fact amassed were not legally theirs but their husbands'. The commercial networks that women developed within and beyond the limits of their families reveal how female status both helped and hindered their trading activities. These activities also combined the domestic and the imperial; as their letters and business papers make clear, women's participation in trade brought the British Empire directly into New York's homes and families.

To say that white women were regular traders in the Atlantic market is not to assert that they became financially self-sufficient. Women as a group never became fiscally independent even in an open market. Instead, ironically, these family relationships that appeared to trammel women were precisely the ones that gave them access to trading networks.[2]

The complex relationship between gender and commerce that is apparent in early eighteenth-century New York was related to a wider unsettling of gender ideology in the British Empire. For much of the eighteenth century, popular and political discussions of Britain's colonial project were predicated on ideas of sexual difference. Expansion and maintenance of the empire were masculinist projects whose hope was to make Britons feel more secure about their masculinity by comparing them favorably to effeminized natives and slaves.[3] Yet in an empire whose ideology was also predicated on the idea of open trade, the participation of women (at least white women) in transatlantic markets was an accepted corollary to imperial ideology.

The networks of imperial commerce in which both men and women traded were created through the family network and particularly through marriage. Commercial credit and familial credit were often one and the same.[4] For most women, these family connections really did represent how the commercial empire functioned. Exceptions arose, of course, and some women traded without family connections, but even for these traders, their experiences in the market were shaped by the gender conventions of the eighteenth-century world.

Just as men's dependence on other men for credit could be fraught with risk, so could the credit relationships between men and women. Women also both enjoyed and extended credit, although in circumstances quite different from those of men; they used *preexisting* connections, usually of family. As we will see, women may have been limited to some degree by the laws of marriage, but those same limitations were part of the kin-based system that allowed women to participate in and influence the imperial system. Their participation in imperial trade through these family networks could be profitable, but it was also attended by certain risks never encountered by their male counterparts.

Coverture and Gendered Commerce

Most general histories of New York have duly noted the presence of female traders. For the most part, such women have been seen as hold-overs from the days of Dutch settlement, when Dutch women were famed for their trading abilities. Early modern Dutch property law, in contrast to English common law, allowed women to own and transfer property regardless of their marital status. This approach to a "family business," in which women were equal partners, led to women's active participation in seventeenth-century transatlantic trade.[5]

The introduction of coverture to New York's law code in 1664 both damaged women's property rights and productively shaped their partici-pation in the market. Under English common law a married woman had no independent economic or legal status: she could not take on debt, sue or be sued, or fulfill contracts. Her husband, on the other hand, had total control over any property she brought to the marriage unless there was a prenuptial agreement. As the British legal commentator Sir Wil-liam Blackstone explained, "By marriage, the husband and wife are one person in law: that is, the very being or legal existence of the woman is suspended during the marriage, or at least incorporated and consoli-dated into that of the husband: under whose wing, protection, and *cover*, she performs every thing; and is therefore called . . . a *feme-covert*."[6] Clearly, a married woman's legal inability to borrow against credit and a creditor's inability to collect a debt from her in court might well have had a chilling effect on her ability to conduct commercial activity. How-ever, coverture also represented the incorporation of a woman into her husband's financial and in some cases commercial networks. The com-ing of the English did not spell immediate doom for the women of New Amsterdam.[7]

To explore the place of white women in Britain's commercial empire is not to engage in a debate over whether women's status improved or worsened during the eighteenth century. Instead, the more revealing question is how coverture shaped the experiences of women who traded in the British Empire. Questions of coverture in colonial courts have been well and carefully researched, and most historians have found that it was used effectively to exclude women from the financial realm. Credi-tors did not want to lose the chance to recover their loans legally. Unlike local transactions, though, transatlantic trade was not impeded by the same concerns over timely debt collection. In international trade net-works, coverture was rarely invoked for two reasons, one legal and the other familial.

Nearly without exception, London merchants did not sue in local courts. Rather, they cut off credit.[8] Most merchants clearly preferred that bad debts never go to court, so they tried to keep a negative balance with their debtors as a cushion.[9] Other disputes might be handled through arbitration, which a New York merchant claimed was the route to the "most speedy & just determination, rather than be put to the expence [*sic*] of two or three lingering Law Suits that may be spun out for Years in the way the Law is here."[10]

Even when coverture would not have informed the decision to bring a debtor to court—in the case of a widow or a man—merchants rarely went to court to collect, preferring instead to try to maintain their trading relationships. Thus, when Waddell Cunningham found himself holding a bad debt from Richard Fulton in Halifax, he did not try to recover the money in court. Rather, he asked another Halifax merchant to try to recover the money for a commission. At the same time he wrote the debtor a stiff note reminding him of the "trouble" to which he was putting the New York merchant and implying that Cunningham was unlikely to do business with him again. Cunningham's curt note moved directly and sarcastically to the matter at hand: "Sir: You may remember when you give [*sic*] your note to Captain Deane, it was to be paid immediately. But certainly you have let that part of the bargain escape your memory, or you would not give me so much trouble to send your note by so many hands."[11] Cunningham was clearly annoyed by the time and effort it took for him to recover his debt, but he threatened Fulton with losing his business rather than with a lawsuit. This refusal of international traders to use the courts to recover debts makes the formal use of coverture relatively marginal to understanding women's role in international networks.

When one considers family networks as the basis of imperial trade, it becomes clear that focusing only on the restrictive nature of coverture cannot explain the dynamic relationship between gender and markets. The legal restrictions placed on married women did not force them out of the international marketplace altogether. Rather, the most significant impact that coverture had on British transatlantic trade was on the structure of family networks. That is, coverture reveals not the ways in which women's participation in the market was limited but the ways in which it was channeled.

Contemporary fears about credit dictated the cultural work of gender in the marketplace. Civic humanists such as Alexander Pope understood from the beginning that commercial markets were intimately linked to issues of dependence.[12] These early modern theorists, moreover, regularly associated ideas of the feminine with dependence, particularly economic dependence. Many early eighteenth-century Britons feared that the webs of dependence and credit created by the commercial empire opened the door to luxury and effeminacy.[13] Eventually, as Britain embraced the power of commerce as a facet of its imperial expansion, the market came to be a "space of manly fortitude."[14] As the link between commerce and status, credit was only as meaningful as the relationships of those extending and receiving it. Performances of both rank and gender completely permeated the granting of credit and credibility. Good credit was based on appropriately gentlemanlike behavior. At the same time, however, the idea of credit, especially in its inverted form of indebtedness, was often seen as feminine. However, what these early modern theorists did not quite recognize was that the webs of credit were not so much effeminizing as reliant on familial gender hierarchies of coverture and female dependence, both legal and customary. In other words, webs of credit were structured on webs of dependence.

Granted, women's importance in the British Empire and its economy was partly symbolic. As Britannia, the female figure represented "national virtue and martial potency." Moreover, the presence of women in certain social situations also indicated cultured civility and sensibility. Yet during the first two-thirds of the eighteenth century, women's place in the British Empire was far more than symbolic. Before the 1760s white women's role in the British Empire was as much to facilitate trade as it was to demarcate class and race.

As we will see, print and other representations of New York women depicted them as active economic participants in the British Empire. Moreover, these women contributed a different sort of cultural work to the eighteenth-century empire. Instead of drawing the boundaries between colony and metropole, they helped construct an image of a mercantile empire in which women and men wove trading webs across the Atlantic. For New Yorkers, the ocean between ports in the British archipelago and ports in North America was less a barrier than a highway. Their family ties, oppressive as they may have been in legal terms, provided the routes.

Women and Trade

When it came to international trade, the presence of women in credit relationships and distribution networks mediated both the values and practices of gender in the British Empire. Despite the persistence of coverture in New York law, male merchants did not treat women as invisible entities. In addition, many women who were not bound by coverture (and who thus had no legal restrictions on their ability to hold property) supported themselves and their families through trading imported goods. Even married women acting as "deputy husbands" or trading under their husbands' names were part of these networks. Nor were the women the only beneficiaries of their trade; the men who acted as their agents or suppliers also benefited. Far from intentionally trying to uphold patriarchy through international commerce, most male traders never inquired into a woman's married status—to their occasional detriment, as some women used this legal loophole to their advantage. Elizabeth Fairday managed to convince the New York Mayor's Court on three different occasions that she could not be held liable for her debts because she was married at the time she contracted them. In another case, an importer of Madeira was able to convince the court that the woman he sued for nonpayment should be forced to pay, but only after he proved that her husband was a bigamist and thus she was not truly a *feme covert*.[15]

More common is the case of the wife of Arendt Schuyler. Although there are no records of Swantje Van Duyckhuysen Schuyler's business, by 1695 her husband had moved from Albany to New York City, where he was made a freeman of the city and became known as a trader. By 1710 he had bought a farm in New Jersey, from which he made a fortune in copper mining. Sometime after the purchase of his farm, he accused another well-known New York merchant, Samuel Bayard, of owing money to him "for that which his [Schuyler's] wife had sent." Bayard replied that he had indeed paid him, but in New Jersey bills; if Schuyler did not want this form of payment, Bayard added, he would be happy to credit him on his account. Clearly, the original transaction had been between Swantje Schuyler and Bayard, but Bayard and Arendt Schuyler understood that the accounts were held in Arendt's name, not Swantje's. Such cases show that even when coverture was formally upheld, it was not a minor barrier to women trading.[16] Certainly, patriarchy and coverture were essential parts of British transatlantic trade, although not merely as ways to limit women's economic power. More significant, instead, are the ways that women's relatively dependent places in their families—as sisters, nieces, and mothers as well as wives—colored British eighteenth-century capitalism. These family relationships structured not only women's places at home but also their networks abroad.

Customhouse records from the early eighteenth century show how women participated in various segments of the market, especially through their familial connections. In a six-year period at the beginning of the century, for example, customs officials recorded that the widow Helena Rombouts exported large quantities of furs to London; the value of her exports exceeded most if not all of those of other merchants on the ships on which she traded. Rombouts also imported large quantities of rum from Nevis, Barbados, and elsewhere in the West Indies.[17] When Andrew Douglass of Surinam died in 1707, his estate recorded fifty-seven pounds of molasses and rum that he had exported for Rombouts on her account.[18] These records date from more than a decade after the death of Rombout's husband Francis, thus proving that she negotiated her transactions for at least that length of time. In other words, these transactions were not exchanges that Francis had initiated and Helena completed after his death; they indicate instead that she continued to use and expand her husband's trade. As the wife of a New York merchant and the daughter of an Albany fur trader, Rombouts no doubt had extensive connections through both her marriage and her natal family on which to draw as she sought trading partners in London and the West Indies. As a woman with capital, she was able to parlay her position as a wife and daughter into successful trading ventures.[19]

The names of other women, about whose families we know little or nothing, are scattered throughout the customhouse and other records. The sources are too spotty for their numbers to be quantified, but the qualitative evidence makes it clear that women imported the same goods as men, sometimes in tiny quantities and sometimes in amounts that made them the merchants with the most to lose on any given ship. Women such as Catherine Apple, Amity Clutterback, and Helena Cooper exported furs and imported dry goods, rum, and "shot."[20] The goods and amounts they traded did not noticeably differ from those of men in the import/export business.

An unusually clear example of the ways women's economic activities were hidden in the archive comes from the records held by the New York merchant Christopher Bancker. Bancker nominally held an account for Lieutenant John Pinhorne. His remarks in the business's journal, however, reveal that this account was used by both John and his wife Gertrude. In June 1749 Bancker noted that he had paid some cash out of John Pinhorne's account "to his wife." Gertrude claimed some of Bancker's profits in cash with some regularity throughout that summer. Gertrude may have been using her family connections to the West Indies for some of her business.[21] Later in June, for example, Bancker noted a credit to "John Pinhorne and his wife" of "250 Spanish milled pieces 8/8 received from cuacoa per the sloop *Three Brothers* John Rivers master £100, minus £2 freight." Further evidence that Gertrude was a primary actor in the business dealings of the couple comes from Bancker's note the following fall that he had paid out to a third party from the John Pinhorne account "for a bill of exchange drawne on his wife for £20 Sterling."[22]

The same restrictions brought about by coverture mean that it is difficult to determine whether a legal motion for debt or breach of contract resulted from women's economic activity or men's. The terminology of the records also disguises women's participation in the market; most of the sources that historians traditionally use to discover employment—court records and city directories—rarely identify women by their occupation. Rather, even while women's own testimonies in court cases demónstrated their active involvement in trade, often on their own or in partnership with other women, these same witnesses defined themselves by their husbands' occupation. Their reticence was the result of the fact that their own profit-seeking endeavors did not have the recognizable apparatus of apprenticeship or other hierarchical configurations that constituted men's work. Thus, women's work did not seem to constitute an identity.[23]

Yet even when historians' sources hide the presence of women in trade, it is clear that the traders' contemporaries understood perfectly that these women were economic actors. Thus when Ann Elizabeth Schuyler, a merchant with an extensive trade network, was robbed in 1735, the court records identified her simply as a "widow," although the same case made it clear that the goods were stolen from her shop.[24] Although Schuyler did not define herself as a merchant, her business interactions with other women and men made it clear that trading was how she spent her time. In another case, the importer Cornelius Lodge was presented by a grand jury for using false measures to sell his merchandise. Lodge argued to the court, however, that he was not responsible because "his wife used a Yard not his."[25] In fact, although the historical record occludes women's economic activities, their exchanges were never hidden from their families, neighbors, and trading part-ners.[26] Coverture, in other words, may be almost as important for shaping later interpretations of eighteenth-century commerce as it was for its participants.

One midcentury trader exemplifies most of the trading and familial networks that the British Empire offered to women. Mary Spratt Provoost Alexander became one of the wealthiest women in New York, thanks to her elite family connections and her trading acumen. Alexander parlayed her Dutch and English origins into an immense fortune. Her Dutch grandmother, Cornelia DePeyster, was a major merchant in her own right; in 1695 she was rated as one of the wealthiest people in New York. Alexander's mother, Maria Shrick Spratt, ran her husbands' mercantile businesses after their successive deaths. When Shrick married her second husband, John Spratt, in 1687, in lieu of a mutual will they signed a prenuptial agreement to join their fortunes: "all the 'advantages, conquests, and benefits' which shall be made during the time of their matrimony shall be held in common." When one spouse died, the other was to receive half of the estate (the rest would go to their children, including Mary).[27] This traditionally Dutch way of thinking about the family fortune boosted the trading enterprises of both mother and daughter.

Alexander's first husband, Samuel Provoost, was a Dutch merchant who left his fortune to his widow absolutely when he died in 1719. Two years later she married her second husband, a Scottish émigré in search of a fortune. Despite his British origins, James Alexander was not necessarily more patriarchal than Provoost had been, as James's will also left everything to Mary absolutely. Long before her second husband's death in 1756, Alexander used her financial and personal capital to become one of the most successful traders in the city. As both a merchant and a shopkeeper, she participated in both local and international markets, importing large amounts of dry goods, china, and groceries from the London merchants Samuel Storke and David Barclay and retailing her imports to residents of New York City, Albany, and New Jersey.[28]

Although other aspects of Alexander's affairs closely resembled those of other women merchants, her wealth brought parts of her business into a realm quite different from those of small and middling traders. With a sufficiently high volume of trade, she could consolidate her imports through just one or two London factors. She was able to reduce her shipping costs considerably by purchasing a one-sixth share in a sloop. Most of all, she focused her attention on imports and retailing rather than on exporting local goods.[29]

At Alexander's death in 1760, David Barclay and Sons drew up an account of the previous three years of her business. From 1758 through 1760 they laid out £10,901.10.3 on her account. Much of this was for annuities they purchased for her, but 57 percent of the disbursements, or £5,692 of £9,873, was for goods sent to New York. They sent shipments ranging from £206 to £1,308. She steadily repaid her debt by sending over endorsed bills of exchange. Although she had to spend time dunning her local customers for debts as small as a few pounds, Alexander kept her account with the Barclays free.[30] At the end of 1758 she had over £300 in credit, and at her death the Barclays disbursed over £15,568 back to her heirs.[31] Alexander was not only wealthy; in addition, her exchange patterns were identical to those of male merchants who routinely imported goods on large credit from British mercantile houses.

Nonetheless, despite the unusually large sums that constituted Alexander's business, her transactions were still limited and shaped by coverture and by the overlap of her business transactions with those of her husband. Business papers indicate that Mary's profit was occasionally paid into James's account, as when in 1737 Alexander's factor Samuel Storke credited fifteen barrels of rice and a box of skins marked "M[ary] A[lexander]" to James's account.[32] On the other hand, James occasionally made note of the occasions when he collected money for Mary or on her account, such as the £4.4 he "Rec'd for my wife of Tho.

Harding" in 1742 or the £12 John Can paid "to my wife on her account" the year before.[33]

At her death in 1760, Alexander's obituary gave equal weight to her commercial success and her family connections. After referring to her as the "relict" of the Honorable James Alexander and the mother of the "present Earl of Stirling," it observed that "She was for many Years past, a very eminent Trader, in this Place."[34] Alexander's success may have been unusual, but the style of her obituary is not, as the two other obituaries in the same issue of the paper show. The death of the wife of the merchant Henry Cruger is reported in two lines, with no mention of her name; her identity is entirely subsumed in his. Benjamin Nichol, however, "one of the most eminent Lawyers on the Continent," earned fourteen lines of text. Though the great bulk of Nichol's obituary concerns his public life, it concludes by noting the loss to his family of "a most excellent Husband, Father, and Master." For both Nichol and Alexander, their family and business lives each merited a mention in their obituaries. Yet the description of Nichol's private life continues the panegyric of his public life; his family members remain unnamed, and their status as wife or child can be ascertained only from the description of Nichol himself. Alexander's obituary, on the other hand, carefully names the specific men in her family by whom she would have been known. Like Mrs. Cruger, she is identified, at least in part, through her familial relationships, and these are noted first. Yet this stock description is immediately followed by the reference to Alexander's unusual identity as a trader. As extraordinary as her obituary is, its two halves are typical of the cultural structures underlying women's trade in New York. Alexander's eminence as a trader may have been the result of her fine business acumen or her grandmother's fortune, but it was always structured through her relationships with the male legal actors of her family, especially her husband.

Ann Elizabeth Schuyler's extant account book, covering the years 1739–42, offers a snapshot of a middling trader's accounts. Her credit was much smaller than Mary Alexander's; every spring she sent between £22 and £45 in specie to Bernard van der Grift in Amsterdam, compared to the several hundred pounds of more complex bills of exchange that Alexander sent to her bankers. Schuyler managed to trade on a smaller scale by leasing room in other merchants' trunks when ships sailed from London. In August 1740, for example, Roderigo Pacheco sent her four different shipments of goods, ranging from £9 to £157, on four different ships. Schuyler also exported foodstuffs twice each year to Curaçao, which allowed her to build credit that could be used for her imports.

Schuyler's husband, John Schuyler, was also a merchant with business connections of his own. Whether Ann Elizabeth, after his death in 1722, used the connections that he had established for her own business is difficult to assess; she left few other papers. It is clear, however, that she took every opportunity possible to extend the reach of her commercial activity. Schuyler's account book reveals the myriad ways a woman could participate in the market. She gave cash for bonds, swapped goods with other merchants (including James Alexander), sold merchandise for other women, and occasionally accepted payment in produce. At times ship captains paid for their own or their wives' purchases with other imported goods. Schuyler extended credit for up to two years, but most of her customers repaid their loans within six months. Compared to Alexander's trading patterns, Schuyler's, like those of most middling traders, had to depend on a wider array of partners and shipping options. Her methods of payment also were far more diverse and haphazard. Yet, while Schuyler could not afford to specialize, her wide-flung trading network testifies to the number of markets that were accessible to middling women.[35]

Other records hint at the relationship between Schuyler's trading practices and her male relatives. It appears that after her husband died, she went into business with her son Brandt. When he died in 1752, she advertised that those to whom his estate owed money "or also against Ann Elizabeth Schuyler" should bring in their accounts to "the said Ann Elizabeth Schuyler" to be paid. Likewise, those indebted either to Brandt Schuyler's estate or to her were asked to pay up. Presumably, upon her son's death, the partnership dissolved.[36]

The fuller record of Margaret Vetch, another middling merchant, shows how networks, within and beyond the family, structured eighteenth-century women's trade. In 1700 Margaret Livingston had married Samuel Vetch, a Scottish adventurer, smuggler, and political striver. When his commitment to the "Glorious Enterprise" of wresting Nova Scotia from France required frequent trips to London, Margaret began trading in his absence. Her commercial ventures were first recorded in 1707, when she imported a small shipment of dry goods; in 1709 she sent beaver skins to Boston. Vetch then followed her husband's political career to Boston, Nova Scotia, and (in 1717) London, but in 1732, when he died there in debtors' prison, she returned to New York and reestablished herself in trade. Even before her return she had already begun to import rum from London to New York, perhaps in an attempt to pay some of her husband's debt. She appears to have been trading in dry goods again by 1737. In 1742 her nephew in Boston tried to collect a debt from one of her agents in that city. In 1744 the merchant-shopkeeper Nicholas Bayard paid her his full debt, amounting to over eighty-four pounds. In 1748 she imported wine, and in 1753 she wrote to her agent in Jamaica advising him on the selling of her candles. In

1752 she and thirty-eight other shopkeepers (one of whom also did business with Ann Elizabeth Schuyler) agreed to give the shopkeeper Obadiah Wells one year to collect his debts without fear of arrest. She died in 1758 at the age of seventy-seven after half a century of economic activity. At her death, her grandson William Bayard sold the remainder of her stock in dry goods, including "a large quantity of the best Silks, of all sorts [and] golden and silver lace."[37] At a time when the market in fine fabrics and fashion was gathering steam, Vetch had wisely stocked up. (See Figure 3.)

Throughout her career Margaret Vetch had family contacts in London for her dry goods, in Boston for the selling of her furs, in the West Indies for her rum, and presumably in southern Europe for her wine. One could imagine Vetch in her last decade running a bilateral trade to the West Indies, exporting spermaceti candles in return for rum. With the profits from selling rum to New York tavern keepers whose businesses were too small to allow them to handle their own imports, Vetch might have purchased yet more goods to be sold in the West Indies. Vetch's business dealings were notably diversified; for other candle shipments she requested her agent to send the proceeds to merchants in London.[38]

A letter to a fellow merchant in Jamaica hints at the number of connections one needed for eighteenth-century commerce. Vetch was well attuned to swings in the market, and she could change her plans accordingly. In 1753 Vetch shipped some goods to her agent in Jamaica, Peter Dubois. Upon receiving them, he informed her that he could not profitably sell the candles that she had sent. Vetch's response indicates the extent of her knowledge both of the Atlantic markets and of the people she needed to take advantage of those markets. She wrote back to Dubois, "am Sorry markets are so Dull, and Candles give so low a price, which makes it difficult to advise what to do, as I am informed they give a good Price at Antigua." She directed him either to send the candles to her nephew Henry Livingston in Antigua or to leave them with James Banyan in Jamaica. Presumably all three men had had some experience with Vetch's business. Moreover, it is clear that Vetch had access to the same information as other merchants did; her business transactions did not suffer from her ignorance of "dull markets."[39]

These three women traders—Mary Alexander, Ann Elizabeth Schuyler, and Margaret Vetch—were all members of old New York families, but the family connections they used in establishing their businesses were not identical.[40] Alexander, for example, had access to the impressive business networks of the women in her family. She also inherited both trade connections and cash from her first husband. Margaret Vetch likewise used her extensive natal family connections to sustain her trad-

Figure 3. This portrait of Margaret Vetch and her first child, Alida (named for her grandmother), painted while Margaret's husband was still alive, evokes the ties between trade and family. Collection of the Museum of the City of New York.

ing networks. However, her resources, unlike Alexander's, came primarily from the men in her family. Vetch's father, Robert Livingston of Livingston Manor, had become one of the wealthiest and most powerful men in New York, and his wife Alida was renowned as one of the finest businesswomen in the colonies. Unlike Alexander's mother and grandmother, however, Alida Livingston did not smooth the way for Margaret to become an eminent trader like herself. Like other Dutch trading families, the Livingstons provided business education not for their daughters but for their sons, sending them to trade under the eye of a relative or associate. While the Livingstons did not provide their daughters with either the capital or the specialized training for commerce that they gave to their sons, Margaret nonetheless benefited from her natal family's connections in the world of trade. When she returned from London to New York in 1732, her brothers and their sons were established in trading ports around North America, Europe, and the West Indies; Margaret had no trouble taking advantage of her connections to her male relatives.[41]

Similarly, a woman might inherit capital but move beyond her nuclear family to invest it in trade. In the same 1724 letter in which he asked for goods for children to use to "play merchant," Cadwallader Colden wrote to his London supplier about Elizabeth Hill, his widowed aunt in Philadelphia. He placed a first order of dry goods for her, to be paid on her account, and explained that she had "a considerable Sum of Money by her which she intends to employ in Trade if she be not discouraged in the beginning." Hill used her nephew and his agent to establish her initial trading networks.[42]

As Vetch did with her nephews, Judith Jay joined forces with her brother Peter to engage in trade. When they exported flour to Jamaica in 1726, they shared the costs and risks equally. As the children of an established mercantile family (their mother, Anna Maria Bayard, was related to the Van Cortlandts, Van Rensselaers, and Schuylers, all well-known trading families), the Jays easily made initial connections.[43] Nonetheless, Peter, not Judith, kept the family books, recording therein Judith's account, including the commission that he charged her. Peter acted as the middleman for a number of female New York merchants, including his cousin Elizabeth Schuyler. Judith was able to trade to the West Indies and Europe in amounts similar to those her brother invested, but only through her connection with him.[44]

The notion of women's legal and cultural dependence on their husbands and other male family members had its parallel in the patterns of women's business ventures. Most commonly, women in trade inherited both their businesses and their connections from their fathers and husbands. Preserved are the names of at least seventy women who traded in international imports; fully half of these seventy were clearly related to families with commercial interests. Elizabeth Crommelin, for example, who advertised in 1741 that she sold Florentine olive oil, was the granddaughter of Daniel Crommelin, a Huguenot refugee who had lived in both New York and the West Indies. Daniel and his son established a trading house in Amsterdam in 1733, from which they directed and supported New York business until Daniel died in 1768. Given the extremely limited trade between British ports and Italy, Elizabeth Crommelin likely got her Italian oil via her family networks in Amsterdam.[45]

Helena, or "Lena," Cooper continued her husband Caleb's import business for nineteen years after he died. Caleb's last recorded imports were in April 1705, three months before his death.[46] The imports attributed to Helena in July and August of 1705 were presumably from orders that Caleb had placed, but the thirty-four gallons of rum she imported in November 1707 were certainly ordered by Helena herself, as were the several shipments of even larger amounts that she received in 1708.[47] When Helena Cooper died in 1724, her business was so extensive that her son and daughter ran a year's worth of advertisements in the local paper to ask fellow New Yorkers to settle their claims on her estate.[48]

Helena Cooper, Helena Rombouts, Ann Elizabeth Schuyler, Margaret Vetch, Mary Alexander, and Elizabeth Hill: all of these businesswomen were widows. Moreover, many widows carried on the family business so successfully that their sons later became major merchants in their own right, benefiting from their mothers' commercial contacts. Flora Breese, whose deceased husband John had been a leather dresser, not only sold "all sorts of skins dressed and dyed" that had come from his stock but also imported mineral dyes such as "Allum, copperas, Raspt Logwood, etc." Twenty years later Sidney Breese was selling imported looking glasses and dry goods in the city. Presumably his mother's business had provided him with an entry into the world of commerce. Elizabeth Phenix, who had been married to the ship captain Alexander Phenix, provided Nicholas Bayard with sugar for retail in 1743, and she advertised goods for sale in 1760. Her son resigned from the chamber of commerce in 1772.[49]

These familial networks grew out of women's dependent status throughout the early modern world. Everywhere women were almost invariably known through their relationships with their male family members. The cultural vestiges of coverture meant that many women were known as "widows" long after their husbands had died, so that Margaret Vetch was still "Widow Vetch" to her cousin Ann Elizabeth Schuyler four years after Samuel Vetch had died.[50] These tags limited women's identities by classifying them as appendages to their male relatives, even those who were dead.[51]

It is unclear to what extent widowhood changed a woman's involvement in the international market. On one hand, far-flung business connections may have marked a new departure for a woman who now needed to support herself without the help of her husband. On the other hand, many of the women whose names show up in custom records or account books only after their husbands died may have been trading all along under their husbands' names. Although for many women widowhood marked a sharp downturn in their standard of living, especially if they inherited involved estates, recent analysis indicates that a middling woman could support herself without a husband's income. She could not do so, however, without his (and her natal family's) business contacts. Margaret Vetch's fur trade offers a good example. Vetch's brother in Albany, Philip Livingston, had supplied her with skins to sell in 1709, and yet Philip and Margaret clearly ran separate businesses. When Philip suggested to a merchant in Boston that he could draw on Margaret's debt for the skins for credit, the merchant replied, "I showed your Sister Vetch your Letter but she made answer that she was owing you no Balance . . . but rather to the Contrary." The same relationships that subordinated women to their male family members also offered middling and elite women a foothold in the market.[52]

Family connections, however, do not entirely explain women's business dealings. Although the social practices of trade were strongly influenced by the fiction of coverture, capitalist trade was not structured on gender difference. While the connections made through family ties facilitated women's businesses and their links to the larger world of imperial commerce, they were never women's only networks, as the Beekman papers show. Like other importers, James and Gerard Beekman often served as middlemen for small New York traders who wanted European goods. Their ledgers substantiate not only the ability of women to operate beyond family networks but also the inherently gender-blind nature of capitalism.

Gerard Beekman acted as a middleman for Mary Elliston and Peter Clopper. In 1759 Beekman informed his London agent that he had drawn on him for £550 in bills of exchange: £250 for Clopper and £300 for Elliston. Beekman held similar accounts for women in New York, Philadelphia, Rhode Island, and Ireland.[53] Gerard was not unusual in offering credit to female trading partners. His cousin James Beekman, for example, extended credit to three women out of every seven customers to whom he provided goods in 1755. His biggest customer, Elizabeth Bend, bought £700 of goods before 1755. Moreover, as the Beekmans' biographer has noted, women and men bought James's goods at roughly the same volume; his ledger does not suggest that all women were forced into small stores where they sold only remnants. Beekman needed both women and men in order to sustain an acceptable volume of business, and they needed him and other merchants as suppliers. None of the women to whom James provided credit was a relative.[54]

The Beekmans' accounts, like those of the three female merchants, demonstrate that women's economic networks were extensive, varied, and profitable. Given the existence (if not the practice) of coverture, their market interactions could never have been identical to men's. However, their participation in the marketplace was clearly expected and encouraged. It is the relationship of gender ideologies to the practices of a commercial empire that thus explains how women participated in the international market and yet rarely became financially independent.

Women's Representation in Courts and Print

Eighteenth-century New York was remarkable for the fluidity of its ideas about women's proper behavior. The expectation that women were and should be economic actors persisted long beyond the English conquest of the city in 1664. Women did not suffer loss of status or respect for openly engaging in the marketplace. Yet, New York was not a gender-free zone. As was true everywhere in eighteenth-century British America, certain differences between men and women were assumed to be both natural and necessary. Oddly, however, given the legal system's formal commitment to coverture, fiscal competency was not a gendered concept. Instead, the underlying conditions that supported the idea of coverture—women's dependent status and especially their weaker and sexualized bodies—pervaded legal and printed representations of women. Both legal cases for slander and literary newspaper articles show how the city's residents imagined and represented women in commerce. The emphasis on female bodies within this world of gendered commerce points to the perils faced by some women traders.

Historians have noted that most defamation suits brought by women in early New England and the Chesapeake resulted from insults to their sexual probity. Such cases are equally evident in the provincial New York courts. In 1723 Francis Judkin and his wife Anne brought a complaint against John Delap for claiming that Anne was a "common whore" and that Delap had had "carnall copulation with her." Similarly, Jane and William Osborne together brought a slander suit against Mary Webb for implying that William was not the father of Jane's child. Mary Webb had scornfully insulted William Osborne's control over his wife's sexuality by mocking, "Cuckold Dogg goe home and See what grows there for George Bragg gave your wife a Silver tanckard for knocking of her." In reply, Jane and William Osborne together accused Webb of slander.[55] It is not surprising that such slanders against a woman's virtue focus most often not on her financial identity but on her physical activity.[56]

Yet many provincial New Yorkers also envisioned the city's women as economic actors, and their economic activity and credit are the focus of at least some of the defamation cases heard by the New York Mayor's

Court. In 1720 the unmarried Mary Schamp accused Alexander Phenix (Elizabeth's husband) of slandering her. She claimed that he had harmed her good name by proclaiming (in Dutch) that "you have Already done two false Oaths so you can do well one more." Schamp took offense at being called a liar, especially since she claimed that "by her honest Care pains and Industry she . . . acquired to herself an honest and competent livelihood." Impugning her honesty, Schamp insisted, not only was an attempt to destroy her "good Name Estate and Living" but also forced her to pay out certain sums of cash, presumably to creditors. She sued for nineteen pounds in damages and won, but the court awarded her only six pence.[57]

Four years later Roger Groves sued Anne Elderton in a similar case. The plaintiff, a hatmaker, claimed that after Elderton had said "Groves is a Cheat and has Cheated me," his business fell off precipitously. Groves likewise complained that Elderton had both generally undermined his "good name fame Creditt and reputation" and specifically cost him the patronage of a particular customer. He claimed damages to his business of two hundred pounds. Again, the court found for the plaintiff but awarded only six pence in damages.[58] In both cases the jury agreed that the plaintiff's economic credit had suffered but not to the egregious extent that the plaintiff claimed. Although Schamp and Groves might not agree, the most striking facet of their two cases is that the juries did not discriminate on the basis of gender; economic reputations of women and men were equally valuable—and vulnerable.

Sometimes the threats to women's bodies and their credit were explicitly interwoven. In 1750 Cathrine Williams complained in the *New-York Weekly Journal* that "several slanderous Tongues" in addition to destroying "both my Credit, my Livelyhood, and good Name" had also threatened her life. Though she refrained from defining her "Livelyhood," she specified the slanders against her ("they have even gone so far as to call me a wicked Woman [that is, a prostitute], and a Thief, which is not so"), and she measured her fear in economically revealing terms:

To the loosing of my Livelyhood: £5000;
To the loss of my character £6000;
for fear of being killed £1000.[59]

Williams feared for her personal safety; she feared much more for her economic vitality; but her reputation, her standing with neighbors and creditors, equaled the sum of her two fears. A woman such as Williams depended for trade on relationships outside of her family, and this independence came at a heavy price. Like an overseas merchant, Williams did not turn to the courts for redress when trading relationships had gone sour; she relied on public opinion as she could best shape it in the newspapers. In the same advertisement Williams identified herself as a widow, a woman once dependent on and still defined by her husband. These threats were not against a disembodied or ungendered trader but rather against a dependent female body.

Men were not immune to physical threats in the course of their trading business, but bodily harm was not always accompanied by an injury to their reputations. When Arendt Schuyler accused Samuel of owing him and his wife Swantje money, in addition to the demand for repayment, "the said Schuyler swore severall oaths & curst & damnd this deponent & immediately gave this deponent a violent blow in the face and that the Blood gushed out whereupon this deponent commanded the peace & sent for a Constable in the meantime the said Schuyler kept striking punching & pushing this deponent after the peace was said commanded as aforesaid that after the Constable came the said Schuyler swore severall [illegible] & said that if it was not for the law he would have the hearts blood of this Deponent or to that effect."[60] This violent encounter is nonetheless also a simpler matter than the vague threats against Cathrine Williams. Schuyler may have been collecting debts on behalf of his wife, but at no point did the creditworthiness of any of the parties enter into the situation. Bayard was assaulted, nominally for not paying a debt, but he was not slandered. The attack on his body was not mirrored by an attack on his reputation.

Like their representation in the New York courts, the representation of women in print was consistent in its attribution of physical vulnerability and yet fluctuated in granting or denying them the appearance of intellectual and financial ability. At times public sympathy for women's position was evoked by casting them in the sympathetic role of the oppressed. A favorite depiction of women in print was as the helpless widow, especially one who had been reduced to poverty by her profligate spouse. This image inevitably aroused eighteenth-century pity. William Livingston, editor of the *Independent Reflector*, made frequent use of the "widow and orphan" motif to highlight the "Abuses and Encroachments" of church and state. As an indication of the myriad uses to which such an image could be put, Livingston's politicized widow most frequently protested taxes for road repair.[61]

In the New York press even the financially capable widow was used to symbolize the limits of female power. Possibly because they knew so many widows in trade, the writers of the *New-York Weekly Journal* published a jab at the governor in the voice of New York's "she-merchants," who identified themselves explicitly as "widows of the city" who "Pay our Taxes, [and] carry on Trade." Their complaint, however, was that they were politically powerless.[62]

By no means were women always represented as merchants in the New York papers. More typical were parodies that mocked female pretensions to politics, rational thought, or independent living. Most of all, these spoofs emphasized women's dependence on male family members. One week after its fictional letter from the widowed "she-merchants," the *New-York Weekly Journal* included a companion letter from "young maids" complaining that men's fascination with politics left them neglected and bored. The large number of vaguely and occasionally virulently misogynistic poems and articles about women's attempts to find husbands are typical of an early American press that took women's dependence on men for granted. The papers occasionally reprinted still more blatantly antifemale articles from London papers, such as one that lamented the end of the Roman custom of keeping women permanently under the control of male guardians (though the Romans had made the custom a mere formality seventeen centuries earlier).[63] The partial reprint of a 1731 poem by George Lyttelton encouraged women not to become engaged in trade but to be engaged to a man:

> The important Business of your Life is Love:
> To this great Point direct your Constant Aim,
> This makes your Happiness and this your Fame.[64]

Like Lyttleton, who urged women to give up the business of trade for the business of love, the papers also imagined the marketplace as an all-male space. In a jeremiad against gossip, the *New-York Weekly Journal* reprinted an article from the *South Carolina Gazette*, whose author, quoting Daniel Defoe, compared a "merchant's credit and a Virgin's virtue," both of which could be ruined by loose talk. A man's reputation might be sullied in a tavern and a woman's at the tea table. Articles such as this one defined commercial credit in purely masculine terms.[65]

Cultural constructions of women's nature were neither consistent nor coherent in New York's court decisions and newspapers. On the one hand, women's claims to a commercial reputation and financial independence were taken for granted. On the other hand, cases for sexual defamation and articles about the "Fair Sex" drew on ubiquitous and stereotypical images of women as subordinate to men and confined to their sexualized bodies. These contradictory representations undergirded the conflict between a theoretically ungendered "open" market and its strongly gendered practice. The clash between the two made women vulnerable at the very moment when they were successfully participating in their trading networks.

The Dangers of Trade

The dangers that New York's most successful women traders faced were correspondingly the most extraordinary. The story of Mary Alexander's death threat illustrates the risks of success for these women in British international trade. One winter's night in 1734, as Alexander and her husband James walked their guests to the door, they found an unsigned letter lying on the floor. While James read it aloud, the rest interrupted with exclamations of horror. The letter read:

To Mrs. Alexander, in NEW YORK.

Mrs. Alexander,
    I am one who was formerly accounted a Gentleman, but am now reduced to poverty, and have not Victuals to Eat, and knowing you to be of a generous Temperament, desire you would comply with my request, which is to let me have Ten Pistols to supply my Necessaries, and carry me to my native Country. This is a bold Request, but I desire you would comply with it, or you and your Family shall feel the Effects of my Displeasure; unless you let me have them, I'll destroy you and your Family, by a Stratagem which I have Contrived. If that don't take desired Effect, I swear by God to Poison all your Tribe, so surely that you shan't know the Perpetrator of the Tragedy, I beg for God's sake that you would let me have the Money, and hinder me from committing such a black Deed. I know you can spare it, so desire you would let me have it.
    Saturday night about 7 o'clock, leave it by the Sellar Door wrapped up in a Rag and about an Hour after I will come and take it; put it on the Ground just where I put the Stick; If you don't leave it I advise you not to Drink your Beer, nor eat your Bread if you value your Life and Healths; for by my Soul I will do what I've mentioned, if I find any Watch to Guard me in taking of it, I'll desist and not take it, but follow my intended Scheme and hinder you from acting more on the Stage of Life: If you comply I'll never molest you more, but if not I'll hazard my Life in destroying yours, and continue what I am.

Mary was overcome with shock. She sat down "much altered and concerned," unable to imagine that she had "such an enemy in the world." The guests tried to reassure Mary, reasoning that the letter's only purpose was to frighten her and James. Angry, Mary said that the letter should be made public and printed, but her husband said that he "would consider well of it before he did that." Besides, one of the guests added, "there were so many things printed in Zenger's journal already."[66]
    The reference to "Zenger's journal" was natural in the Alexander household since James Alexander was one of the people bankrolling John Peter Zenger's *New-York Weekly Journal* in order to have a place to criticize the governor in print. Just a few months later Zenger's paper would be burned by the public hangman at the start of the printer's famous trial for libel. Though the letter would soon become a part of

New York's factious politics, it was originally addressed to Mary Alexander, the merchant, rather than to her husband, the politician. It was a demand for money couched as a double threat against her livelihood and her life.[67]

Mary Alexander was distressed that someone would threaten her life. She was not surprised, however, that someone would ask her for cash. She was a married woman, but she controlled her own financial decisions. This letter, tossed onto her hallway floor, literally brought the components of the British Empire into her house. The author's identity has never been discovered, but it seems likely that the "native Country" to which he wished to return was presumably somewhere within the web of British commerce.

The winter of 1733–34 was a hard one for New York. The city was squarely in the middle of an eight-year recession: shipbuilding had ground almost to a halt, imports had dropped 11 percent from the previous decade, and coinage was in short supply. The result was a "serious shrinkage of trade."[68] The previous summer a ditty in the *New-York Gazette* had asked rhetorically:

Pray tell me the cause of trade being so dead
Why Shops are shut up, Goods and owners all fled,
And industrious Families cannot get Bread?
I'd also fain know what makes Money so scarce
When to St A——e and elsewhere we may have free Commerce?[69]

In such an economic climate a man who had been once "accounted a Gentleman" could easily be "reduced to poverty." The language of mercantilism in the letter suggests that the writer's failed fortune was a result of bad business. A return home would allow him a fresh start, presumably on the basis of fresh credit.

Moreover, hard British currency was not easy to come by in the colonies, and it is not surprising that a man threatening his reader with death did not ask for a bill of exchange or a letter of credit, for which he would have needed to give his name. It is nonetheless notable that he asked to be paid in Spanish coin. Spanish pistoles and doubloons were common and accepted currency in New York, but they had not lost their foreign associations.[70] The letter leaves no doubt that the author thought of Mary as a solvent and internationally connected merchant.

The author's commercial failure and Mary's commercial success shape the gendered content of the letter. As a recent and groundbreaking analysis of masculinity and mercantile subjectivity puts it, "business failure, like cuckolding, feminizes the merchant by reducing him to ineffectual supplication." Supplication is not necessarily ineffectual, and a poverty-stricken businessman might indeed regain his former status, but the resumption of that independence depends on the kindness of his fellow businessmen, and the powerless position from which the failed merchant must make his entreaties puts him on par with a structurally powerless woman. The letter's feminized author, then, must have found it all the more galling to request help from a masculinized woman, and it is all the more understandable that his (embarrassing) request for help came in the form of a threat. In an attempt to assert his masculine power over a woman, even one wealthier and more successful than he, the writer threatens her with violence to her body as well as her business.[71]

As a twist on the practices of coverture, even Mary's death threat was soon transferred to her husband. When William Smith included a reprint of this letter in his *History of New York* in 1776, it was addressed to James rather than Mary.[72] Contemporary historians have gone no deeper into the sources than Smith's own account, thus ignoring the fact that the letter was never intended for James.[73] Smith's revision, however, is unsurprising; because Alexander was a married woman, her legal personality was subsumed under her husband's. Certainly, her husband's prominence led to the publication of the death threat. Her husband, his associates, and later historians all assumed that this letter was about the very male factional politics that divided New York. Eighteenth-century politics, particularly as they were practiced in New York, were entirely masculinist, shot through with sexualized innuendo and occasional violence.[74]

Yet, if the letter was intended as a political threat, the author couched his threats in the language not of politics or law but of commerce. James Alexander hypothesized that it might have been sent by a disgruntled political foe to whom he had served a writ the previous day; despite a long investigation, however, and the publication of several pamphlets on the subject, James's theory was never proved.[75] Even if it had been proved, questions still remain, including why the letter was addressed not to James but to Mary and why it was phrased as an appeal from one merchant to another.

Despite the factional politics in which this letter almost immediately became embroiled, the colony's governor offered a reward of fifty pounds and a pardon to anyone who could give information about the threat. New York's grand jury and governor took the threat seriously.[76] So did the city's mayor, Robert Lurting, who told James that in his place he "would have taken Care, to have got some Body to watch, to see if they could discover any Person, to come to the place . . . in order to take up the Money." James dismissed Lurting's concerns, telling him that "he was not at all afraid, tho' his Wife was very much scar'd, yet he did not fear anything of that kind."[77] James, interpreting the letter through the prism of factional politics, saw it as part of eighteenth-century street theater, akin to the public hangman's burning of John Peter Zenger's newspaper. Even the letter's author had used theatrical metaphor, threatening to "hinder" the Alexanders "from acting more on the Stage of Life." Whether or not the author intended to carry out his threat, his letter reveals the anger and failure a commercial empire could spawn. Mary Alexander's gender was not peripheral but central to the dangers of commerce in the British Empire.

Women's participation in the eighteenth-century marketplace was both gender-neutral and deeply gendered. As Mary Alexander's experience illustrates, the result was to upend gender hierarchies in the world of commerce while keeping them for family politics. White women were able to create and exploit effective trading networks that gave them access to credit and information, often over an extended period of their lives. They were likewise able to collect debts and to protect their commercial reputations. For married women, coverture posed only a limited threat to their potential success. In many ways the market treated these women in just as disembodied a fashion as it treated the men who took part in commerce, except that their networks were initially or primarily the result of their or their husbands' family ties.

The paradox of eighteenth-century trading networks is that the practices of an apparently gender-neutral capitalism bolstered gender hierarchies. Nothing as crude or obvious as coverture limited women's participation in the market. Rather, cultural and structural ideologies that few eighteenth-century New Yorkers could discern continually worked against women's ever achieving great financial power. As New York women traded under their husbands' names, asked their nephews to arrange loans, or bickered with their brothers over payments, they appeared to act as "deputy husbands," holding together the household by doing men's work when there were no men to do it for them.

Yet the effects of these women's trading enterprises went far beyond their family economies. Family hierarchies, and particularly the legal subordination of married women to their husbands, structured women's trading networks. In turn, women's extensive participation in the transatlantic market shaped the culture of Britain's commercial empire. The empire was not constructed through the active exclusion of its female subjects. Instead, transatlantic commerce welcomed the participation of women traders at the same time that coverture and similar gender ideologies shaped trading networks for both women and men.

The ways coverture informed women's experiences in the marketplace were not entirely benign, however. The gendered bodies that gave female traders access to family credit networks also provided a target for misogynistic and sometimes violent attacks. The dangers of the British economy were to the intertwined integrity of women's credit and women's bodies. Even wealthy merchants such as Mary Alexander found their lives threatened. Cathrine Williams, who published her death threat in the newspaper, found the economy of the British Empire even more dangerous. Williams was accused of being a "wicked woman" and a thief. As we will see, such charges were a persistent theme in accusations against poorer women. Livelihood, character, and life itself were inextricable for female traders.

Chapter Three

The Informal Economy

In the first two-thirds of the eighteenth century, New York tavern keepers were frequently accused of running "disordered" or "disorderly house[s]."[1] The New York Supreme Court indictment against Elizabeth Anderson in 1754 is typical of these accusations: "Elizabeth Anderson late of the said City of New York Huckster is a woman of notorious and ill fame, and keeps a common disordered house of Bawdry and Tipling And that the said Elizabeth frequently harbours and entertains in her said House Negro Slaves and divers other persons of Idle and suspected Character . . . permitting them by Night as well as by Day to remain drinking and behaving disorderly to the Great Disturbance of the Inhabitants residing in her Neighbourhood to the evil Example of all others in like Manner offending and against the peace of our said Lord the King his Crown and Dignity."[2] Much more than a simple complaint against a sleazy neighbor, this indictment against Anderson is a complex condensation of the ways that race, sex, status, and the law conjoined to create a particular and discrete economy.

Anderson was identified as a "huckster," a woman who sold small amounts of goods from a small shop or temporary stall. From her tiny shop Anderson hawked groceries, including oranges and limes provided by a seafaring relative. The citrus fruits that Anderson sold marked her involvement in the Atlantic market, although at quite a different scale from that of Gerard Beekman. The other accusations against her—of illicit sex, excessive drinking, and interracial socializing—although less obviously related to the world of trade, are equally revealing about how New York's poorest residents participated in the world of Atlantic exchange. The charges against Anderson describe many of the aspects of poor New Yorkers' commercial lives: drinking establishments run by women but frequented by men (often these establishments were not licensed by the state) and customers who were slaves and other servants of color.

More often noted in criminal court records than merchants' ledgers, these cheap shops, unregulated taverns, secondhand goods, and interracial exchanges formed a commercial world through which poor and enslaved New Yorkers could participate in the burgeoning Atlantic consumer economy. Yet with opportunity came risks—to one's reputation, freedom, and personal safety. The combination of undocumented goods, seedy taverns, interracial clientele, and inelegant behavior put the women and men who participated in this informal economy under constant suspicion. Given the hostility with which New York authorities viewed this market, it should not be surprising that most of the evidence for this economy comes from the criminal court records. Yet many more people were accused of participating in the informal economy than were proved to have worked in it. Though these records might tell us little about criminal activity, they do reveal how poor urban dwellers channeled the flow of goods from international merchants into their own lives.

Although court records might indicate that this economy was entirely illegal, many of these transactions occurred in a gray area between illicit and strictly legal. Because so much of this economy was either unregulated or conducted in violation of the state's regulations, it is best thought of as an "informal" economy. Sociologists have coined the term "informal economy" to describe a sector of the contemporary economy that "is unregulated by the institutions of society, in a legal and social environment in which similar activities are regulated." Activity within an informal economy is therefore not necessarily illegal; the simple lack of regulation may in some cases be an infringement of the law (selling alcohol without a license, for example), but the activities themselves may be perfectly legal. Although the term "informal economy" is anachronistic, it captures most simply the nature of the market sector within which many poor and enslaved New Yorkers worked. Unlike, say, "black market" or "underground economy," this term passes no judgment on the legality or morality of its participants' activities; the focus remains on the economic exchanges rather than on elite opinion of those exchanges.

Although sociologists generally speak of the informal economy in terms of its production and labor, it is the end point of production, consumption, that plays the most prominent role in the construction of status in the eighteenth century. Scholars tend to think of poor populations primarily in terms of their labor and ability to produce goods, but nearly all inhabitants of the imperial British world were also consumers. Enjoying food, cloth, accessories, and other goods made outside their local context was a vital way that those who were not a part of the city's elite participated in the commercial British Empire. Sometimes poorer New Yorkers found that the best or only way to be able to buy these imperial goods was through the informal economy.[3]

Unregulated trade, primarily the pawning of clothes and the sale of alcohol, pervaded provincial New York. Yet the very nature of these exchanges makes precise economic data impossible to find. When the criminal court records do take the informal economy into account, they reveal a world of economic activity inhabited by New Yorkers too poor even to get into debt since no one would give them credit. We will therefore never know precisely how the informal economy was connected to the formal economy in *fiscal* terms. It is possible, however, to see how they were linked in *cultural* terms. They were two parts of an eighteenth-century trend toward greater consumption. The informal economy maintained a space in the marketplace for those who were excluded—by reasons of status, race, gender, or credit—from buying and selling in the formal economy.

Poor white women were the linchpins of this informal economy. They were the ones who bought and sold, who looked for tiny openings in any market to sell or buy just one more item, who ran the risk of illegal trading with slaves or in stolen goods. These trades took place in small taverns and shops, often involving alcohol, often with a biracial clientele, and almost always unregulated by license or inspection. Over it all hung an aura of illegality, exacerbated by the suspicion of transgressive sexuality and riotous living.

These trading networks among New York's poor and enslaved were primarily local. They rarely depended on the complex systems of trust, family connections, and international trading networks to which confidence artists, merchants, and shopkeepers were so indebted. Yet, like those New Yorkers who participated in the formal economy of transatlantic trade, those who bought and sold in the informal economy were closely tied to the larger British Empire and especially to British Atlantic trade. The story of credit and connections seen in the world of New York's commerce is continued in the darker and smaller shops and taverns of this port city. Status, both apparent and actual, structured the form of New York's formal economy. The informal economy took those markers of status and upended their meaning by making them accessible to New York's nonelite classes.

The elite New Yorkers who constituted the city's courts interpreted these transactions as illegal, immoral, and dangerous. For the participants, however, this particular commercial world was a creative and legitimate—if not necessarily legal—part of the world of goods. The result of these economic practices, moreover, was a shift in both the traditional status divide between black and white and the meaning of status goods.

The details of New York's informal economy are preserved most extensively in the records of the colony's courts of law. Accusations of theft, fencing, illegal trading, and unlicensed retail document the hazards of economic life for hundreds of New York's poorer inhabitants. The legal nature of these documents, however, while offering the chance to clarify, at least in part, the types of people and activities that comprised the informal economy, inevitably align our perspective with that of the predominantly middling and elite citizens who brought the cases to court.

The sizable presence of women defined the informal economy. On both sides of the early modern Atlantic, women on the economic margins often supported themselves through trade. In Europe they traditionally participated in a variety of economic activities, especially tavern keeping and selling goods; in New York also, they looked to the market to make ends meet.[4] This "economy of makeshifts," as one historian has termed it, did not differentiate between criminal and legitimate activity. It ran the gamut from small shops and taverns to market stalls to peddlers; many of these sites of exchange dealt in both secondhand and stolen goods. Moreover, poverty in the eighteenth century did not necessarily exclude one from enjoying consumer goods or even fashionable items, but it meant that the method of obtaining these items might seem unorthodox to members of the elite or the middling sort.[5]

The careful preservation of court minute books, both in the colonies and in England, has made it possible for scholars to estimate with some certainty the relationship between social groups and accusations of crimes. Although women's historians tend to look primarily at crimes that obviously involved women, such as rape, infanticide, and sexual slander, these were not the crimes for which most women were brought into court, either as perpetrators or victims, particularly in the cities.[6] Instead, property crimes represented women's most common offenses against the law. Unlike at least one urban county of England, where property offenses formed the largest category of accusations against both men and women, in New York larceny ranked first among women but not among men. Among men, property offenses ranked third, behind crimes of violence and violations of public order.[7] In New York, as in other cities, women were prosecuted for stealing far beyond their proportion of the criminal population. In New York City women were involved in over 26 percent of the prosecutions for theft. Given the fact that women made up slightly less than 10 percent of all criminal prosecutions, this fact is particularly striking. Theft was the largest single category of women's crime; at 36.1 percent, it represented more than one-third of all the prosecutions against women in New York.

The informal economy had intricate connections to more legitimate traders. In 1759, for example, Abraham and Rachel Elberson were accused of receiving indigo from a slave named Jupiter, who had probably gotten the indigo from his owner, the merchant Francis Lewis. Lewis was hardly beyond reproach; he regularly smuggled goods into New York without paying customs duties.[8]

In addition to accusations of theft, New Yorkers were prosecuted for receiving stolen goods. Fencing was not a felony according to common law, but by the eighteenth century fencers were treated as accessories after the fact and could be prosecuted for misdemeanors.[9] These criminal relationships were often biracial and bisexual; the collaboration between thief and fence was frequently between a black seller (often a man) and a white receiver (often a woman). Mary Holst was accused of receiving gold and silver rings from a slave named Pompey, and Mary Smith was accused of receiving stolen money from a slave named Somerset.[10] White women and black men worked together not just in disorderly houses but also throughout the informal economy. White women and black men came together to buy and sell a large number of items, including jewelry, housewares, and eyeglasses.[11] In what might have been a preparation for a Christmas party, Winifred Douglas was accused of encouraging a slave named Harry to steal two gallons of Madeira out of John Moore's cellar on Christmas Eve.[12] An Irish woman named Jane Kelly was convicted of acting as an accomplice to a slave of James Alexander's named Cuffee, who was sentenced to hang for robbing his mistress Mary Alexander's shop.[13] In a similar case fifteen years earlier, Ann Butler had been found hiding in an outhouse of Stephen DeLancey's home, having robbed his home and convinced his slaves to run away.[14] Their interactions could also be explicitly criminal.

Combinations of thieves and receivers, of course, were not limited to black men and white women. Elizabeth Clarke was whipped for knowingly receiving stolen goods from a white sailor, and Mary Ellis was indicted for receiving stolen napkins from Phyllis, a slave of John Watts.[15] Even slave women could be indicted for receiving.[16]

Of course, these accusations of theft were not necessarily true. When the same Elizabeth Clarke, Abigail Arden, and Samuel Brown were accused of receiving stolen goods in 1737, only Clarke was found guilty.[17] Women who ran small shops and taverns were in particular danger of being accused of illegal trading, theft, fencing, and other forms of illegal trade. The secondhand market on which these women relied and the slaves who played an active role in its trading networks colored this economic activity with the suspicion of theft. However, a charge of larceny was easier to make than to prove; of all crimes, theft was the one of which women were both most frequently accused and most frequently acquitted. Nearly one-quarter (22.6 percent) of larceny accusations against women were found to be groundless. Even in cases of women with "infamous" reputations, the courts often judged them to be innocent, although they banished them from the city nonetheless. In 1740, for example, a special New York Court of General Sessions admitted that it did not have enough evidence to convict Mary Cullen of stealing a sheet, but it ruled that "foreasmuch as the said Mary Cullen is . . . a person of ill fame it is further ordered that the said Mary Cullen to within forty eight hours after discharge depart this city and if she return again that she be apprehended and receive such punishment as the justices in their discretion shall order and direct."[18]

Women in New York's informal economy rendered themselves suspicious through their relations with slaves, but they also invited suspicion if they lacked the stable relationship of marriage. Susannah Hutchins, for example, who pleaded guilty to selling liquor to slaves, was identified primarily as a "Single woman [who] is a woman of evil behavior and conversation and a great disturber of the Peace." The court implied that the lack of a male head of household contributed to the "evil Rule and Government in her said House."[19] Some historians have argued that single women were imagined to be sources of disorder, likely to "seduce husbands from the home and hearth to the tavern and bawdy house."[20] Yet such an explanation is only partly correct. As the next section of this chapter will show, taverns and bawdy houses were indeed sources of social anxiety, and women, married or not, were often implicated in that anxiety. However, seduction is not the crime of which the city's women were accused. Unlike their New England counterparts, New York women were rarely brought to court for the sexual crimes of prostitution, lascivious carriage, or even bastardy.[21] Property crime was the accusation they were far more likely to face.

The Disorderly House

Exchange in the informal economy commonly took place in the sorts of establishments, dubbed "disorderly houses," that Elizabeth Anderson was charged with keeping. The term encapsulates both the activities that defined the informal economy and the struggle for its interpretation that separated its participants from its critics. Disorder was in the eye of the elite beholder, and a poor but enterprising tavern keeper would never have defined her house as disordered; here then, more than anywhere else in New York, the meaning of the informal economy was created, contested, and preserved.

States often take an interest in controlling the allocation of the legal authority to engage in commerce. In New York this interest led to the creation not only of specific regulations and rules but also of a new and curiously ambiguous legal category: the disorderly house. This general term had no strict definition; it could encompass "not merely houses where fights and brawls took place, but brothels, places where inordinate drinking was done and at unseasonable hours, unlicensed alehouses, 'tippling' houses and dives where slaves, Negroes, servants, apprentices and sailors were entertained and often given credit when they could not pay cash."[22] Many of these activities were illegal, such as selling liquor without a license, selling liquor to slaves or apprentices, or allowing gaming. Yet tavern keepers were rarely brought to court on these specific counts; much more often they were accused of the much vaguer charge of keeping a disorderly house. Most frequently they were accused of "entertaining" slaves, despite the fact that the provision of entertainment was not a crime; rather this general term covered the illegal activity of selling slaves liquor. Unlicensed taverns in New York were termed "disorderly" precisely because they were places where whites were willing to drink with, talk with, and otherwise "entertain" blacks. Throughout the British period New York's neighborhoods were not stratified by class, so wealthy merchants and poor tavern keepers often set up shops, made their homes, and brought their clients into close proximity.[23] Thus, neighbors often complained about such taverns, but the city never eradicated them.

These sorts of taverns and private houses both flourished and were prosecuted in New York because of their close association with trade. The credit that tavern keepers offered and the liquor that they sometimes sold, especially to men of color, made them both essential and suspicious partners in New York's larger economy. Most of the extant evidence for these "disorderly houses" has been preserved in a set of sources with a clear bias toward elite entertainment practices and commercial "order": legal records. Prosecutions for disorderly houses were almost always made by defendants' more respectable neighbors. Carefully read, however, even these sources can reveal the complexities of the connections between race, gender, and commerce among New York's working poor.

After theft, the second most common crime for which New York women were prosecuted was the keeping of a disorderly house. Nearly 15 percent of the women accused in the New York Court of General Sessions were brought up on this vague charge. Moreover, relative to accusations of disorderly houses in general, taverns run by women were especially likely to be accused of being disorderly; 40 percent of the cases involving disorderly houses prosecuted women, despite the fact that they operated only 15–30 percent of the licensed taverns between 1757 and 1763.[24]

Of course, men were liable to this charge as well. Peter Hampton was indicted in 1753 for running a disorderly house. The magistrates accused him of running a brothel in which he allowed "divers suspected persons of evill name and fame to have carnall knowledge with whores, and by procurement, and persuasion of the said Peter Hampton . . . fornication and whoredom then and there commit." Yet taverns and stores run by women, especially those who were or were thought to be widowed or single, were particularly likely to be presented to the courts as "disorderly." Even Peter Hampton's wife was added to the indictment three months after he was charged.[25] In 1723 Judith Peters, "reputed wife of Thomas Peters," was accused of entertaining "divers male slaves" in a "tippling house."[26] When it was a woman under prosecution for keeping a disorderly house, the charge implied either prostitution or interracial socializing or both. Sometimes she was suspected of participating in or condoning sexual activity, using the business as a brothel. Thus, Catherine Cooper, a widow, was accused in 1760 of being a "woman of evil behavior and conversation" who kept a house in which she "entertained, harbored and supported divers servants apprentices, vagabonds and other idle and suspected persons."[27] More explicitly, Catherine Turner was accused of keeping a disorderly house in which "Men and Women in her said House at unlawfull Times . . . remained drinking, tippling, whoring, and misbehaving themselves unlawfully."[28]

Neighbors often complained that a disorderly house had both suspicious sexual activity and interracial socializing. The widow Elizabeth Green, for example, was jailed for eight days in 1710 for permitting "sundry negro Slaves to assemble and meet together to feast and revel in the night time and then and there did keep and maintain a disorderly house."[29] Even when a woman claimed that she did not know a black man was enslaved, the court could still fine her.[30] Interracial socializing and interracial theft seemed to go hand in hand, especially when a slave exchanged stolen goods for alcohol. As early as 1704 the tavern keeper Anne White was indicted for "receiving stolen goods from the slave of Capt. Peter Mathews and for succoring aiding harboring and entertaining the said slave etc."[31] The widow Catherine Elbertse pleaded guilty to an indictment six years later that she had sold alcohol to slaves "for her own private and unlawful Gain" and then "from the said negro Slaves did wickedly and deceitfully receive take and convert to her own use sundry sums of money and other goods and with them the said negro slaves did then and there knowingly willfully wickedly and deceitfully buy sell and trade to the Evil Example of Others."[32] The court dealt harshly with any attempts to "buy sell and trade" between white women and black slaves, especially for "private . . . Gain."

The disorderly house came under particular suspicion of connections with theft. London observers Daniel Defoe and Henry Fielding both blamed disorderly houses for the increase in robberies, and in New York the local newspapers called for more careful oversight.[33] An angry or overzealous neighbor could easily turn the fear that a tavern dealt in stolen goods into a legal nightmare for its owners. John Webb, for example, was already identified as a "victualler" when he became a freeman of the city in 1710. Two years later his liquor license was temporarily suspended while he and his wife Anne were investigated for "entertaining and trading with Negro slaves" as well as allowing "suspected people of evil conversation there drinking swearing and playing at unlawful games (to wit) at Cards Dice and Other unlawful Games at all hours."[34] Their neighbor Abigail Cogan had claimed that Anne and John "Receivd Goods Bonnets and Other things of Negro's."[35] The Webbs were convicted of running a disorderly house and lost their license.

The Webbs brought a defamation suit against Cogan, claiming that they had always been "without any suspicion of Trading or dealing with any slaves have always used and kept themselves Innocent." Initially the Webbs won their case and ten pounds in damages. Cogan, however, won her appeal, arguing in part that there was no proof that the Webbs' business was damaged by her accusation while the case was under review. In fact, only three months after the Webbs were convicted of trading with slaves, the New York Court of General Sessions unanimously requested the mayor to grant John Webb another license as long as he produced certificates from two of his "principal" neighbors that he was now keeping an orderly house.[36]

The two courts decided that the Webbs had been running a disorderly house and that Cogan's description of it as disorderly had not caused them any economic harm. It seems likely, therefore, that the same people who had been frequenting the Webbs' tavern did not care whether or not the tavern keepers were pawning goods from slaves; that was a concern of the neighbors rather than of the patrons. The Webbs' messy drama neatly captures the complex nature of the disorderly house, which existed not only in the neighborhoods of New York but also in the minds of its inhabitants.

Goods

As with the accusations for disorderly houses, the sources that describe the goods circulating through the informal economy come from prominent members of society with elitist relationships to the world of goods. The enormous increase of consumer goods in markets around the British Empire had become obvious by the first quarter of the eighteenth century.[37] These items bore a complex set of meanings for those who consumed them. On the one hand, in provincial outposts such as New York, fashionable consumer imports implied a close connection to the wider British Empire; on the other hand, the very idea of fashion attempted to create a certain sense of distinction between the city's elite and others. Thus poorer people's possession of many of the consumer goods that were intended to mark elite status was an immediate cause for suspicion among the city's legal elite. They often assumed that such goods could only have been stolen.

A closer look at the goods exchanged in taverns and shops shows how poor people, not just those of middling rank, participated in the world of goods. Historians of the consumer revolution have assumed that middling and wealthy people were the first to desire and purchase luxury goods. According to this theory, as goods became increasingly affordable, the desire for them slowly made its way down the social ladder.[38] The informal economy in eighteenth-century New York, however, demonstrates otherwise. Poor and enslaved people did not wait until they could afford to buy new cloth before they participated in the consumer marketplace; instead, they joined a vibrant informal economy of secondhand goods sold in taverns that may have helped fuel even the middle-class consumption of imports. The desire among New York's poor for consumer goods, even if those goods were not brand new, created and energized the secondhand market, and the existence of this market, by providing a new outlet for used goods, energized the formal economy.

Pawning, fencing, and receiving all brought poor New Yorkers into the consumer economy. People with limited disposable income, such as slaves or poor white women, did not think that fashion and consumerism were out of their reach. Runaway slave advertisements, for example, are excellent guides to the fashionable clothing and accessories that slaves acquired, including wigs.[39] Other examples show that slaves also owned consumer goods that members of the elite thought should be limited to the wealthy. When constables and justices in New York searched the homes of slave owners looking for evidence of the conspiracy in 1741, they arrested two slaves for having items "thought improper for, and unbecoming the Condition of Slaves."[40] However, what officials thought was "unbecoming the Condition of Slaves" and what slaves themselves desired to own were two very different things. Historians have not been accustomed to thinking of slaves as consumers; their lack of personal freedom seemed to imply a lack of economic freedom as well. However, the evidence of runaway-slave advertisements and court records indicates that in one important area some urban slaves took for themselves the freedom of choice. Consumer choice was one of the most important characteristics of the new consumer market, but urban slaves could and did consider more choices than those goods advertised in the newspapers.[42] The secondhand-clothes market in which they participated as both suppliers and purchasers increased yet further the quantities of available goods.

Although the secondhand market may not have offered quite the dizzying array of new goods found in more respectable shops, the variety of goods stolen for resale indicates that a wide selection was available for nonelites.[42] New York appears to have been a convenient entrepôt for goods stolen from other colonies. A storekeeper from Norfolk, Connecticut, printed an advertisement in the *Pennsylvania Gazette* that two men were thought to be making their way southward with a haul of, among other things, stolen lustrig, ribbons, stockings, and shoes. The advertiser informed his readers, "They have been pursued to the City of New York, where they have disposed of some of said Goods, and 'tis supposed are in the Jerseys or Pennsylvania, or gone towards Maryland."[43] By one of his associates, the leader of one of Philadelphia's gangs of robbers sent to New York some of his haul, consisting of "two silk Gowns, two other Gowns, three fine aprons, a Tea Chest, some Cambrick Handkerchiefs and other Things."[44] Thieves from neighboring colonies recognized the vibrancy of New York's secondhand market, since they sold off at least some of their goods in the port.

Others came directly to New York to partake in the secondhand market. In 1738 Jane Robinson, "late of Newcastle, on Delaware," confessed to stealing "a Bonnet, a straw hat and a punch Bowl," and a month later she was accused of stealing a new piece of linen, a child's linen dress, several caps and more linen remnants, an old child's cloak, and a new boy's coat—all from different sources. At the end of her trial the court said that "there was also found upon the said Jane Robinson a dozen of new knifes and forks with horn handles, upwards of nine yards of new garlix linen an old fashioned silver spoon and a silver bodkin and other goods supposed to be stolen."[45] If the confession was genuine, Robinson's extensive haul certainly indicates her skill as a thief, but it presents other questions as well. One wonders, for example, what Robinson intended to do with a punch bowl; its resale value depended on finding another member of the informal economy who felt a need for such a specialized item.

Thanks to a useful study of the English clothing trade in the long eighteenth century, we now have extensive evidence of a healthy trade in secondhand clothing. Women in particular were active participants in this economy, largely because of the ways in which women's domestic and business work came together in dealings with secondhand clothing; "without formal training, women's homely practices assumed commercial value, intersecting with the market needs of the community."[46] Yet almost all of this commercial activity took place below the level of the regulated economy. As a result, "women seemed to earn disproportionate disapproval for independent, unsanctioned economic activities."[47] The combination of the nature of the unregulated clothing trade and women's central place in it led contemporaries to think of the exchange in secondhand clothing as "disorderly." In New York as well as in England, women's commercial activity often seemed suspicious.

These secondhand consumer goods probably indicated comfort, fashion, and status to their owners in ways similar to those of their original owners when new. Yet consumer goods—especially cloth and clothing— had another and quite specific meaning in the informal economy. These goods frequently served as currency among shopkeepers, tavern owners, and customers.

Clothing was clearly a vital commodity in New York's informal economy. Statistics for New York are almost impossible to come by, given that the court clerk only sporadically recorded the items alleged to have been stolen. However, an analysis of the available numbers indicates that of the ninety-five larceny cases mentioned either in the minute books of the New York Supreme Court or Court of General Sessions or in the newspapers and that specifically list the items that had been stolen, fifty-five included clothing or cloth.[48] In 1700 and again in 1701, for example, an Indian woman named Amy Carr was convicted of stealing first two smocks and then a "child's mantle."[49] Many thefts were as small as Carr's or smaller. William Dickson was accused of stealing a "small piece of osnaburg" worth ten pence, while Elizabeth Clarke and Mary McCarty were accused of stealing a "remnant of calico" worth six pence. Other thefts, however, involved such finery as a blue cloth coat with gilt and velvet buttons.[50]

J. M. Beattie's carefully gathered numbers for England indicate that in urban areas clothes represented the largest single category of stolen goods. Garthine Walker has found a similar phenomenon in Cheshire; not only were clothes and linens the objects most likely to be stolen by both men and women, but they also represented a much larger proportion of items stolen by women than by men.[51]

Previous scholars have suggested that people stole clothes out of the "pinch of economic necessity."[52] One cites the example of an enslaved woman who stole cloth to make clothing and claimed in her defense that "she stole the goods because she was almost naked and her mistress would give her no clothes."[53] Undoubtedly, material circumstances could drive people to theft. When Samuel Powell, tailor and servant to Francis Mesnard, stole a coat in January 1737, he may have been compelled by the cold to find some warmer clothing.[54]

However, the pinch of necessity does not suffice to explain the ubiquitous records of stolen clothing with little or no practical use. While James Thomas might have stolen a gown and petticoat for someone else's use, Isaac Moore's theft of two pairs of silk stockings represents more than a need to cover his legs.[55] Silk stockings were valuable imports as well as useful articles of clothing, and the wearing—or stealing—of such stockings signaled a connection with the larger world of foreign luxury goods that have not historically been associated with poor laborers. The man who stole four coats the same day as well as a silk handker-chief will not have worn them all himself; some of them were obviously for resale.[56] One woman, indicted and hanged for grand larceny, stole "one blue boy's striped linen waistcoat of the value of four shillings . . . one figured callico short gown of the value of one shilling . . . two small blue striped linen gowns each of the value of two shillings . . . and four small-figured callico gowns each of the value of one shilling."[57] A band of soldiers and sailors conducted raids on dry-goods shops, stealing a variety of cloth such as "one piece of brown Broad-Cloth, and one ditto of a Lead Colour, a half Piece of red Duffils, a Piece of white Linnen, another of Stuff, and several ready-made Shirts and Trowsers."[58] Elinor Holmes stole a silver spoon and a piece of silk, both of them iconically luxurious consumer goods and neither a necessity of life.[59] The uninten-tional symbolic effect of stealing these sorts of items was to distribute goods that marked elite status widely across social hierarchies. Practi-cally, however, these goods were stolen for quite another purpose.

Clothing represented not only a currency of its own that could be traded for liquor, rent, or even a search warrant; it also could be sold for hard currency. As a result, even slaves, themselves property, could participate as consumers. They even had "disposable" income. Thus the informal economy in general and the secondhand market in particular had extensive implications for poor New Yorkers. They could buy the status goods that were intended to be markers of the elite.

When they revised the liquor laws in 1737, members of New York's legislature indicated their knowledge of and discomfort with the ways that poorer residents used cloth as payment for drink. In that legislation the assembly carefully spelled out the terms and meanings of "credit." By this new legislation it became illegal to "take or receive directly or indirectly from any such servant or apprentice any Cloathing or any other goods Chattles Wares or Merchandizes in payment for any Such Strong Liquors or in pawn or Pledge to Secure any SUCH payment." Acknowledging the prevalence of clothing in these transactions, the law-makers separated this item from the merchandise, tools, and instru-ments with which it had been grouped in earlier laws.[60]

This same law, which made it illegal for tavern keepers to take cloth-ing in exchange for drink, admitted that the pawning of clothing or other goods by servants for alcohol was a "common practice," but it was done in "so Secret a manner that no Person is privy to it but the said Tavern Keeper or Inholder and Such Servant or Apprentice." Legisla-tors nonetheless tried to clamp down on the practice in any way they could. Suspecting that tavern keepers might be running more compli-cated commercial operations than the simple exchange of goods for liquor, lawmakers also made it illegal for tavern keepers to extend credit beyond six shillings for liquor or "other Tavern Expenses."[61]

Participants

A close focus on the markers of the middling and elite economy gives a false impression of poor white women's exclusion from the world of the market.[62] The New York Mayor's Court, where suppliers sued debtors, offers little evidence of women's economic activity. However, other court records, including those in which women and men were accused of criminal activities, give a fuller picture of the extensive role of commerce in poor women's lives. In urban centers such as New York, women were particularly prevalent in retail trade. Some shopkeepers were able to use their husbands' trading connections to stock their shops. Women without such family connections, however, were still able to sell goods and drink, although usually at a modest level. Most of these small, backstreet shops and market stalls left little trace in the historical record.

The illegality of a transaction was as much constructed by the regulations of trade as by an individual's activities. Because the city set legal stipulations on who could buy and sell and in what settings, it was easy for poorer people to be caught in the trap of illegal trading. The New York City Council used licenses to decide who could trade licitly and who could not. Not surprisingly, peddlers, the most irregular of traders, were carefully regulated. In 1714 the New York General Assembly began to license hawkers and peddlers throughout the province except for within the city. The act was intended to restrict the numbers of wandering sellers, since each peddler had to pay ten pounds per year for the license; half of that sum had to be paid before the government would issue a license, and one had to apply for that license in writing. The fine for trading without a license was set at thirty pounds. Hawkers and peddlers were prohibited altogether from trading in New York City.[63] All these restrictions on trade were intended to control the participants in the market.

Itinerancy and the unregulated nature of the trade in marginal and secondhand goods no doubt contributed to the suspicion of peddlers. In 1750 "sundry merchants and shopkeepers" complained to the city's Common Council that peddlers were operating in the city without licenses. They pleaded that "Hawkers and Pedlars . . . (who may properly be called Vagrants having neither home nor habitation and who neither watch nor pay taxes)" still peddled goods in the streets of New York despite the ban against peddling. The merchants claimed that they suffered significant financial harm from these peddlers; since "they are in no ways obliged to pay any part in the publick expenses of this city they can sell considerably cheaper than the merchants or shopkeepers that are obliged to pay rents and contribute this proportion to the public taxes and watch of the city."[64] The wealthy storekeepers who signed this petition were rightly anxious about the possibilities that an entrepreneurial peddler could exploit. Obadiah Wells, for example, received a peddler's license in 1735, and by 1752 he had become a shopkeeper with such extensive contacts that when he declared bankruptcy, nearly forty merchants signed a creditors' agreement with him.[65] Established shopkeepers eagerly upheld licensing regulations as a way to decrease competition. Moreover, as their parenthetical jab at "vagrants" makes clear, these shopkeepers saw legal regulation as a means of socially controlling the marketplace.

The city's lawmakers were particularly vigilant about controlling women's commerce. Peddlers, hawkers, and hucksters were often women. As a result, unlike most other New York laws, those concerning peddlers were explicitly gender-inclusive. The request for a peddler's license had to be "in writing under his or her hand or under the hand of some Person by him her or them AUTHORIZED." Women were intended to be covered under the law. In fact, one of the laws specifically granted a free peddler's license to a woman who would otherwise have been entirely destitute.[66]

Neither as a peddler nor as a shopkeeper with a fixed place of business, however, could a woman simply open up shop in New York. Instead, every nonitinerant seller of merchandise—that is, "every Merchant Trader or Shop Keeper"—was also regulated and licensed. Although the licenses were relatively affordable at only £3.12,[67] at times, as with liquor licenses, the Common Council occasionally waived the fees for poor women. In 1704 Jael Ratier was given "Liberty to follow any Lawful Trade or Employment within this Corporation for the better Obtaining A livelihood for her and her family during her well behaving her self any former law of this Corporation to the Contrary Notwithstanding."[68] Mary Lawrence obtained a free license in the same year; she established a small store of odds and ends, mainly dry goods, in the business district of the Dock Ward.[69] When she was robbed in 1722, she testified that the stolen goods consisted of "sundry pieces & remnants of Callicoes, three remnants of silk muslin, one muslin handkerchief, one piece of silk handkerchief containing eleven handkerchiefs, some remnants of chequered holland, some cotton handkerchiefs, some remall (thin silk) handkerchiefs, some pewter basins, four or five pewter porringers, a pewter chamber pot, some mill'd woollen caps, a hatt, some shoe buckles, three pair women's stockings, a bag of buttons."[70] As the variety of this merchandise attests, shopkeepers such as Lawrence traded in small amounts of a large number of items, some of which may have been the ends of bolts that she bought or scavenged from wealthier shopkeepers.

Like women's shops, the taverns that women ran ranged from the very humble, run directly out of a woman's home, to the quite genteel, such as the "spacious elegant new Coffee-House" operated by Mary Ferrara.[71] For women who were poor but not utterly without money, the city offered tavern licenses at a reduced rate. In 1757, for example, women received nearly one-third of all the city's tavern licenses. Of those licenses that were offered at a discount, however, women received a full two-thirds. Clearly, the city encouraged retail as a way for women to support themselves.[72]

Some women saw their fortunes fluctuate over the years. Elizabeth Jourdain was widowed in 1703, but over the next few years she established herself comfortably enough as a tavern keeper to host the Governor's Council meetings when council members contemplated an attack on Canada. The council, however, never paid its bill, and several years later, in 1717, Jourdain asked the General Assembly of New York to settle "the publick Debts of the Government," including "lodging Soldiers, and entertaining Gentlemen of her Majesty's Council at her house, on the affair of the Expedition against Canada." The assembly passed a law to pay off the public debt, but the debt to Jourdain apparently went unpaid. That same year Jourdain applied for and received from the city a free license to sell liquor. Her name reappears in court documents for 1727, when she unsuccessfully tried to avoid the excise tax by pleading "extreem poverty," and for 1736, when she received yet another free liquor license. Jourdain is a typical example of a woman who, for more than thirty years, ran a retail business that repeatedly came close to insolvency.[73] Like Ann Elizabeth Schuyler or Helena Cooper, she began her career as an independent businesswoman with all the advantages of a trader. When her husband, a mariner, died in 1703, he left an estate of 145 gallons of rum and two hundred pounds.[74] Either through bad luck or poor management, however, Jourdain had to struggle to make ends meet.

Participants in the lower echelons of New York's commercial economy might find themselves running afoul of the state's restrictions even if they were not dealing in stolen goods. Some of these limitations on trade were relatively simple; in 1724 Mary Ellison was accused of buying a pair of military breeches from a soldier against army regulations.[75] Other people who tried to work in the commercial market were hindered from trading in New York by an extensive array of legal prohibitions. Slaves in particular were altogether forbidden by law from engaging in trade. In fact, the regulation of slaves in New York was primarily directed at curtailing their economic activities. As early as 1702 it was illegal to trade with slaves at all.[76] When the legislature revised the slave code in the wake of the 1712 uprising, it turned first to controlling exchange. The first provision of the new code made it illegal to trade with any slaves, either by buying or selling, without the express permission of the slave's owner.[77] The revised act "for better regulating" slaves in 1730 recognized the extensive network of illegal trade between free and enslaved New Yorkers and spelled out even more explicitly the prohibition against doing business with slaves. The preamble thundered, "notwithstanding Sundry Laws passed heretofore in this Colony for the purposes abovementioned several evil disposed Persons having nothing in View but their private gain do Clandestinely trade and traffic with Slaves." This act also made it clear that it was illegal to "sell any rum or other strong Liquor to any Negro Indian or Mulato Slave or Slaves or shall buy or take in pawn from them any wares Merchandises apparel Tools Instruments or any other Kind of goods whatever."[78] White servants and apprentices were also legally limited in their economic dealings. The assembly declared it illegal to sell "strong Liquors to Servants and Apprentices and from giving Large Credit to others."[79]

The New York slave code had two primary goals. First, it tried to reduce both alcohol consumption by slaves and the gathering of slaves in taverns. In the midst of the 1741 trials, a petition that was presented to the assembly and printed in the newspapers claimed that "upon strict Enquiry the great Number of Publick Houses in which Negroes have been entertained and encouraged to buy Rum and other strong Liquors has been a principal Instrument to their Diabolical Villainies."[80] Second, it tried to restrict the commercial activities of slaves and whites who would do business with them. It was this second goal that subsequent regulation worked hardest to attain.

Women who ran taverns often managed two sorts of businesses under the same roof: retail shops and drinking establishments. Traditionally, tavern keepers, acting as pawnbrokers, took goods in kind for drink.[81] In these smaller, more marginal shops, women often bought and sold secondhand goods as well as new candles or cloth remnants. These same women and men often pawned goods that had been legally acquired, thereby injecting more secondhand goods into the market. Women's participation in pawning, and particularly in the pawning of clothing, was extensive. Furthermore, women frequently ran the small taverns in which these exchanges—both legal and illegal—took place.

Such exchanges, whether above or below the law, were thought to be women's work. Although occasionally a man might be indicted for receiving stolen goods, the exchange of secondhand goods was usually assumed to be the responsibility of women. In 1742, for example, Philip Anderson and Elizabeth Allen were accused of stealing "some soap an apron some salt meat six coursehatss [corsets] and a blanket," and Henry and Elizabeth Bell were accused of knowingly receiving stolen goods from Anderson and Allen. Elizabeth Allen admitted to stealing the meat and the apron; the two men were found not guilty, and although Elizabeth Bell pleaded her innocence, the court found her guilty. The court clearly assumed that the transfer of the stolen goods was a transaction between two women and that the men were not involved.[82]

The secondhand market was not necessarily illegal, however, or even disreputable. Indeed, such activity seems to have been so common that few people bothered to take notice of it unless it was also accompanied by some suspicious person. Some retailers sold both new and old dry goods. Ann Elizabeth Schuyler, an established and well-respected merchant for over thirty years in New York City, occasionally sold a pair of "worn Gloves" or "worn hose."[83] Although no records appear in New York noting the sale of used dresses or coats by secondhand dealers, evidence from England shows a flourishing and extensive secondhand market in this period, both in London and in the smaller cities.[84] Other women advertised their ability to refurbish used clothing; Elizabeth Boyd, for example, offered "to graft Pieces in Knit Jackets and Breeches, not to be discern'd, also to graft and foot stockings, and Gentlemen's Gloves, Mittens or Muffatees made out of old Stockings, or runs them in the Heels."[85] Although the legitimate secondhand market seems to have been less fully developed in New York than in Britain, where some pawnbrokers and retailers even protected themselves with insurance, New York women clearly participated in all aspects of the clothing industry.[86]

The journey of a piece of Bristol cloth illustrates some of the confusions inherent in poor women's attempts to clothe themselves. In October 1722 Gertrude LaRoux, a widow and shopkeeper, was robbed. The thief took "a double gown of Callico & a piece of Bristol stuff of about forty yards, a piece of Indian Sattin of about three yard." A week later La Roux thought that she saw a piece of the Bristol at the house of Cornelia Pickett. Pickett told a magistrate that on the previous day a woman she knew named Anne Sawyer had brought the cloth to her so that it could be made into a "loose gown." Sawyer had told her that she had bought it "at a shop in town" at a good price. When the clerk of the city council, David Jamison, questioned Sawyer, she admitted bringing the material to Pickett's house. She claimed, however, that she had bought the material from an Indian slave of William Dobbs, who she had thought was a freeman.[87] The courts did not believe Sawyer; she was sentenced to jail for felonious stealing. The judges clearly believed that she had not merely received the goods but stolen them.[88]

Again, because much of the evidence for this informal economy comes from court records, it is easy to overemphasize the illegality of such transactions. Especially with secondhand goods, the line between legal and illegal was not always obvious even to the participants. If Sawyer had bought the cloth from an unknown man, she might have surmised that it had been stolen, given its inexpensive price. Her own suspicions might have led her to lie to Pickett that she had bought the goods "at a shop." Just as the free or enslaved status of a seller or buyer was not always clear, so the origin of the goods was often in question, and the desire to pawn them could easily outweigh the concern to verify the transaction's legality.

Not only was the line between legal and illegal frequently unclear, but it was also flexible. Women in late eighteenth-century London were often accused of theft, but most of these defendants claimed that what was being prosecuted as a theft was actually an act of "borrowing gone awry."[89] Similarly, Englishwomen who accepted clothes in pawn did not always examine their sources closely. The person trying to pawn the goods, moreover, might have had his or her own ideas about whose goods these were. Women occasionally pawned articles from rooms that they were renting, under the impression that the bed sheets, for example, were temporarily theirs to hock for a short-term loan. Likewise, servants and apprentices did not always agree on the ownership of property; a journeyman breeches maker sold his master's sample breeches as secondhand clothing after he had worn them to a fair.[90]

In New York ownership was not always clear when slaves, servants, and apprentices took goods and pawned them, and this fact led to confusion over the legality of the behavior of the women who received such goods. Thus women sometimes bought clothing from enslaved men and thought that the transactions were legal. Gerritie Cure admitted to buying a shirt from Bristo, a slave of Robert Walter's, but she pleaded that she had not known it was a crime. The court claimed that the shirt had been stolen from Walter, but Bristo may have considered the shirt his own; Cure certainly did.[91] Some slaves clearly considered clothing their own to dispose of as they pleased, but owners and magistrates disagreed.

Personal Costs

Elizabeth Anderson would at first seem to be exactly the sort of female criminal likely to run a disorderly house. Eleven of her neighbors, some of New York's most prominent merchants, wrote a petition to the supreme court claiming that she was "a person of notorious ill fame and reputation" and asking "for [their] Common Safety" that she be removed "or at least that she be taken to lay some restraint upon her

Behavior." As an example of her inability to keep an orderly house, one neighbor claimed that "at Two o'Clock in the Morning, [he] heard a general noise . . . and in the midst of it, murder cry'd."[92] Three weeks later both New York papers reported that Anderson, "a loose and profligate Wretch," was whipped thirty-nine times for theft. The *New-York Weekly Post-Boy* hinted that the story behind the theft had some complicated nuances, since Anderson was whipped "not only for stealing but swearing and Robbery against the Challenger of the very Thing which, upon trial, was proved she stole herself." Anderson's story, however, is much more complex than the *Post-Boy* implied, and it vividly demonstrates the dangers of the informal economy.[93]

Elizabeth Anderson was a relatively recent immigrant to New York City. Widowed in Ireland, she had been left destitute except for a brother "in good circumstances" in Boston. On his advice, she and her daughter came to New York, where "he might have a Better Opportunity to assist her in some little way of Business." Despite the inconvenience of distance, then, Anderson's brother saw New York City as an advantageous place for a single woman to support herself and her daughter. Accordingly, Elizabeth Anderson "hired a small shop or shed with a Chamber over it not a foot wide in a good Neighbourhood . . . and sold Bread Beer Candles Cheese in small Quantitys by the penny Lemmons Oranges Limes potatos and other such small Commoditys."[94]

Her daughter Mary had just turned fourteen when she caught the eye of a few young elite men who boarded nearby. John Lawrence, Charles Arding, and Cornelius Livingston were the younger sons of local elite families, and they all used to stop by Anderson's store to buy fruit. Elizabeth Anderson suspected that they might have "ill designs" on her daughter Mary, and she tried to keep her out of the shop when the men were there. However, Anderson's vigilance extended only so far. When she received a message that Mrs. Ferrara, the men's landlady, wanted some oranges, she thought nothing of sending her daughter on the errand, even at ten o'clock at night. Ferrara ran the Merchant's Coffee House, one of the busiest and most respectable public houses in New York. Anderson was probably more pleased to have Ferrara's business than worried about Ferrara's lodgers. Mary Anderson was shown into a parlor, where four men—the three elite youths and another named Cornelius Oudenaarde—were sitting. Anderson stood in silence for a moment while the men "held down their heads and sneered and winked upon one another." Mary asked them if they had not ordered some oranges. One of the men said that the oranges were not what they had wanted. Mary, not perceiving any double entendre, turned to leave, but at that point two of the men got up and locked the door. Charles Arding then grabbed her and tried to force her into a bed in an adjoining room. Mary screamed and fought, and Arding let go of her. Then John Lawrence tried to rape her. He pushed her down an entryway and first offered her silk fabrics in exchange for sex. She refused, and he "pulled down his Breeches and used Violence towards her," as the attorney general later characterized the assault. Mary, desperate, pulled her skirt forward through her legs and held the hem in her teeth. Lawrence continued to fight her for a few minutes but eventually gave up and let her go.

Mary, although upset and "disordered," did not tell her mother what had happened until the next day, when Livingston came to the shop to ask if Elizabeth was planning to make a complaint to the king's attorney, William Kempe. Only then did Elizabeth demand that Mary tell her what had happened. Mary Anderson then filed a complaint and found Kempe sympathetic. Infuriated, the men swore revenge. They embarked on a plan of prosecution so extensive and wide-ranging that it would have been worthy of a Restoration comedy, had it not been true. As the attorney general explained in his brief, "no Schemes have been left unattempted, no Falshoods nor Inventions omitted to blacken their Character, nor no practices untryed to deter the carrying on this prosecution against the defendants."

The power of commerce in New York City is nowhere clearer than in the fact that these four men chose to exact their retribution through the medium of trade. The revenge that Lawrence, Livingston, Arding, and Oudenaarde chose clearly demonstrates the fine line between legal and illegal activity in colonial New York's informal economy. They attempted to force Anderson into illegal exchange by trying to trick her into receiving stolen goods and trading with slaves, all under the cover of other transactions. Lawrence, Livingston, Arding, and Oudenaarde arranged for two unknown young men to approach Anderson's shop and sell her some secondhand clothes. When Anderson refused to accept the clothing, they offered her one of the articles, a cloak, as a gift. She refused that as well, possibly on the grounds that she did not deal in dry goods, because one of the men then said that he "had something for her in her own way." He then offered to sell her potatoes cheaply if she would keep the transaction secret. This offer she also refused.

Unable to trick her into accepting suspicious goods, the young men moved to another sphere of women's economic activity: keeping taverns. They insisted that she sell them some liquor. She protested that she had none to sell them, but they caught sight of a small bowl of punch that she had made for herself on the counter. The two men grabbed the punch, tossed down a few coins on the counter, and called to some slaves who were at the doorway to come in and drink it. If they had done so, the young men could have had grounds—entirely trumped up—for accusing her of "trading with Negroes," the common term that covered the crime of selling liquor to slaves. However, Anderson saw what they intended and drove all the men, black and white, from her store. As they left, they punched her in the face. Physical violence was a part of the revenge, but it was not the primary vehicle.

This incident made Anderson very cautious for a while. When another black man tried to sell her some cheese, she lured him to a nearby alderman's house and handed him over along with the cheese as evidence of the attempted deception. She was determined not to be caught breaking the regulations of retailing. Colonial laws that forbade trading with slaves might be infrequently or inconsistently enforced, but Anderson knew that she was already under suspicion.

The next, and successful, attempt at revenge led to the downfall of the Andersons, and it did so because of the centrality of clothing in the informal economy. One day a poorly dressed woman whom Elizabeth Anderson did not know came into her shop and begged for some food. Anderson "out of Compassion" gave her some. The woman told her that she had a sick husband and starving children at home and pleaded with Anderson to trade her some food in exchange for a petticoat in pawn. Later on, when Anderson was in jail on suspicion of keeping a disorderly house, her own house was robbed. Her daughter Mary had some suspicion of who might have stolen the goods. She then went to a constable to request a search warrant, but because she did not have the cash to pay for one, she offered a cloak that had been worth three shillings.[95] A cloak, like the poor woman's petticoat, was a common cloth substitution for cash.

Mary Anderson at the time suspected a trick, but she could not convince her mother. Elizabeth Anderson insisted that the woman really was in terrible need, and hence she agreed to the trade. The woman never returned to redeem her petticoat, so Elizabeth began to wear it herself. Then she made a real mistake, and Lawrence and his friends took their revenge. Charles Sullivan, "a person of ill Character" but an acquaintance of Elizabeth's, invited her into his house to rest on the way home from a walk and saw the petticoat. When he admired it and asked where she had gotten it, Anderson lied, saying that it was her own and that she had brought it from Ireland. At this Sullivan denounced her as a liar, claiming that it had been stolen from his own house. Anderson, knowing that Lawrence wanted to accuse her of receiving stolen goods, quickly backpedaled and told him about the poor woman who needed food. She pulled it off and offered it to him, begging him to forget the entire incident. Sullivan then threatened to prosecute her for the theft unless she found this mysterious poor woman. To ensure that she would look for the reputed thief, Sullivan took her cloak, its silver clasp, and her silver shoe buckles as security.

Anderson did try to find the woman, but she learned that the woman had actually been a friend of Sullivan's and that she had now left town. Although Anderson went back to the alderman and told him the entire story, she had run out of luck. Sullivan, spurred on (so Anderson certainly believed) by Lawrence and his friends, prosecuted Anderson for theft.

The young men easily manipulated the court system to work in their favor. In 1732 the New York legislature had provided for a court of "special sessions," in which persons accused of misdemeanors could be tried summarily without a jury and sentenced to a corporal punishment.[96] Lawrence and his friends brought her before the New York Court of Special Sessions, and although her daughter told the court the whole story of the poor woman and the petticoat, the recorder, Simeon Johnson, was not convinced. Instead he threatened Anderson, berated her for beginning a prosecution for rape against Lawrence, and ordered her to be whipped. The attorney general charged later that "Arding and Lawrence gave the Executioner Money to whip her severely and she was whipped most inhumanly, till she fell several times into Convulsions."[97]

Outraged by the summary judgment against Anderson, Kempe put his utmost into the trial against Lawrence, Arding, Livingston, and Oudenaarde. The newspapers mocked his concern, gloating that the court found Anderson guilty of theft "notwithstanding all the Interest that was made by her friends."[98] Kempe had put his own interest in jeopardy as well, for in October of that year he was indicted in the New York Supreme Court for maladministration, and the incident on which the prosecution based its case was Kempe's championing of Elizabeth Anderson.[99] The attorney general's best, in the end, was not quite good enough. When the attempted rape case came to trial in April 1755, the jury acquitted all four men the same day.

As one gender historian has pointed out, cases such as the Andersons' show the terrible vulnerability of working women and the privileged position that elite men held in early America. The brazen insouciance of Livingston and his friends and their immediate acquittal bear out this interpretation. It is not enough, however, to explain the entrapment of Elizabeth Anderson as a part of the making of early American patriarchy.[100] Although the attempted rape of Mary Anderson is an unambiguous story of an effort to assert power through gendered violence, the attempted destruction of Elizabeth Anderson shows a very different use of power. The physical violence that the gang of men used was only partly successful; they achieved true success by harnessing the power and the system of trade.

The tale of Elizabeth and Mary Anderson's persecution also sheds an entirely different light on both the informal economy and larceny. Those elite young men took the world of the informal economy that could be so liberating for slaves and poor white women and made it a constantly threatening and dangerous place. The elaborate plots to trap Anderson reveal the small shop in the informal economy as a place under siege.

Most of all, these connections between slaves, secondhand clothes, and white women show how the goods that were thought to be clear signs of eighteenth-century status were not restricted to the wealthy and the elite. In taverns that were often no more than front rooms or in tiny shops "above stairs," women and men, both free and enslaved, pawned and fenced goods that had little practical value in their hardworking lives. Punch bowls and velvet cloaks became currency in their own economy, to be exchanged for a drink, a room, or even a search warrant. Nor did consumer goods simply represent cash, for those who accepted these goods in pawn sold them again to customers who desired luxury goods. Such a desire fueled both firsthand and secondhand production of consumer goods. However, not everyone benefited from this loose and underground economy. The possibilities it offered for improving one's personal lot could come at a price. Fourteen-year-old Mary Anderson was the victim of an attempted gang rape; her mother, in trying to defend her daughter, was whipped until she lost consciousness. Every attempt the Andersons made to survive in their "economy of makeshifts" was viewed with hostility and suspicion by members of the elite and the courts.

There were other, wider implications to the informal economy as well. By redistributing used and stolen goods, making them accessible even to the poorest of New Yorkers, those women and men who worked in the informal economy inadvertently undermined the meaning of those consumer goods meant to indicate status. As both buyers and sellers, these poor and enslaved New Yorkers entered into a wide world of Atlantic goods and commerce. At the same time, their involvement in this market ended up undercutting exactly the sorts of status divisions that consumer goods were intended to create and support. These men and women rarely intended to create a social revolution, however, and their trading and purchases in this market often came at great personal costs to themselves. Moreover, status distinctions did not disappear with the emergence of a secondhand consumer market. Instead, elite New Yorkers found other ways to turn the presentations of their bodies into markers of distinction.

Chapter Four

Masters of Distinction

In the early summer of 1731 the *New-York Gazette* convened a "court of manners" for its readers, printing semiserious essays on topics such as tea tables and the taking of snuff. Within this discussion appeared a farcical petition from "the young Tradesmen and Artificers of the City of New-York" who were looking for wives. These middling young men complained that the "gay and splendid Appearance" affected by the "young Ladies about our own station" was so intimidating that the men did not dare to approach them, fearing that they could not "distinguish [the women] from People of the best Estates in Town." A man who addressed a woman of higher status might unintentionally give offense to the local elite, but without clear visual cues of rank, how could he confidently address the object of his affections? So the women of his own lower rank became unapproachable, "thus guarded with an Air of Quality, and entrenched behind double Rows of china-Ware, and covered with Silk and Satin without."[1]

As the *Gazette*'s mocking essay makes clear, by the early 1730s the widespread distribution of consumer goods such as fashionable clothes and tea equipages had become a matter of some concern. No longer could one depend on silk, satin, and china to distinguish "People of Condition" from the lower strata of society. The bachelor tradesmen may have hoped that middling women would choose to "distinguish themselves from People of Condition" by simplifying their dress and social habits; members of the elite, however, could not depend on the lower classes to limit their own consumption and maintain the outward distinctions of status.

In its next issue the *Gazette*, tongue firmly in cheek, offered a solution to this social conundrum. The "Court of Manners" ruled that the artisans should save up their money, buy their own tea sets, and hire a "young Lady . . . to teach them the Laws, Rules, Customs, Phrases and Names of the Tea-Utensils; in all which (by a close Application) they may soon arrive to a great Proficiency, which will certainly render them polite and agreeable to those whose Favour they solicit."[2] Elite manners and etiquette, the paper implied, were accessible to anyone willing to pay for the lessons. The result would completely elide the distinction between elite and common social status. Although the idea of hiring an expert to teach uncouth New Yorkers the finer points of ceremony may have seemed humorous to the editor of the *Gazette*, the city's elite did not find the prospect of learning manners from hired hands particularly funny.

Eighteenth-century New Yorkers of all ranks were eager to partake of the world of luxury goods and the distinctions that came with them. Members of the political elite in particular, wanting to assert their position in the British Empire, eagerly pursued the status that these goods symbolized. However, secondhand luxury goods were so widely available that these commodities began to lose their cultural distinctiveness; their distribution through both the formal and informal markets of New York's commercial economy destabilized the very hierarchies of social status they were intended to reinforce. Proper comportment at exclusive public gatherings such as balls and dinners thus assumed an even greater importance in signifying rank. As members of the political class jockeyed for appointments and favors from the imperial government, public displays of gentility became markers of their close ties to the power of the British Empire. As middling artisans feared the loss of suitable spouses to the artifices of elite display, elite New Yorkers anxiously strove to maintain the markers of their own distinct status. Nowhere were these anxieties played out more carefully than in the arena of formal manners and public gatherings.

The city's distance from the London metropolis meant that New Yorkers were forced to learn the performance of gentility from traveling dancing masters, who claimed to possess expertise not simply in dance but in all modes of refined comportment. A dancing master was a peripatetic one-man finishing school; he moved from city to city on the imperial periphery selling an education in dance, poise, manners, and whatever social graces the local elite felt they needed. Yet, in relying on itinerant hired hands to teach gentility, elite New Yorkers undermined the very status they sought to assert, for though the knowledge that the dancing masters imparted enabled members of the elite to publicly display their distinction, its availability to anyone who possessed the wherewithal to pay for it contradicted its exclusivity, thereby undermining its value to confer social status. In this way, as peddlers of gentility, dancing masters were both eminently desirable and inherently dangerous. The social contradiction that they embodied endangered the dancing masters themselves; their intimate but fraught connection to a provincial gentility that had to be purchased through instruction forced these teachers into the rough-and-tumble world of New York's cultural and imperial politics.

Like the con artists who relied on the commercial economy for their schemes, New York's dancing masters exploited the system of commercial gentility. The sales of financial credit and social credit were all part of the city's dangerous world of commerce. Yet, while New Yorkers were equally interested in the goods that con artists and dancing masters purveyed, the dancing masters' services created a deeper anxiety, for their fraud was transparent and accepted: by purchasing gentility, New Yorkers acknowledged the importance and the instability of their own status.

Gentility in Transition

Just as the eighteenth-century world of credit was caught between two ways of doing business, so the world of status distinction in this period was a system in transition. Until the end of the seventeenth century, social status was assumed to be conferred by birth and property in England. Ownership of land in particular was fundamental in claims of high status. By the early years of the eighteenth century, however, these entrenched and explicit markers of elite rank had begun to shift. Especially for the "lower gentry," the meaning implied by the term "gentleman" had become increasingly uncertain; gentility now referred as much to polite behavior as it did to birth. Even members of the wellborn country elite came to embrace these new ideals of gentility in support of their declarations of high status. As one historian of politeness has phrased it, "To be a gentleman or a lady was, to a noteworthy extent, to make a cultural rather than sociological claim about oneself."[3] These cultural claims needed to be made; assertions of gentility were necessary for both commercial and social credit.

The enormous mobility of the eighteenth-century Atlantic world had further jeopardized the reliability of social stratification, especially in port cities. With so many people moving beyond the worlds where they had been known, other markers of status besides reputation had to be pressed into service. As we have already seen, the world of goods formed a large part of New York's new recipe for status. Yet the secondhand market in consumer goods undermined any straightforward associations between commodities and status. Thus, New York's larger commercial culture necessitated the use of sociability to create elite status. For elite New Yorkers, sociability was the literal practice of social position; it became the way by which rank could be both displayed and asserted, since status was claimed by its performance. In other words, the way one acted in social settings was a marker of how one wished others to read one's status.[4] To achieve the desired results, knowledge of this appropriate behavior had to be purchased.

Although elite New Yorkers were united in their desire to separate themselves from the plebeian masses, desire for power and status kept them at each others' throats for much of the eighteenth century. Provincial New York's frenzied party politics was notorious. As members of the city's leading families jockeyed for position, they turned to any weapon they found at hand. Although New York's factions were known as the "Court party" and the "Country party" (with political terminology that mimicked the artistic dichotomy between court dances and country dances), their differences rarely centered on issues of policy or ideology. Instead, political disputes were formulated through family and individual loyalties. The elite men embroiled in these disputes distinguished themselves by attacking not their rivals' concepts but their gentility. Performance of status, then, rather than political content or ideas, structured the province's partisan politics.[5]

Most famously in the 1730s, several particularly witty partisans used satire and the public prints to portray each other as fawning dogs or oversexed apes, creating a brouhaha that culminated in John Peter Zenger's dramatic trial for libel.[6] Less cleverly but much more frequently, partisans used both the places and the forms of sociability to proclaim rank, loyalty, and honor. Most of the city's satirists in the 1730s published their work in the *New-York Weekly Journal.* When one of the paper's anonymous contributors wanted to address the question of factionalism more broadly, he turned to the language of politeness. He advised that "men should strictly keep to good manners" in their political wrangles. Indeed, the author continued, proper behavior would be the primary criterion of success in winning a political dispute: "Besides people that are not concerned, when they come to hear or read these disputes, will certainly say: that side that is managed with the most good Manners has been managed by Gentlemen."[7] Good politics in the eighteenth century were indistinguishable from good manners.

Manners were as fundamental as goods to the creation of politeness throughout eighteenth-century Britain and just as accessible through the marketplace. The display of elegant consumer goods did not on its own produce status; one also needed to display an elegant posture, an elegant bow, and elegant dance steps. The "gentle" way of using the body was by no means natural; it had to be properly learned. Aspiring colonists needed to purchase the services of a dancing master to teach them how to behave in polite society.[8]

Both the mobility of New York's residents and the frequent swings of fashionable behavior destabilized most indicators of elite distinction. The uncertainty of knowing precisely who belonged in polite society led members of the elite to turn to the dancing masters for help. They hoped that a more explicit presentation and use of the elite body would cleanly demarcate the genteel from the rude. At the same time, however, that dancing masters were able to help New York's elite negotiate the worlds between old and new forms of status, they also created a new problem for their clients. A claim to polite status that was dependent on manners learned from a dancing master was inherently a status based on knowledge bought and sold in the marketplace. The new gentility thus forced elite people to purchase a status that they wanted to but could not acquire elsewhere.

The professional life of dancing master Henry Holt demonstrates the imperial and commercial webs in which dancing masters lived their lives. Holt first made his presence known in New York through an advertisement, published in 1737, announcing his plan to hold a ball at Stephen DeLancey's former mansion, which he had taken for a dancing school. To prepare his potential audience for the evening, Holt offered dance lessons twice a week in the afternoons. For his qualifications Holt claimed that he had been taught by one of the "most celebrated Masters in England" and had danced "a considerable Time at the Theatre Royal in Drury Lane." These credentials disingenuously implied that Holt had just arrived from London, which was not true; for at least the previous three years Holt had lived in Charleston, running another dancing school as well as a theater company. Earlier in 1737 he had settled his accounts in South Carolina and moved to New York. Holt was that eighteenth-century creature of the market, an itinerant peddler of gentility. He moved from place to place and advertised in order to create and satisfy the demand for a dance teacher.[9]

On the other hand, Holt's itinerancy could also work against him. Colonial Americans who had already established themselves did not look favorably on itinerants and often worried that they would become a drain on parish or city funds. Most dancing teachers were seen as little better than elegant charlatans. Sometimes the very appellation of "dancing master" was enough to arouse suspicion. In 1732 the *Pennsylvania Gazette* reported a search for a suspected murderer "who professes several Businesses, as Butcher, Dancing Master, etc." If butchery and murder were virtual synonyms, the teacher of dance became guilty by association; a man who called himself a dancing master might be capable of anything. Wisely, then, Holt constructed his advertisement to imply that he had come directly from the source of true culture, London. In order to avoid the odium of itinerancy, he omitted mention of his years in Charleston.[10]

Holt was not the first to attempt a career in New York's dance market, but he was the first to succeed. Francis Stepney, a man before his time, came to New York in 1687. Members of the city council suspected that he had been forced to leave Boston for "ill-behavior"; besides, they added, he had no "manuall occupation whereby to get an honest livelyhood." Unwilling to consider the teaching of dance a reputable way to earn a living, they required him to pay a large sum in security to the council simply to stay in town, and they refused to let him practice his trade. New York did not yet have either the need or the demand for dance instruction.[11]

The advent of public balls in the early eighteenth century signaled a shift in the council's attitude toward dancing masters, if not their view of itinerants. By 1716 Boston had an established dance teacher, and before the end of the 1720s the *New-York Gazette* was advertising the sale of a house "commonly called the Dancing School." In the 1730s George Brownell tried the New York dance market. Brownell was at least as roving an itinerant as Holt, and he too hid his previous experience. In addition to providing Benjamin Franklin with his first math lessons, he had taught dancing in Boston as early as 1713. He first advertised his talents in New York in 1731, claiming additional expertise in "Reading Writing Cyphering, Merchant Accompts, Latin Greek etc." This wide set of skills still did not convince Brownell to refer even once in print to his experiences in other colonies. Brownell must have had at least some professional success; his clients included the ten-year-old Phila Franks, daughter of an elite family and the future wife of Oliver DeLancey, and Alexander and Elizabeth Colden, the upper-class but country-bred children of an equally distinguished family. Brownell came to New York in 1731 and had left for Philadelphia by 1736. In 1737 Holt arrived in town. From that point on, New York usually had at least one dancing instructor, although turnover was high until the end of the 1750s.[12]

Dancing masters sold their offers of gentility by advertising their wares, thereby taking advantage of both an expanding market and an expanding print culture. Advertising likely allowed George Brownell to make a comfortable living in all three northeastern cities, while Francis Stepney, thirty years earlier, had been unceremoniously ejected from them. Itinerancy and dependence on a fluid and possibly elastic market, however, was a clear departure from the polite culture these men tried to teach, and this produced a surprising paradox. New Yorkers who strove for politeness were forced to learn their manners from hired hands. Like con artists, dancing masters were able to ply their wares in a world structured by commerce and the social relations it engendered. At the same time, their elite customers were sensitive to the possibilities that their teachers were not all they seemed to be. Unlike tailors, for example, who were also necessary partners in elite self-presentation, dancing masters had to look much like gentlemen even when they were not. Dancing masters may have known their material, but since they were not genteel themselves, their attempts to embody their subjects inevitably had to meet with failure. The very nature of their profession made them dubious if necessary guides to the new and continually changing gentility of the ballroom.[13]

The Practice of Gentility

The ballroom, and ballroom dancing in particular, was an ideal site for the performance of the commodified gentility that marked an elite New Yorker. In a remarkably explicit exposition of the relationship between status, commerce, and dancing assemblies, New York's newspaper revealed the importance of manners to the city's merchant class. Although the intended audience of the article was clearly men, women too had an essential role to play in the creation of genteel status.

This new definition of gentility ran into opposition on multiple fronts. Some essayists, for example, fretted that Britons spent too much time acquiring manners. One popular ultra-Whig tract reprinted at midcentury in New York thundered that in Britain's "comfortable Cities" one finds "a motley Race of *English* Traders burlesqued into *French* dancing-masters."[14] In the previous decade a similar but more local criticism made its way into New York's public consciousness In November 1732 the *Boston Gazette* published an editorial inveighing against dancing in general and dancing assemblies in particular. Its editor railed against dance as a manifestation of extravagant luxury that was "hastening the ruin of our Country."[15] His critical eye saw little distinction between a trader who mastered a dance and a traitorous dancing master.

In a direct response to the Boston editorial, the *New-York Gazette* published an explicit defense of the rise of gentility in the colonies and emphasized the importance of dancing assemblies for the creation of status. The editor of the New York paper, William Bradford, argued that far from being a bad influence on state and society, balls were in fact a force for good. Not only did they bring provincial manners closer to those of London, but they also smoothed political differences and re-established class differences. The Boston editorial had implied that the constituent parts of such a monstrous entity as a dancing assembly were "irregular enormous and unnatural." Rather huffily the New York rejoinder explained that the members of an assembly were "Women of the most celebrated Beauty and distinguished Virtue" and "Gentlemen of the best Sense, improving Conversation and unspotted Honour"—in short, New York's commercial class.[16]

Moreover, the close ties of the city's elite to other parts of Britain through their commercial networks were the basis for these assemblies. Bradford disparaged the Boston editorialist's "ill Manners" and "low and narrow Way of thinking" as that of a rusticated colonial whose attitude only dissociated Britons from their empire. The *New-York Gazette* further explained that anyone of any note in England attended such assemblies and that New Yorkers and other dancers were simply trying to "revive and restore in America" the manifestations of politeness so pervasive in Britain. Dancing made one more British as well as more polite.[17]

Bradford did not claim that the men and women who attended assemblies were aristocratic by birth. Rather, following the lead of the London literary magazine the *Tatler*, he implied that merchants as well as courtiers could be gentlemen.[18] Without disdaining high birth, he made it clear that politeness did not depend on lineage; since not everyone who wished to be genteel could have blue blood ("we would all be well bred if we could"), most people were forced to "endeavour at the Appearance of being so," a goal that one could successfully obtain by "Example, Custom, and habit." Dancing assemblies were the surest and most compendious route to such a goal, for they were "the Promoters and the Patterns of Vertue, Manners, good Sense, and good Behaviour, the first Introduction to a general Complaisance, to good Neighbourhood, and to a vertuous, genteel, unaffected, easy Commerce between the well bred of both sexes." The education that one received at a ball, therefore, could compensate for the limitations of one's birth.[19]

The *New-York Gazette* emphasized the fellowship of civil and genteel society. Assemblies, the paper argued, did not simply provide polish for the individual; they also created a whole world before which the individual was required to perform. People had no choice but to behave properly when "they found the numerous and judicious Eyes of a genteel Assembly turned upon their Conduct toward each other," and, being members of that genteel assembly, they helped to strengthen as well as to portray its social codes. Behavior that might be effective in a situation intended to emphasize traditional family-based hierarchical differences had no place in a sociable gathering, "for a Churl or a Shrew may make a commanding, insulting and important Figure among the Servants and Dependants of a Family, though both would be exceedingly contemptible, if the same wretched Character distinguish'd itself at a play or a Ball." In the polite world, good behavior was monitored by one's peers, which gave a "standing Discouragement to, and a severe Reproach and Satyr [Satire] upon the Sot, the Clown, and the outrageous Party-man of every Denomination."[20] Bradford implied that other members of the elite would discipline bad manners at an assembly.

The New York paper revealed its Whiggish orientation toward the virtues of commerce and trade in its discussion of the ballroom's benefits. In light of New York's particularly factious politics, it is not surprising that the *Gazette* lingered longingly over the possibility of "Reproach and Satyr" on the "outrageous Party-man." However, the *Gazette* had a particular fear about the pernicious dangers of party divisions. In a horri-fied tone the paper recounted a parable of a "Tory Fox-hunter [who] would rather drink with his own Groom than hunt with a Whig Lord though he had the best Pack of Dogs in the Kingdom and lived in uni-versal Hospitality." The confusion of class boundaries could go no fur-ther than servant and master sharing a sociable glass. The ball, argued the *New-York Gazette*, not only could save the British Empire from the dangers of class leveling but also could temper political differences.[21]

Bradford was quick to point out, moreover, that not just any club or society had the restorative powers of the ball. The editor recalled that in the bad old days of party strife, "every Bowling Green had its party and every little Club a Set of Members who were bound to think, drink, speak, and sing as some hothead Leader was pleas'd to direct." These all-male clubs contributed to the divisive party politics that in turn com-pelled the hunter to prefer a drink with his groom to a shooting party with his elite peers. Only civil discourse between the "well bred of both sexes" could reestablish class boundaries. The *New-York Gazette* never implied that women alone were enough to make a society polite (as nineteenth-century theorists of gender ideology would eventually argue). Rather it was the heterosociability of the ball that created "a Peo-ple polite and Vertuous."[22]

Gentility was not the exclusive province of either men or women; it involved "easy Commerce between the well bred of both sexes." As several historians have demonstrated, gentility erased differences, including sexual difference, between all those who had at least the "Appearance" of politeness and brought them together into a harmoni-ous egalitarianism. Politeness was not necessarily based on birth and breeding, since it could be acquired with practice and hard work. Although polite society rested on a clear distinction between the refined and the rough, in theory there were no differences among the genteel or between men and women in particular. In a polite gathering, more-over, women were more than merely "arbiters of sociability and deco-rum" who judged dance and dress. The gentility of the ballroom depended on heterosociability.[23] As James Forester's "The Polite Philos-opher" noted in 1758, the "most *Effectual* method of arriving at the Summit of Genteel Behavior . . . [is] by conversing with the *Ladies.*"[24]

William Bradford's emphasis on the assembly characterized the way that New Yorkers thought about the exhibition of their status. Formal public dances had been popular in New York since their first appearance in 1713, but they became increasingly important among the elite who sponsored and attended them in the years following. In addition to pro-viding entertainment and pleasure, balls and assemblies served two fur-ther purposes in colonial New York City. Primarily, they created and maintained distance between people of different ranks through their celebration of a commodified polite culture. In addition, they subordinated local political conflicts to a backdrop for the performance of gentility. Government-sponsored balls helped connect their male and female participants to a wider British Empire. Such entertainments were by their very nature heterosocial occasions; the bonds that elite white male New Yorkers formed with the empire required women's partnership.

The *Gazette*'s essay is an idealist fantasy. It accurately describes a gentlemanly standard of British imperial manners: open to merchants, nonaristocratic, heterosocial, and nonpartisan. These manners were meant to be both learned and displayed in a ballroom. However, New York's assembly rooms were rarely places in which men could perform their elite status without either partisanship or the invisible help of the dancing master.

New York may have had a public dancing assembly as early as the 1730s, and with the opening of the New-exchange assembly room in the middle of the century, the opportunities for elegant dancing and socializing had become increasingly common. Musicians such as the oboist Charles Love occasionally sponsored balls there after concerts, and New York's elite organized a series of public assemblies that met regularly.[25] These bimonthly public balls occasionally replaced the state-sponsored balls, as when in 1758 the assembly's managers advertised that the second ball of the season would take place on the king's birthday, "so to be continued once a fortnight, till the first Thursday in May."[26] Governor James DeLancey thus refrained that year from sponsoring a ball in honor of the king's birthday. The managers understood that these balls were no mere diversion; as they noted in print several years later, they were "sensible of the advantages of so useful and polite an entertainment."[27] In providing a place for women and men together to perform their gentility and imperial allegiances, these assemblies played an essential public role.

Gentlemen's clubs also offered balls that indicated the members' polite sociability, allegiances, and connections, and they shaped New York's image as a genteel city of the British Empire. In 1757 the New York St. Andrew's Society gave a ball "at which a large and polite company of both sexes assembled. The ladies in particular, made a most brilliant appearance; and it is thought there scarcely ever was before so great a number of elegantly dress'd fine women seen together at any one place in North-America." The British military officers in attendance had clearly expected to be scornful of the women's taste. Instead, "they were most agreeably surprize'd and struck with the charming sight."[28] Five years later the British military commander Sir Jeffrey Amherst held a similar ball for ninety-six couples on the anniversary of Saint George. The New York newspaper's correspondent reported proudly that the company arrived "all very richly dressed; and 'tis said the entertainment was the most elegant ever seen in America."[29] The participants and the reporters alike preened themselves on New York's debonair preeminence in a British province.

Balls were a physical and visual division between the elite and the non-elite. Removed from the context of balls, however, dancing was not an elite or exclusive pastime. Dancing at parties or in taverns was an established tradition; in England, Morris dances and maypoles long antedated the Tudors.[30] In the seventeenth century dancing became suspect under the Puritans, and even in New York it was forbidden on Sundays.[31] However, eighteenth-century gentility put dancing in a new setting, surrounded it with luxurious goods, and made the rarefied result inaccessible to large numbers of people. At that point, balls became not only acceptable but also genteel.[32] Special assembly rooms for the dancers, mahogany tables for the cards, and silver serving pieces for the food all turned a spirited gathering into a fashionable event.

Still more important than the tangible goods and the brilliant setting of the assembly room were the intricate steps of the dance. Two types of dancing had existed in England at least since the time of Queen Elizabeth: pairs dancing and country dancing.[33] Dancing in pairs, sometimes known as "court dancing," was originally a complicated series of steps reserved for the aristocracy. Louis XIV developed court dances in the middle of the seventeenth century in order to keep his courtiers too busy to plot against his absolute monarchy.[34] By the eighteenth century pair dancing was symbolized above all by the minuet. This was the first dance that inaugurated most British balls, and this was the dance that established one's gentility and standing for the rest of the evening. The most prestigious couple of the assembly was invited to lead off the ball; after them, other pairs would follow, one at a time. Couples did not share the dance floor with each other but performed in front of the entire company. The challenge, both for women and for men, was not only to perform the minuet gracefully but also to be able to keep up with its constantly changing steps.[35] Those richly dressed "principal inhabitants," both male and female, had to know each choreographed turn, step, and wave of the arm. One New York dancing master estimated that it took two months to learn the minuet.[36] As this all-important dance could not be self-taught, a dancing master became essential to the social success of elite New Yorkers.

No longer simply a gathering that included a person who happened to play a fiddle, the ball quickly became an elaborate affair. Balls were far more than mere get-togethers. At a ball one might dance, dine, play

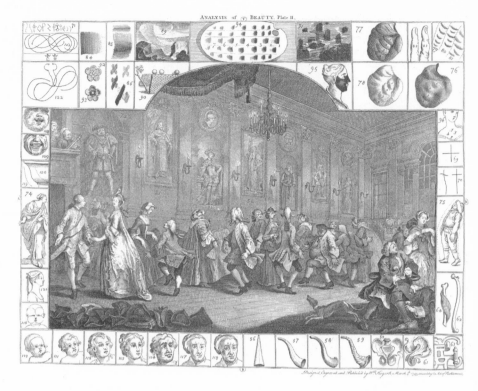

Figure 4. William Hogarth, *The Analysis of Beauty*, plate II: *The Country Dance* (1753). The tall couple in the left foreground are the epitome of eighteenth-century grace, with straight but not stiff postures and softly curving arms and legs. McCormick Library of Special Collections, Northwestern University.

cards or music, or even learn a new dance made for the occasion by the resident dancing master.[37] Even more important, balls allowed participants to make claims to status through a demonstration of their proper use of fashion, objects, and bodies. Furthermore, through the performance of dance, even those participants who may have been able to purchase the dress of polite guests could be separated into those who were truly genteel and those who were only pretending. Even a country dance could distinguish the capable from the clownish; William Hogarth, in his etching *The Analysis of Beauty*, plate 2: *The Country Dance* (1753), makes a clear contrast between the one graceful couple and the rest of the boorish dancers in the room (see Figure 4).

Far from London, provincial New Yorkers took it upon themselves at least in part to learn the proper movements. Booksellers sold collections of dances such as *Genteel Collections of Country Dances, Minuets, Marches, and Hornpipes* and John Playford's *The Dancing Master: Directions for Dancing*.[38] When he was in his thirties, the wealthy businessman James Alexander wrote down several new dance steps in a little notebook as an aide-mémoire. Alexander clearly used his notebook to keep up with the newest dances in Europe, most of which had been composed after he had moved to New York.[39] Other etiquette books, such as François Nivelon's *Rudiments of Genteel Behavior*, with its elaborately engraved plates of minuet steps and the proper way to hold a fan, appear not to have been sold in the American colonies (see Figure 5). For a more reliable education that went beyond learning variations on old dances, aspiring New Yorkers needed to employ dancing masters.

No figures in New York City were more central to the quest for civility than the dancing masters. Anyone of any age with pretensions to gentility went to a dancing master for instruction. The curriculum of the dancing masters offered more than the minuet; these men also taught all areas of "deportment"—posture, carriage, grace, and manners—that would be on display at a ball or other public event.[40] New Yorkers craved this education for themselves and their children. Oliver DeLancey's wife Phila Franks had started taking dance lessons with George Brownell before her eleventh birthday.[41] In 1731 Alice Colden justified sending her son "Sandie" and daughter "Bettie" to school in New York from their home in the country in terms that speak to the overlap of urbanity and gentility. As she wrote to her aunt, "we have allowed them a litle of that [dance lessons] likeways pewrly [purely] to make them know how to cary their body in company and to rubb off some of the countrey air which they have a good deal of in their cariage."[42] As James Alexander's notebook of dance steps shows, country dances were pleasant and good to know, but court dances such as the minuet instilled a more gracious form of bodily comportment. These dances needed to be learned properly; as the children of an elite family, Sandie and Bettie Colden needed a dancing master in the city to teach them what their country upbringing could not provide.

Dancing masters offered to tailor their lessons to any potential client. Most dancing schools were clearly intended for children, for whom there seemed to be little embarrassment about the process of learning gentility. When William Turner announced the opening of his dancing and fencing school, he promised to teach "those polite accomplishments, in the newest taste and most approv'd method." John Trotter, who in 1768 claimed he had been teaching in New York for over twenty years, promised to teach the minuet "in the nicest taste." Learning to dance for adults was another matter, and dancing masters seemed to recognize the potential shame. Thus they suggested discretion through pri-

Plate 1.

B.Dandridge Pinx.

L.P.Boitard Sculp.

According to Act of Parliament

Figure 5. François Nivelon, *Rudiments of Genteel Behavior*, "Standing." Notice a gentleman's posture: this fine line between stiff formality and relaxed ease was known as "complaisance." By permission of the Folger Shakespeare Library.

vate lessons. John Riveirs, for example, offered public lessons at his dancing school but also advertised that he would instruct "Any Gentlemen and Ladies who chuse to be taught at their own houses." Likewise, William Hulett held a dancing school but suggested that "Ladies or gentlemen may be attended privately, at their own houses." Men and women who were still in the process of learning ought not to dance in public, as one dancing master made clear when he suggested that his current pupils should continue to "honour [him] with the further protection and countenance of those ladies and gentlemen who have hitherto employ'd him" as "none of them have yet had time to be perfected in their minuets." Adult New Yorkers might find their claims to gentility compromised, this dancing master warned, if they dispensed too soon with his services.[43]

Formal dancing at balls and the superior social status that it demonstrated had explicit political meanings for New Yorkers. These evening entertainments were usually sponsored by the governor in his official residence, Fort George, where they always included numerous formal toasts to the royal family and to the city's noble patrons, such as the dukes of Newcastle and Grafton. Such balls allowed elite New Yorkers to establish their connections to the British Empire by providing forums for the expression of one's political allegiance and one's social claims to an imperial British identity.

Official balls sponsored by the royal governor demonstrated both cultural and political power. Newspapers often reported the balls in formulaic terms that emphasized their fashion, elegance, and patriotism. In 1734 the governor and his wife gave a "splendid ball" where, the *New-York Gazette* reported, one could find "the most numerous and fine appearance of Ladies and Gentlemen that had ever been known upon the like occasion."[44] In 1735 the *American Weekly Mercury* described a ball for the king's birthday at which "the appearance of gentlemen & ladies was very splendid, there being a great many of them in new cloaths, very rich, in honour of the day."[45] That same year, for the queen's birthday, the governor hosted a ball at Fort George, which the *New-York Gazette* admiring described as "a very rich and splendid entertainment for a vast concourse of the best gentlemen and ladies of the place."[46] Every official ball ended formulaically with "all imaginable demonstrations of joy," but one account explains more fully the nature of the guests' enthusiasm. At the celebration of George II's birthday in 1734 a ship happened to arrive from London that same morning. It brought "no small addition to the general joy and satisfaction of the day" with its report of the royal family's health and the news that "the Kingdom enjoyed at present all the blessings of peace, plenty, and a flourishing trade under his majesty's most glorious and auspicious administration."[47] The genteel ball and the commercial empire worked hand in glove.

These balls also served an explicitly political purpose. Public and open celebrations of secular holidays and anniversaries had been part of formal English politics at least since the Restoration in 1660, only four years before New York was incorporated into England's North American colonies. State-sponsored birthday parties for the current sovereign as well as celebrations of the anniversary of the coronation were fixtures of New York's social calendar. In the eighteenth century these festivities usually ended with balls. Such balls were explicitly designed to excite the participants' loyalty to their sovereign and their country. In New York such balls had the added effect of uniting a politically factious elite in the common cause of the British Empire.[48]

A newspaper account of a 1717 celebration in New York of George I's birthday shows the political and traditional nature of these commemorations:

At noon upon Drinking his Majesties, the Prince and Royal Family's Healths, a Round of the Guns in the Garrison was fired and was answered by the Vessels in the Road, the Soldiers (who with the Officers all in new Cloaths made a hansome Appearance) fired three Vollies as did our Militia, who were under Arms, together with a new Artillery Company, being all in Blew Cloaths with Gold laced Hats, the company consisted of Masters and Mates of Vessels, at night there was a bonfire and Plenty of Wine at the charge of the Corporation, there were rockets and other fireworks fired from the Walls of the Garrison, the whole Town was illuminated and the whole was concluded with a fine ball and hansome Entertainment by his Excellency the Governor.[49]

Much of the celebration—the bonfire, the free drinks, the artillery salutes on land and sea, the soldiers' uniforms, the fireworks, the illumination—was intended for the whole town. Based on the accounts of similar celebrations, however, the ball and entertainment given by the governor were clearly intended only for the elite. The lunchtime toasts to the health of the royal family were usually made by the governor, his council, other principal "gentlemen" and merchants, and, on occasion, their female relatives. As reported in the newspaper's summary of the events, the day began and ended with the governor. As the representative of the king, he ensured that the celebration's public festivities were bounded by these displays of imperial loyalty. Such celebrations, then, were intended to remind even those residents of England's most diverse colony of the power of their monarch.[50] At the same time, the distinction between the ball and the bonfire physically marked the separation of the gentle and the vulgar. Genteel amusements could keep provincials from feeling like rustics, and a dancing master could keep them from looking like boors.[51]

The ball for King George's birthday was only one of many such celebrations in the early part of the eighteenth century. In August 1713, in order to commemorate the end of Queen Anne's War and the new peace between Great Britain and France, the New York Common Council voted to provide a bonfire on the green in front of the fort, twenty-five gallons of wine, and "Illuminations and Other Demonstrations of Joy." The city disbursed £15.6.6 for the festivities. Like most other public celebrations, the day concluded with a ball, the first ever in New York. Although the council did not specifically mention the ball in its minutes (probably because balls were under the specific purview of the governor), in its own report of the event the *Boston News-Letter* dubbed the evening "Another Ball for Peace."[52]

Most of the elements of these rituals were hallowed by a long English tradition that British New Yorkers deliberately replicated in their new homes. Since at least the time of Queen Elizabeth, bonfires, alcohol, and fireworks were essential parts of public celebrations. While none of these elements was exclusively British, "distinctively in England they were harnessed to the needs of the state, to be deployed on its significant moments and anniversaries." In both England and New York, then, customary expressions of rejoicing were explicitly political events. Elizabethan and Stuart England developed all the varieties of traditional political jubilation except the ball. Only the ball seemed to be an eighteenth-century innovation.[53]

By the 1730s New Yorkers had begun to use balls to celebrate a wider array of political events than the sovereign's birthday or coronation day. In 1733 Governor Cosby sponsored the first New York celebration of the Prince of Wales's birthday. The celebration followed the pattern of other state-sponsored celebrations: the province's politicians and the "principal Gentlemen, Merchants and Inhabitants of this City" paid their respects to the governor, reviewed the royal troops, and enjoyed the salute from Fort George's cannons. They then drank toasts to the royal family.

In keeping with the mixed-sex sociability fundamental to polite entertainments, even the daytime celebrations included women. The company was invited "to the honour of waiting upon his Excellency's lady, the Hon. Mrs. Cosby and daughters in the with drawing room [*sic*]." Then again in the evening "the gentlemen and ladies of this city were present at a most splendid entertainment." The newspaper reported poetically that the night's ball "lasted as long as the regard which his Excellency's family always pays to the succeeding day, admitted."[54] For this celebration, the behavior of the drawing room was an essential part of the entire day. The governor's council, the members of the legislature, and other merchants and "inhabitants" paid their respects to the female representatives of the king as well as to the governor. A successful ball was predicated on the harmonious interaction of the two sexes; here, too, heterosocial elegance marked a proper celebration.

New Yorkers had little trouble acknowledging both the social and the imperial aspects of a ball, for both politics and dance were public rituals of order. The newspapers even turned this link into an allegory. In 1748 the *New-York Post-Boy* opened its October 3 issue with a poem that it claimed modestly was "but by Way of Simile." The poem compared the negotiation of the treaty at Aix-la-Chapelle that ended King George's War between England and France to a dance:

> Have you not seen at Country Wake
> A Crew of Dancers merry make?
> They figure in, and figure out:
> Go Back to Back, and turn about:
> They sett; take Hands; they cross; change Sides:
> (Each Movement a Scrub Minstrel guides)
> Around the measur'd Labyrinth trace
> 'Till each regains his former Place.
> So certain Potentates (two Couple)
> Leagu'd in Alliance, hight quadruple:
> After a Maze of Treaties run,
> Are e'en *just where they first begun*:
> I won't affirm who led the Dance,
> Yet for the Rhyme, suppose it *F——e*)
> But this I dare, at least, to say.
> *Old E——d* must the Piper pay.[55]

The anonymous author's political goal was to emphasize the uselessness of the treaty by pointing out that, just as in a round dance, the parties ended where they began. Dance perfectly encapsulated the relationship between two hostile countries: they advanced and retreated; they began; they shook hands; they attacked; they reversed their positions. The lofty imperialism of the two powers is brought low by the country setting, the inelegant ("scrub") musician, and the last line's crassly idiomatic reference to payment. Yet the dance is also intricate and formalized; both England and France knew the steps despite their complexity ("Around the measur'd Labyrinth trace"). Indeed, the steps were driven by outside forces that were beyond the control of either party ("Each Movement a Scrub Minstrel guides"). The language of the dancing body was also the language of imperial diplomacy.

Local dances brought home to New York's elite the political implications of balls, but these "splendid entertainments" did not always resemble the idealized version given by the local papers. Gentility on the ground was not quite the panacea for the province's famed factionalism that the newspapers had envisioned; in fact, partisan conflicts were so ordinary a part of political celebrations that the newspapers noted the occasions on which they seemed relatively subdued. In 1737, for example, the *New-York Gazette* reported that a celebration for George II's birthday displayed "demonstrations of Joy and Satisfaction, more than of late, in that all distinction of Party and Faction being Removed."[56]

Sometimes balls reinforced party divisions rather than eliminating them. In 1736 and 1748 New York's newspapers reported the occurrence of "competing" balls. In the earlier incident factional politics in New York were at their height, with Governor William Cosby and Judge Lewis Morris leading the two sides whose clash had begun as an argument over pay and soon grew into the famous Zenger libel case. In the later incident, Governor George Clinton was likewise engaging in a fierce partisan battle. However, party politics were neither restricted to men nor played out only in the courtroom and council chamber; the heterosocial ball was also an ideal venue for performing one's party loyalties.[57]

A dispute over the date of the Prince of Wales's birthday in 1736 provided an excuse for the competing balls. William Bradford, the official government printer, claimed that the birthday fell on a Monday, but the English papers put it on a Tuesday. The governor's supporters planned a Tuesday ball at Robert Todd's tavern, while the opposition prepared one on Monday at the Black Horse. The debate ranged among women as well as men. Archibald Kennedy, one of the governor's closest advisers, wrote to his friend Cadwallader Colden, "It is certain the Ladys declare openly of the Side of the Black Horse where there is to be a Grand Supper next Monday being the Princes Birthday according to Mr. Bradford's Acct."[58]

Bradford did not publish an account of the governor's evening at Todd's tavern, but Zenger's *New-York Weekly Journal* reported on the opposition ball at the Black Horse. So glowing was Zenger's description that he nearly ran out of superlatives: the evening was celebrated "in a most elegant and genteel Manner," with a "most Magnificent Appearance" of guests as well as a "most sumptuous Entertainment" after the dancing; in sum, "The whole was conducted with the utmost Decency, Mirth, and Chearfulness." From this gleaming scene of gentility and entertainment emerge two noteworthy figures. First, Euphemia Norris was chosen to lead the ball in "two new Country Dances made upon the Occasion."[59] As the daughter of the opposition party's leader and the wife of Captain Matthew Norris, who had recently been elected master of the Freemasons' lodge, Euphemia neatly represented the conflation of familial and political loyalties that constituted New York's factional politics. Second, Zenger also reported that "The Honourable *Rip Van Dam*, Esq. . . . began the Royal Healths." Van Dam was the previous acting governor, and his salary had precipitated the first dispute with the current governor. The careful mention of both Van Dam and Norris left no doubt of the political nature of the evening or of its oppositional politics. It is likewise noteworthy that Zenger deliberately chose a man and a woman to make the political and social affiliations of the antigovernor ball clear. Van Dam took the traditionally male role of offering the toasts, but that alone was not enough. The evening at the Black Horse was founded on heterosociability, and its political impact was due in part to the prominent display of harmonious power sharing between the sexes.

The second set of competing balls took place in 1748, when tensions were again at a peak, this time between Governor Clinton and a faction headed by James DeLancey. The description of the evening was somewhat more evenhanded: the governor entertained "some of the Gentlemen of the council" and other dignitaries with "a most extraordinary glass of wine (such as is rare to be met with in any private home)." Nevertheless, the opposition ball again received most of the attention. It was given, the account claims, by those "gentlemen that had not the honour to be invited to His Excellency's ball." They nonetheless "resolved not to be behindhand in their demonstrations of loyalty." This "Most elegant" entertainment managed the feat of lasting from six in the evening until five in the morning "without the least incivility offered or offence taken by anyone, which is scarce to be said on the like occasions." Again social superlatives—"most extraordinary," "Most elegant," "without the least incivility"—reinforce the competitive nature of the ball, where gentility was a sign of loyalty. Even in England by the middle of the eighteenth century, balls had become a standard element of election campaigns. Far from reducing political divisions, they were employed to exacerbate them. Like the British campaign balls, these competing dances in particular served to connect women and men with their local politics. At the same time, by putting these balls in the context of "demonstrations of loyalty" to the sovereign, dancers made manifest the connection between sociability, gentility, and empire for both women and men.[60]

The Problem with Dancing Masters

The discomfort that the city's elite felt with the intimate relationship between polite manners and dancing masters is captured neatly in a Dean Swift satire reprinted in a New York paper in 1748. Swift offers a long series of puns as heckling bystanders watch a counterfeiter brought to the gallows; whereas a cook jeers, "I'll give him a *Lick* in the *Chops*" and a farmer mocks, "I'll *Thrash* him," the dancing master threatens,

"I'll *Teach him Better Manners.*"[61] The piece offers no wordplay from the dancing master, only the uncomfortable acknowledgment that learning manners from a dancing master was some form of punishment akin to a punch in the mouth. The threat "I'll *Teach him Better Manners*" simultaneously affirms the legitimacy of the codes of social conduct and denies to some the right of inculcating those codes in others. The process of teaching manners was fraught with ambiguity and anxiety. If one was to make a good showing at a town ball, one had to know how to dance properly, and for that, one needed education from a dancing master, who thus became an important guide to New York's marketplace of gentility. Yet in the context of this imperial world, the dancing master's putatively apolitical status was as unstable as his social status. Almost inevitably, in times of political stress, the dancing master was caught up in the maelstrom of New York's factional politics.

The dancing masters to whom the elite turned for their lessons found themselves in precarious positions. At a time when gentility was not wholly established as a social order, the dancing masters in turn became yet more unstable guides. The shifting foundations of rank made the dancing master and his lessons both more desirable and more problematic. The close intersection of sociability and politics in New York further tainted the dancing master with suspicions about both his local and his imperial loyalties. He became a figure both essential and circumspect.

Even as they depended on dancing masters, New Yorkers also feared what they could teach. In 1754 the *New-York Mercury* published a satirical poem with commentary entitled "The MONKEY who had seen the World," explaining the perils of an education acquired by an unintelligent or immoral traveler. Like the Aesopic monkey of the fable, who comes home schooled only in the vices of the lands that he has visited, "Little Clodis Friskabout" is described in the commentary as a youth who traveled to London and there learned all the unbecoming practices of a "*compleat Gentleman.*" Among his other accomplishments, Friskabout attended balls, where he "distinguish'd himself . . . in that most polite Accomplishment *Dancing* whereof he is now compleat Master." Like other fops and fribbles, the writer continues scornfully, Friskabout "can move a Minute [minuet] after the newest Fashion in *England*; can quiver like a Butterfly; [and] is a perfect Conneisueur [*sic*] in Dress."[62] To the host of a New York ball such as Governor Cosby or Jeffrey Amherst, dancing an up-to-date minuet with the grace of a butterfly was the mark of an elegant and respectable man; to the author of the *Mercury*'s satire, such a talent, far from confirming one's noble character, was merely one element in a combined package of eye-catching but socially disreputable behaviors.

The satire also speaks to anxieties over the dangers of excessive education in the arts of gentility. If his experience in London has turned a young member of New York's upper class—and no one with such a name can represent any other part of the social spectrum—into a complete master of dancing, what is to distinguish Little Clodis Friskabout from the decidedly nonelite dancing master who taught him his art? Friskabout's extreme gentility has brought the young gentleman into confusion with the teacher. Members of the elite may have hoped, as a Boston paper claimed, that they and others could sense a certain *je ne sais quoi* "which distinguishes the air of a gentleman from that of a dancing-master,"[63] but the very existence of this hope confirms the unreliability of social stature defined by artistic accomplishment. They were afraid of being mistaken for their social inferiors; conversely, those, such as the dancing masters, who hawked refinement to the upper class were afraid of being targeted for the social mobility that they embodied.

Other sites of genteel sociability besides balls did not always make clear that provincial dancing masters were not on the level of the city's elite. The dance teacher Henry Holt, for example, quickly incorporated himself into the most polite association of New York's social scene by becoming a Freemason. Colonial Freemasonry, like other associations, was a vehicle for achieving a class-bound ideal of politeness. Standards for acceptance were high, and hierarchies, even within the lodge, were sharply drawn. As a result of these social distinctions, nongentlemen such as artisans and even sea captains usually could not become officers in a Masonic lodge. Yet Holt did.[64]

When the dancing master departed from Charleston in 1737, he left behind an already flourishing club scene. Besides Scottish, Huguenot, Welsh, Irish, and German societies, elite men also formed clubs that reached across ethnic boundaries. The longest lasting of these was a Freemasons' lodge, which Charlestonians had organized in 1736, the year before Holt left for New York.[65] The first public mention in New York of Freemasons appeared in November 1737, four months after Holt first advertised his presence there. Holt was likely a charter member of the new society of Freemasons in New York, since by February 1738 he had been elected to the office of junior warden.[66] To achieve the third-highest post in the lodge (below master and senior warden) was not only an honor and an indication of Holt's acceptance into polite society; it also implies that he had a direct role in the foundation of a genteel and polite association. With men such as Holt as leaders of gentlemen's societies, it is no surprise that other New Yorkers were unsure of their ability to tell the difference between teachers of gentility and the genteel.

Most dancing masters, however, had to protect their reputations more zealously than Holt did. Peter Vianey, who taught the minuet and other French dances in a public dancing school, ran a defensive advertisement in the *New-York Journal.* In it he noted that he had recently learned that "he has been mistaken for a dancing-master, whose behaviour to his scholars gave just offence in this city some years ago." He assured his potential clients that not only did he have impeccable recommendations but also he had been in the country only for the last four years. Here, at least, social mobility worked in a newcomer's favor; for Vianey, who was in a more precarious situation than Holt, it seemed the wiser course not to omit but to emphasize his itinerancy in order to salvage his reputation.[67]

The cultural context of Britain's commercial empire completely structured the dancing master's world. Just as commercial reputation was the foundation of the success of any confidence trickster, so it was for the dancing master. A con artist relied on a social environment in which reputation mattered but was hard to verify, and he relied on a process by which he created the false reputation of a trustworthy gentleman trader. Likewise, the dancing master worked in a world structured by an all-too-successful market of goods, in which the distinction between the rude and the gentle had to be demonstrated through the body. Like a successful confidence scheme, dance instruction required the dancing master to masquerade as an elite body even while he was economically dependent on the patronage of his clients. The dancing master had to tread a social tightrope. With too great a difference between himself and his elite students, he became a disreputable teacher of gentility. On the other hand, if he slid too imperceptibly into the genteel world of his adult pupils, he triggered suspicions of trickery in himself and instability in his clients.

To be sure, the dancing master is not simply the con artist's doppelgänger. Politeness and credit were equally intangible and equally necessary components of elite success. No one, however, truly needed the con artist. Yet it was commonly understood that certain manners had to be acquired not from one's equals but from a man of lower social status. New York's merchant class sought out dancing masters with a full knowledge—reinforced by a long tradition of British satire on the dancing master—of their ambiguous status. That knowledge was not, however, reassuring.

So, despite the possibilities for social acceptability, the itinerancy inherent in the dancing masters' profession made them all the more suspicious political figures during wartime. Although white men (and black sailors to a lesser degree) had some freedom of mobility that they could often turn to their advantage, traveling men fell under suspicion far more often than their settled counterparts did. Communities, fearing the poverty that vagabonds brought and the social and economic burden of supporting them, frequently drove itinerants out of town. Eighteenth-century New York also feared, not without reason, that newcomers might be French or Spanish spies. Other colonies encountered the same danger; in 1737 Governor Manuel de Montiano of Spanish

Florida had sent an Ibaja Indian named Juan Ygnacio de los Reyes to Saint Simons in Georgia "to try, using his native wit, to slip in . . . and discover as much as he could of the plans of the English, and of their condition." Juan Ygnacio learned a good deal about the Saint Simons militia before returning to Florida. Caleb Davis, a merchant in Charleston, was a double agent working both for James Oglethorpe, the governor of Georgia, and for the Spanish governor of Florida. Wartime practices made it likely that both sides were engaged in surveillance.[68]

The slightest connection with Catholicism or France could raise suspicions. One New Yorker took out advertisements in the newspaper to quash rumors that he had been drinking toasts to the Catholic Pretender to the British throne; he offered a twenty-pound reward to find the source of the false report. In February 1746 a French passenger from Curaçao was arrested as a spy in New York and examined. One year before, two Moravian clergymen from Pennsylvania were imprisoned "under suspicion of being disguised papists." They were released six weeks later after Conrad Weiser, a well-known Pennsylvania justice of the peace and diplomat, sent a certificate cosigned by the governor of Pennsylvania attesting that the two men were "true protestants."[69]

Dancing masters were particularly susceptible to such allegations of spying. In May 1741 the same Governor Oglethorpe wrote from Georgia to his counterpart in New York that he had discovered "a villainous design of a very extraordinary nature." Oglethorpe feared that in a plan that the southern governor claimed was "too horrid for any Prince to order," "many priests were employ'd who pretended to be Physicians, Dancing masters, and other such kinds of occupations, and under that pretence to get admittance and confidence in families."[70] Rather than providing a link to the court culture of London, minuets and other French dances could become markers of suspicious activity. The minuet was developed in and for the Catholic absolutist court of Louis XIV.[71] As common as the minuet became at British balls, it always carried with it a whiff of popery.[72] If the dance was French, who was to say that its teachers were not as well? In the middle of the French and Indian War, the lieutenant governor of Halifax wrote to the New York Council urging them to arrest a French dancing master on suspicion of being a spy. Three weeks later the dancing master was committed to jail.[73] The ancient rhyme between "France" and "dance" was again used to denigratory effect during the war in 1755, when a couplet from a London magazine was reprinted in a New York newspaper. The doggerel reframes military conflict through cultural polarization, taking dance as the concluding and conclusive mark of an effeminate and overcivilized traitor: "The brave shou'd fight; but for the fops of France, / 'Tis theirs to cook, to taylorize and dance."[74]

For most of New York's elites, their connections to the British Empire were both commercial and social. In his commodification of gentility, the dancing master was a prefect hybrid of imperial commerce and imperial sociability. However, the commercial British Empire was not the only empire in the Atlantic world; in times of conflict, imperial politics also meant wartime politics of hostility against Catholics. In war and in peace, dancing masters across British North America were dubious characters. New Yorkers and other colonists, unable to turn to court culture for an education in gentility, were thus forced to depend on a teacher of all forms of politeness, the dancing master, and he was by nature an unstable guide to gentility. At any time a dancing master might become an object of suspicion.

Yet there is no evidence that New York's dancing masters were ever either spies or confidence tricksters. Instead, these hawkers of politeness were lightning rods for more diffuse concerns over the irresolvable gap between being and looking genteel. Thus, New Yorkers' worries about gentility were not merely that a dancing master might not be quite what he seemed. Instead, they feared that even a gentleman might not be recognized as an elite if he did not perform politely. His very status was in the hands of the dancing master.

Thus the dangers of distinction were not only for the dancing master. The world of New York's commercial culture was also dangerous for men's claims to gentility. Dependence on commodified gentility threatened their sense of what it meant to be a man. As one historian has recently noted, "The prevailing eighteenth-century concept was of masculinity not just as a social but a sociable category in which gender identity was conferred, or denied, by men's capacity of gentlemanly social performance."[75] No wonder the accusation of being a gentleman or teaching manners was so fraught; it was a comment on masculinity itself.

Like the balls for which they educated their clientele, dancing masters in wartime became an issue of more than social status, and their unreliability had implications beyond local factional politics. Dancing masters came to be seen as figures with important connections to Britain's imperial conflicts. The public balls with which dancing masters were so clearly involved had shown New Yorkers the impact that sociability could have on politics. When concerns about rank gave way to fears of invasion, the dancing masters took the fall.

The commercial British Empire in wartime affected more lives than those of elite New Yorkers and dance instructors. In the wide Atlantic world other eighteenth-century itinerants, of all races and nationalities, found themselves embroiled in conflicts over commerce and status. Like Henry Holt and his colleagues, sailors found both possibilities and dangers in the fluid commercial world of New York's imperial port.

Chapter Five

Black Cargo or Crew

In 1713 Stephen Domingo, an Afro-Spanish native of Carthagena in Colombia, was being held in slavery in New York City. Domingo had been sold to a New Yorker by a British privateer as part of the loot from a Spanish ship captured during Queen Anne's War (1702–13). Domingo petitioned the New York Common Council for his freedom, claiming that as a freeborn sailor he could not legally be enslaved by Mr. Perce, the man who claimed to own him.

In eighteenth-century New York enslaved men of African descent rarely achieved freedom merely by asking for it. However, Domingo had a good chance of success, for he had managed to acquire an affidavit from a formidable privateering captain named Charles Pinkethman attesting to his freedom. Pinkethman was a captain of some note in New York—the following winter the city's government would honor him for "having done many Considerable services for this City in the late Warr as Commander of a Pirate ship of Warr called the Hunter"—and his word would have carried a good deal of weight among the council members. A week and a half after Pinkethman gave his deposition, the New York mayor and his council ordered Perce and one Captain Mayon (probably the privateer who had captured Domingo) to respond to the charges.[1]

The final outcome of Domingo's case is unknown. Moreover, this uncertainty is only one of the questions that this brief encounter in the New York council chamber raises. How did a man from Carthagena come to New York? Why did the official record refer to him as a "Spanish Negro Living with Mr. Perce" and not simply call him a slave? Why did a ship captain vouch for his freedom? Why did the officials of New York's government give him a hearing at all?

The brief story of Stephen Domingo offers an unusual glimpse into the problem of slave status in the imperial and commercial context of eighteenth-century New York. The shifting status of Domingo and other black sailors in New York demonstrates how the city's involvement in the wars for trade and empire worked against other eighteenth-century ideals of fixed racial hierarchies. The fate of sailors captured by privateers looking to profit from imperial wars varied greatly and was shaped by the close links between trade, war, and international law. Slavery was by no means the only possible outcome for a black sailor brought to New York City.

For sailors captured during wartime, the implications of living on the margins of competing empires were obvious. Unlike many traders and consumers in imperial New York, black sailors experienced firsthand the actions of the imperial state. They consciously and explicitly declared their imperial identities as they proclaimed themselves French or Spanish subjects. Like New Yorkers on land, however, these sailors' status did not derive solely from their political allegiances. Although the symbols of their status were rarely the consumer goods or elegant dances that we saw earlier, their symbols were just as closely tied to the commercial empire and its commodification of goods. For these sailors, their status derived from the British Empire's attempts to commodify persons as slaves in the context of wars over trading routes.

The freedom suits of these foreign black sailors ultimately compelled New York's courts to rethink their understanding of the relationship between race and slavery. Nearly all of these sailors arrived in New York as the result of privateering during the continuous wars for empire. New York's involvement in privateering is the key to understanding the commercial nature of the empire and its wars, as well as the combination of profit and war that created the black prisoner of war. Once these sailors arrived in New York, few accepted their enslavement passively. As a result, the courts were forced to redefine their justifications for enslavement. They also had to create a range of possible statuses for these foreign nationals. Although slavery was as much a system of law as of labor, black sailors did not find that the legal institutions of the state necessarily worked against their interests. Surprisingly, at times the imperial and commercial culture of New York combined with the empire's legal apparatus to undermine the easy definitions of identity that slavery imposed elsewhere.

Of course, an imperial, commercial, militarized port city on the Atlantic rim and a crop-producing plantation offered two vastly different perspectives on the question of slave status. Few in either situation questioned the enslavement of Africans who had been bought in Africa by slave traders, but the enslavement of foreign black sailors picked up by cruising British privateers was another matter entirely. Unlike plantation slavery, eighteenth-century Atlantic slavery was by its nature shifting and contingent. In these port cities, freedom and slavery were less polar opposites than they were points on a spectrum of status, from independence to apprenticeship to indentured servitude to slavery. In a world in which both Spanish and British colonial officials occasionally championed the causes of impoverished black sailors, blackness and bondage were not synonymous. Though a black sailor faced a great many dangers to his liberty on the open seas, his capture by an enemy ship did not automatically result in lifelong enslavement.[2]

Commerce and Captivity

During King George's War (1739–48) fighting was particularly fierce in the wealthy West Indies, of which Britain, France, and Spain all claimed possession. In the summer of 1740 the British garrison in New York had sent six hundred men, most of them volunteers, in an unsuccessful attempt to capture Cuba.[3] Some of these New Yorkers fought alongside Admiral Edward Vernon, who had taken Puerto Bello in Cuba from the Spanish in November 1739, a naval success that aroused great public enthusiasm for the war throughout the British Empire.[4] New Yorkers were willing to fight the war in one of two ways: some volunteered for the armed services, but many more joined privateering ventures, which offered an attractive combination of patriotism and profit. During the nine years of the war, privateer captains and owners were able to fill more than ten thousand berths with willing enlistees.

In the mid-1730s, a few years before the outbreak of war, Juan Miranda was a sixteen-year-old boy from New Grenada doing his best to be a dutiful nephew. His uncle had asked him to come live with him in Havana, and Miranda was willing to go. Miranda was a Spanish subject, the child of a free white man and a free black woman, and he was ready to see some of the world. However, Miranda's voyage from Cartagena to Havana took an unexpected turn when the Spanish ship on which he was sailing captured several French and Dutch ships trading illegally near Curaçao off the coast of what is now Colombia.[5] They confiscated the cargo and ship and sent the sailors back to Curaçao in the longboats. It can hardly have been a surprise to Miranda and others on the Spanish ship when the Dutch authorities in Curaçao sent out another ship to capture the Spanish cutter. The Dutch brought all the Spanish back to Curaçao and imprisoned them.

The coast guard ship on which Miranda was sailing was patrolling the West Indies against British violations of trade agreements. British captains and governors for their part complained vociferously about the "depredations" of the Spanish, particularly their aggressive seizures of British shipping. Retaliations on both sides heightened tensions. In 1738 Captain Robert Jenkins had claimed that the Spanish sailors of a *guarda costa* had boarded his ship seven years earlier and cut off his ear; the resulting publicity pushed Britain into a subset of King George's War, the humorously named but politically serious War of Jenkins' Ear.[6]

Miranda had languished in prison for over six months when a British captain who sailed a Dutch ship made him a proposition: if Miranda would join the captain's crew for a voyage to New York, the captain would arrange for him to get to Cuba. Captain William Axon cared little about the nationalities of the men on his ship—he was a Briton sailing under Dutch colors—and, like most other ship captains in the West Indies, he was in desperate need of deckhands. One common solution was to seek out sailors in the prisons. Axon thus found Miranda in jail and offered him a place on his ship heading for New York. Miranda may have initially thought that he was bargaining away his labor only temporarily, for he remembered Axon telling him not to be "uneasy with his condition"; he needed to sail on only three or four more voyages with Axon and then he would be sent home "at liberty." However, as Miranda would discover, clearly something was amiss in his relationship with Axon.

Axon was more than simply a ship's captain; he was a privateer.[7] As such, his role was both military and economic. Throughout the eighteenth century, government officials freely gave permission to captains to act as privateers. With its official letter of marque from the city, a British ship during wartime could capture a Spanish or (after 1744) French ship and bring it back with its cargo to a friendly British vice-admiralty court. There the British captain would ask the court to consider his prize legitimate and legally able to be sold, the legal term for which is "libeled." The profits were then shared among the ship's owners, captain, and crew. According to one historian, over 90 percent of prize suits brought before the vice-admiralty courts in North America were declared legal and these prizes therefore able to be sold.[8] (See Figure 6.)

Like other British privateers, Axon served in two complementary capacities. He was an arm of the British navy, interfering with foreign trade during wartime and blocking enemy ports, and he was a businessman on a speculative venture. Although the risks to both body and purse were enormous, the possibility of quick riches kept investors and sailors hooked.[9]

Privateering became increasingly profitable for captains and owners throughout the eighteenth century. Before the Prize Act of 1708, the British Crown in the person of the lord high admiral was entitled to a tenth of the profits of any prize. In an attempt to encourage attacks on Spanish commerce, the Prize Act renounced all governmental claims to profits. Furthermore, after 1744 slaves and other goods were entirely duty free.[10] The Prize Act of 1740 also capped the amount of court fees and charges that a captain had to pay. Thus nearly all of a privateer's take was profit.[11]

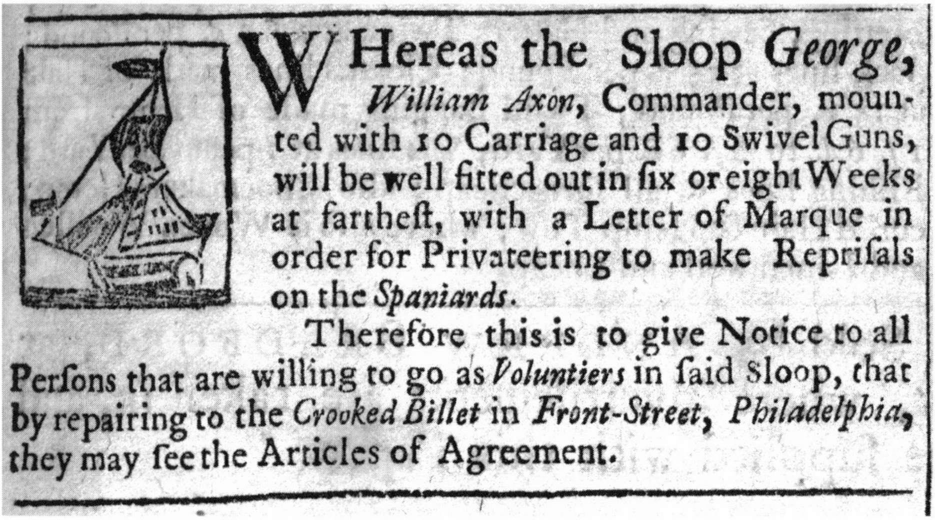

> **W** **Hereas the Sloop** *George,* *William Axon,* Commander, mounted with 10 Carriage and 10 Swivel Guns, will be well fitted out in fix or eight Weeks at fartheſt, with a Letter of Marque in order for Privateering to make Repriſals on the *Spaniards.* Therefore this is to give Notice to all Perſons that are willing to go as *Voluntiers* in ſaid Sloop, that by repairing to the *Crooked Billet* in *Front-Street,* *Philadelphia,* they may ſee the Articles of Agreement.

Figure 6. Privateering recruitment newspaper advertisement. Like other privateers, William Axon could rarely enlist a full crew through advertisements such as these. Note the combination of profits and patriotism, "Privateering to make Reprisals on the Spaniards." American Antiquarian Society.

In their combination of economic and military goals, privateers were essential in defining the nature and scope of British warfare. Before 1763 the stated goal of the British Empire was not territory but a maritime empire based on trade.[12] By emphasizing trade over conquest, the imperial wars created an Atlantic world that was mobile, fluid, and commercial in nature. This world created risks and possibilities for black sailors that were not unlike the risks of all commercial ventures—great gains, great losses, and enormous potential for reversals.

The close tie for New Yorkers between war, trade, and privateering was reflected in the local press. Print negotiated the space between the trade and war, tying the two into a neat package. Through newspaper accounts of battles, privateers, prize ships, and auctions, New Yorkers envisioned a world in which war and trade were refracted through their city. Neither the city's sailors nor its readers imagined that imperial war was a distant conflict between disembodied nations. Gory and precise descriptions of battles had a prominent place in wartime newspapers; during the years that Britain was at war, each issue of New York's two newspapers had at least one article on privateer battles or privateer prizes. The articles explicitly connected war and commerce. When the *Royal Hester* brought into New York two enormous prizes, the newspaper praised the privateer for his success in "reducing the mercantile Interest of France."[13] Accounts of privateers' exploits at sea keenly brought home the excitement of empire to New Yorkers who were safe on land. At the same time, nothing could have made the profitability of empire more vivid.

As the newspapers explained it to their readers, privateering was a business, and a profitable one at that.[14] As soon as the government had issued him a letter of marque, Captain John Lush was the first privateer out of the harbor at the beginning of King George's War. Even before the news could make it into print, the city was abuzz with the knowledge that Lush's cruise had been successful and that he was returning with two prize ships, "one of them very rich." The newspaper reported the rumor but also puffed the possibilities for investment in privateering ventures. As a result of these well-laden ships and Lush's success in capturing them, the *New York Weekly Journal* also announced that "shares are bought and sold confidently by several."[15]

Little in the war-time newspapers compares to the delight with which John Lush's prizes were reported and fawned over. When Lush's first prize ships arrived in the harbor, the *New York Gazette* extolled one as "very rich, being laden with Cocoa, Indigo, and a considerable quantity of pieces of eight."[16] The following March, Lush reappeared in New York with two more prizes, which the *New York Weekly Journal* claimed were "esteemed the richest taken by any Privateer in this War." Most of the cargo was described without fanfare ("Cocoa, &c., &c."), but two items caught the paper's attention: clothes and money. The "rich laced and embroider'd cloathes taken from the *Spaniards*" that the men wore to row their captain to land provided a gorgeous spectacle for New Yorkers; Lush came ashore with "the Guns from the Ships in the Harbour firing and the Docks crowded with the populace." As for money, "each man [had] already receiv'd 425 pieces of eight," and the ship also held the private fortune of a Spanish passenger, amounting to more than twenty-two thousand pieces of eight. The nineteen black Spanish sailors, whom Lush also seized and sold, were assumed to be slaves and were described as "good serviceable Negroes."[17]

By the spring of 1740 newspapers were carrying multiple stories of British bravery and Spanish wealth.[18] A typical issue from May 1740 emphasized the enormous abundance of goods. On the same day, the *New-York Weekly Journal* told its readers, three different privateers and their prizes arrived. First came a Rhode Island privateer, next a privateer from Bermuda, and "likewise the same Day Captain Bayard in the Sloop *Ranger* also came into this Harbour." The description of this victorious trio culminated with the highlights of Bayard's catch, many of which were objects of Catholic ritual. They included a "large Gold Cup" weighing more than two pounds, a "set of Gold Altar plate," a "most beautiful Picture in a Massy Silver Frame," a "Silver Crucifix," and "several other valuable commodities." Only one item in the inventory was not clearly designated for Catholic worship, since it was the ritual object for the temple of international consumption: "a large Silver tea table."[19]

Bayard's prize consisted of far more than Catholic items, but except for the tea table, only those items appeared in the news story. The rest of the cargo was made accessible to the public through an advertisement of Guilian Verplank. He offered for sale "the following Prize Goods just imported by Capt. *Sam Bayard*: Eleven Pipes of Brandy, Two Ditto Wine, Havanna Hides, Tanned Leather, Snuff in small Baggs, Ditto superfine in Canisters, Gum Elemmi, Muscovado Sugar, Powder Sugar, Campech Logwood and Sundry other." The phrase "just imported" was meant to be taken literally, since these goods had indeed just been brought into port. In the context of wartime, however, these "imports" were the result not of international trade but of imperial warfare. Still, the similarities between trade and seizure are worth noting. After all, the privateering voyages were bankrolled by leading merchants, who saw them as just another investment, like bringing in buttons from Manchester.[20] But now "imported" took on a new sense of danger and battle and patriotism.

The papers not only extolled the riches to be gained from Spanish ships but also decried the subhuman behavior to be expected from Spanish Catholics, especially those of mixed race. A brief and bloody story of three Afro-Spanish sailors shows the economic nature of the war (this time from the Spanish perspective) and the anti-Catholic jingoism of the New York press. The three mixed-race Spaniards were sailing in November 1747 from New York on the *Polly* as "passengers," the paper claimed, "with a sole intent that every one should go home to his Native Place of abode." As they neared Jamaica, the trio seized control of the ship. They "murdered all the sloops company" (five in all) and threw the bodies overboard. They then sailed the ship into Spanish San Domingo and told the local governor that they had been enslaved by the ship's crew and had rebelled against the whites in order to gain their freedom. Following the rules of engagement practiced in King George's War, the Spanish seized the sloop and cargo as the spoils of war and kept the money for the Spanish Crown.

The New York paper that reported the capture of the *Polly* and the death of its crew was horrified at the carnage. For the press, this "very melancholy Account" encapsulated the horror of war with foreign black sailors. In case the readers failed to note that King George's War was a war of national, racial, and religious identity, the paper fulminated that "this barbarous Murder" was done by "Villainous and inhuman Butchers of Mankind," by "those Villains whose Blood Thirsty Nature is never glutted until their Savage Hands are embrued in the Blood of some poor Protestant or other."[21] Some black Catholic Spaniards no longer counted as human, and their hands, dark with natural pigment and British blood, were doubly unclean.

As the reports of battles and prizes make clear, the New York papers portrayed the city's involvement in Britain's eighteenth-century imperial wars as a combination of anti-Catholic fervor, access to consumer goods, and hindrance of enemy trade. The newspapers brought together war and trade through consumer goods such as sugar and cocoa. They never mentioned, however, the profits to be made on black sailors.

Because of the nature of maritime warfare in the West Indies, large numbers of foreign mariners ended up in New York. Some occasionally arrived of their own free will to engage in trade, but the regulations on shipping were so strict that their numbers were limited. Much more frequently these foreign sailors were prisoners of war from captured ships. Privateering had the effect of moving people as well as goods around the Caribbean. Sailors from the victorious ship helped guide the prize into a welcoming port; ship hands from the captured vessel often took their place on the enemy ship.

Juan Miranda, however, had not been sailing on a prize ship when Axon met him, and the captain therefore could not simply press him into service on his vessel. It was not until Miranda had languished in prison for several months that Axon made him a proposition: if Miranda would join the captain's crew for a voyage to New York, Axon would arrange for him to get to Cuba. Miranda agreed. However, once he was on board, the captain started to change his story. First he told Miranda that he would have to sail three or four voyages with him before he could return to his uncle. Then he convinced Miranda that instead of sailing he should apprentice himself for seven years to a sailmaker in New York who could teach him this admittedly useful trade. The captain assured Miranda that as a freeman he would have nothing to fear from such an apprenticeship. Miranda agreed to the proposal, and the captain (pocketing the apprenticeship fee) duly handed him over to a New Yorker named Peter Van Ranst.[22]

Eighteenth-century privateering and particularly the practice of capturing dark-skinned sailors made war as well as commerce a vehicle for enslavement. Wars in the Caribbean heightened the imperial identities of French and Spanish black and mixed-race sailors by making them opponents of British privateers. At the same time that privateer captains feared these sailors as military foes, however, they also saw in them a potential expansion of their profit. For a man who appeared not to be white, sailing could be a dangerous trade. As many others besides Juan

Miranda found out, the capture of a black sailor by a white captain was only the beginning of the story.

New York had a particular interest in imperial wars in general and in privateering in particular. In every war, eighteenth-century New York was at the forefront of the privateering craze. When Alexander Hamilton visited the city in 1744, he complained in his journal that "the table chat run upon privateering and such discourse as has now become so common that it is tiresome and flat."[23] Hamilton's disdain for mercantile affairs did not mislead him into overstating the case; New York had indeed wholeheartedly embraced privateering. During King George's War, the city sent out ships on at least 105 privateering expeditions, second in number only to Newport. These vessels, moreover, were far larger than those from Rhode Island, and as a result, New York privateers had the largest share of privateering berths from any of the colonial ports. The larger ships meant not only larger crews but also greater construction costs; New York spent more than any other colony on building ships for privateers.[24]

Sailors, shipbuilders, and investors were not the only ones who actively promoted the British Empire as a means to wealth. The vice-admiralty courts also recognized the financial benefits of encouraging captains to bring their prizes back to New York's port. After Lewis Morris, Jr., became the vice-admiralty court judge in 1739, New York tried and condemned more prize cases than any other court in British North America. Morris's explicit championing of British privateers and his aggressive approach to condemning foreign goods and sailors made New York an attractive port for privateers, who often chose it over other North American courts as a port of return. The overwhelmingly likely fate for a captured dark-skinned sailor was to end up in New York.[25]

Historians have long known that some conflicts of empire, particularly a commercial empire, can be uncovered in the archived records of the colonial vice-admiralty courts. The role of these courts in enforcing the Acts of Trade and subsequent colonial antipathy to them in the period immediately preceding the Revolution tend to dominate any discussion of the vice-admiralty courts in the eighteenth-century Atlantic.[26] However, vice-admiralty courts had other important functions in the eighteenth century. They were the courts through which all privateering business passed, including prize cases. In these cases the courts decided which vessels and how much of their cargoes had been legitimately captured. The vice-admiralty court then "libeled" the goods that they declared to have been legally seized, thus giving the privateer owners the legal right to sell the cargoes. The depositions, testimony, and decisions of these courts are an untouched treasure trove of information about foreign sailors as well as foreign goods. The struggles of sailors and captains for freedom and enslavement were dutifully recorded and filed by this watchdog of British commercial control. Cross-currents of race, profit, war, and empire came together in the vice-admiralty court's proceedings.[27] The privateering records explicitly lay out the commercial nature of the British Empire, its wars, and the combination of commerce and war that created the black prisoner of war.

Slave, Servant, or Prisoner

As he sat in jail in Curaçao, Juan Miranda likely realized that he would have been wise to listen more carefully to the exact wording of Captain Axon's original proposal. The repeated assurances that he should not be "uneasy with his condition" and that eventually he would find himself "at liberty" might have warned the teenager that there was good reason to doubt the temporary nature of his subservient status. When he accepted the terms of a sail-making apprenticeship with Peter Van Ranst, the same uncertainties resurfaced. Before the seven years of his indenture had passed, Axon had perished at sea and the sailmaker Van Ranst had died also, leaving Miranda to the mercies of the widow Sarah Van Ranst and her son Cornelius. When Miranda's seven years ended, Sarah told him that he would be free "soon," but it became clear that she had no intention of freeing him. He stayed with her for another nine years until finally, almost twenty years after his capture at sea, he filed a complaint with the attorney general in 1752.[28]

Miranda came to New York expecting to serve a fixed term as an apprentice. The arrangement was unusual but not unheard of. That he ended up a slave was still less unusual. There were particular risks to having dark skin in the eighteenth-century Atlantic world, and a black or mixed-race sailor was rarely treated like his lighter-skinned colleagues. Privateering captains in particular were likely to see dark-skinned sailors as an appropriate form of potential profit, potential labor, or both. It is not surprising that captains would try to enslave sailors; what is striking is the range of possible outcomes. Enslavement was but one form of servitude in which foreign black sailors found themselves. The length and degree of their unfreedom depended heavily on circumstances beyond skin color.

In the seventeenth century some European prisoners of war, primarily Scots and Irish, were sent to Barbados and the Chesapeake as indentured servants with finite terms.[29] However, by the eighteenth century, use of prisoners for labor had fallen out of favor. As early as 1625 Hugo Grotius, in his study of international law, concluded that "among Christians it is generally agreed, that being engaged in War, they that are taken Prisoners, are not made Slaves, so as to sell them, or force them to hard Labours, or to such Miseries as are common to Slaves."[30] Prisoners of war might be pawns to be traded for other prisoners of war or redeemed in some other way, but international law dictated that they not be used for labor.

As recent work on Britons enslaved on the Barbary Coast in the seventeenth and early eighteenth century has demonstrated, Christians might well be made slaves, although only rarely by other Christians. Britons might have hoped that they would "never be slaves," as *Rule Britannia* claimed in 1740, but until the 1730s they and other Europeans were regularly captured and enslaved by North Africans. Nonetheless, though Europeans might have experienced slavery themselves, they did not enslave other Europeans in the Atlantic world.[31]

The writings of theorists such as Grotius, however, who depended heavily on classical arguments to make his case, did not describe the multiracial world of naval warfare in the eighteenth-century Atlantic. There were so many men of color in this world of privateering that, as one Spanish colonial official put it, "without those of 'broken' color [mulattos], blacks, and Indians, which abound in our towns in America, I do not know if we could arm a single corsair solely with Spaniards."[32] Thus, Grotius's assumption that prisoners of war would be temporarily held and then redeemed was undermined by the racial realities of warfare in the Americas. Men captured in eighteenth-century wars were no longer distinguished by the single dichotomy between Christian and heathen; markers of free status had become more fluid and more dangerous. As one New York governor explained in a letter to the Lords of Trade, "by reason of their colour which is swarthy, they were said to be slaves and as such were sold."[33] Now skin color was the first step to enslavement.

When Captain Dennis McGillicuddy captured a fishing canoe off the coast of Tortuga in 1761, he freed the white man on board but seized the black man, Jean-Baptiste LaVille, along with LaVille's dark-skinned nephew. The two men protested that LaVille was a baptized Christian, but an argument that Grotius might have accepted was now invalid. Both LaVille and his nephew were carried back to New York and eventually brought before the vice-admiralty court.[34]

The distinction that captains of privateers made between black sailors and white ones was clear: black sailors were brought before the courts to be condemned, whereas white sailors were treated as prisoners of war.[35] Often captains did not bother to bring white prisoners back to New York at all, especially after a ruling by the council in 1712 that held a captain responsible for the maintenance of his prisoners.[36] If they were not needed as crew, they were expensive deadweight that consumed the limited supplies on board.[37] Some white sailors were put in local jails;

others were sent off on longboats with a modicum of food and water and allowed to "escape" or simply dumped on West Indian shores.[38] Still others, when they saw British vessels in pursuit, ran their ships onto shore and escaped on foot.[39] Those few whites who were taken to New York were left to find their own way home, sometimes, as Axon promised Miranda, by shipping on the sort of British privateer that had captured them in the first place.

Until the middle of King George's War, white prisoners of war were given total freedom of the city. In 1744, however, Governor George Clinton protested that it was "utterly improper that they should, contrary to all precedents, be suffered to go about at large, viewing our situation and fortification, a practice not suffered by any other country in the time of the profoundest peace."[40] Clinton proposed that white prisoners be committed to jail but that each be given a daily allowance for sustenance. Moreover, he suggested that New Yorkers remember the Golden Rule and the fact that English prisoners were being held in foreign jails as well. Prisoners were then exchanged with British prisoners as soon as possible.[41]

Once home, privateers hoped to convince the vice-admiralty courts that the dark-skinned enemy sailors against whom they had fought were actually the slave property of French or Spanish subjects and thus liable to confiscation, like indigo and cocoa. They knew that the courts would automatically assume that a man of African descent was a slave, as is clear from the vice-admiralty court minute books, which invariably identified the contested sailors as "negro slaves" long before their fate was decided.[42] The New York Vice-Admiralty Court immediately transformed a black sailor from a foreign enemy into a chattel slave.

The color of a black sailor was not always obvious. The infinite variations of complexion among the seamen of the Atlantic meant that the definition of blackness often defied easy reckoning. Courts called on white sailors to identify potential blacks among the foreign crews. For example, early one morning in 1762 the British ship *Prosperous Polly* was sailing out of Martinique when she was taken by a French ship. The French ship put some of her mariners on board the *Prosperous Polly* to make sure that she came back to a French port. Among those sailors was a man named Joseph. He was obviously of African ancestry, at least to the eyes of one British sailor, who also declared that four other men "from their color and curled hair all appeared . . . to be mulattos."[43] On the other hand, a different British sailor and the captain of the French mariners, while acknowledging that Joseph was black, both claimed that there were no mulattos on board. So long as the French were victors, however, what the British thought of them did not matter. For two days the French sailors, including Joseph, sailed the *Prosperous Polly* toward the French possessions in the Caribbean. Then the fate of both the *Prosperous Polly* and Joseph shifted again. A British ship, the *Orleans,* managed to wrest possession of the *Polly* away from its French captors. The *Orleans* in turn put some of its British sailors on board the *Prosperous Polly* to ensure its arrival in a British port. The *Orleans* sailed back to New York with the *Prosperous Polly* in tow, intent on getting the court to libel any French possessions that had been put on board during its two days in French hands. The captain listed Joseph and no one else as part of the cargo. (Joseph easily regained his freedom, but for historical reasons that will be explained below.)

The assumption that any black foreigner could be enslaved often served devious ship captains well. At the beginning of King George's War, Captain James Hill of New York was short of hands for his cruise. The governor of Jamaica permitted British captains to impress into maritime service any Spanish prisoners of war they found in the jail at Spanish Town. Hill took a mixed-race Spanish sailor named Philip Joseph out of the Jamaica jail and brought him to New York, where he remained "in the service" of Captain Hill for seven years. Hill did not bother to make Joseph's legal status explicit, but he clearly intended to hold him in servitude. Joseph managed to find a credible New Yorker who attested to the fact that all of the Spanish sailors in the Jamaica jail were freemen, and the board sent him home to Havana as a Spanish prisoner of war.[44]

Because the vice-admiralty court often assumed that black and mixed-race sailors were slaves and not prisoners of war, these men could neither be traded for white prisoners nor be sent home. Their status was not national but racial. During negotiations for the exchange of prisoners after King George's War between the French and the English, the governor of New France, the marquis de la Jonquière, wrote to his superior in France that although he had returned all the English subjects who were still in his hands, including an "English Indian" who had been bought by a Montreal seminary from the Iroquois, he refused to send back one Samuel Fremont, a "negro." "We have ordered that he remain in the Colony," the marquis explained, "all negroes being slaves, in whatever country they reside." Jonquière further elaborated that in refusing to send back Fremont, "I only do what the English themselves did in 1747," when the English, using the same argument, would not send back the servant of a French naval officer.[45] Yet, Jonquière's bald assertion that "all negroes" were slaves overstated the clarity of the case. Jonquière may have felt that he could know a man's status by looking at him, but as an official he was in the minority. Freedom and slavery were not such stark opposites as the marquis implied. These prize cases forced New York officials to recognize precisely how arbitrary and impermanent slave status was.

Moreover, although the vice-admiralty courts often assumed that blackness could lead to an automatic condemnation, the servitude that some of the sailors experienced in New York was sometimes less than pure chattel slavery. In a striking instance of New York's relatively creative approaches to servitude, some of the first black sailors to be taken prisoner in the eighteenth century petitioned the governor in 1711 for their release on the grounds that they were freemen at home. The governor's council was sympathetic but not softhearted. Unfortunately, neither of the two sailors could "present proof of their freedom," and to do so was "likely to be very expensive and take up a long time." On the other hand, since the council felt that it was "hard against Law and Justice that if they were freemen at the time of their being taken they should be made slaves or being sold as such should continue so," they came up with a compromise: indenture. They declared, "it is the Opinion of this board that the best medium that can be taken in this case is that they severally enter into Indentures to serve their respective master and Mistress for such reasonable Terms as they can Agree on and at the Expiration thereof be free." The council's explicit promise of freedom at the end of the mutually agreed-upon term of service makes it clear that it saw indenture not as a slippery slope to slavery but as a sign of the sailors' original freedom.[46]

When Juan Miranda and Sarah Van Ranst took their case to court in 1756, their dispute over Miranda's freedom illustrated perfectly the uncertainty of slave status in New York. Miranda was sure that he had agreed to a fixed period of servitude. Van Ranst claimed that she owned him as a chattel slave. Each brought witnesses to support his or her claim. Mary Pinhorne claimed that Miranda had "always" asserted that he was free, whereas Jacobus Kiersted, a privateering captain, testified that he had heard that claim only very recently.[47]

Europeans frequently agreed to bind themselves and their labor for a limited amount of time. The extent that Africans did so, however, has been overlooked in light of the far greater proportion of those who were forced to lifelong slavery. For foreign sailors in New York, however, slavery was never necessarily lifelong. In the context of labor arrangements with other foreign blacks in New York, Miranda's argument that he was apprenticed and not enslaved appears even more likely. Slavery was by no means the only form of unfreedom that white New Yorkers could imagine for foreign blacks.

Although there were few British American–born free blacks in eighteenth-century New York, other free foreign blacks besides Miranda did indenture themselves to New Yorkers.[48] In 1751 another young man from Curaçao, Francisco Gosé, signed a four-year indenture with John Ebbets "for diverse sums of money and also for other good Causes."[49]

He carefully attached the proofs of his freedom when signing his indenture and made sure that he was identified within the document as a
"free Negro." That both the courts and servants took care in defining
free status shows the extent to which everyone realized the ease with
which that status could be subverted.

Thus it was not only the formal terms of Miranda's servitude that were
unclear. Miranda's own experience, in which his status was uncertain for
at least seven years and probably twice that long, demonstrates the tension between freedom and labor that existed throughout the early modern Atlantic world. Many people, including white men, worked under
less than optimal conditions and were rarely in total control of their own
bodies and labor. They worked as indentured servants, suffered forced
transportation, and were pressed into service in the Royal Navy. In the
words of a recent scholar, "freedom in colonial America existed along a
continuum from the slave, stripped of all rights, to the independent
property owner, and during a lifetime an individual might well occupy
more than one place on this spectrum."[50] As a young man, Miranda
might not have found slavery in New York very different from indentured servitude.[51]

As in Miranda's case, often no one, white or black, made a sailor's
status unambiguously clear to fellow New Yorkers. When Jean-Baptiste
LaVille was captured by the *Mars* in the West Indies, he was fortunate
enough to find on board two French officials who were willing to vouch
for his free status. He then arranged with the captain, Dennis McGillicuddy, that in exchange for serving on the crew during the return cruise
to New York the captain would drop him and his nephew Pierre off in
Hispaniola on his next voyage to the West Indies. LaVille decided not to
take the trouble to get formal affidavits of his freedom from the Frenchmen on board.

They returned to New York, where LaVille and his nephew spent the
next few months wandering freely around the city. In November the
Mars set out for Martineo in the West Indies, and the captain ordered
LaVille to go on board as a crew member, although the captain refused
to let the nephew sail and left him as an assumed slave in New York.

When the ship arrived in Monte Christi, LaVille decided that he
should go home and not return to New York for Pierre. He may have
surmised that in Hispaniola he could find documentation that would
allow him to free his nephew. He went to the captain and reminded him
of his promise. Rather than immediately setting LaVille onshore, however, the captain began to prevaricate. When he told his cocaptain, Dennis McGillicuddy, that LaVille wanted to disembark, McGillicuddy flew
into a rage. He seized a cat-o'-nine-tails and with it chased LaVille into
the hold of the brig. LaVille outran him, but that was his only victory.

The brig returned to New York with LaVille on board. When they returned to the city, the cocaptain was still angry. He refused to let LaVille visit his nephew, and within a month McGillicuddy had filed a libel claiming that LaVille and Pierre were the property of French subjects and could be sold as slaves.

LaVille vigorously defended himself against McGillicuddy. He insisted that not only had he never had a chance to collect documentation of his freedom—since he had been on board the *Mars* during most of his imprisonment—but also he would have obtained affidavits from the French officials before they left New York had he known it would be necessary. He insisted throughout his depositions and answers to the libel that he had always been free, that other whites had vouched for his freedom, and that even one of the ship's owners had believed that he was free.

John Morin Scott, his appointed lawyer, ably defended LaVille. He considered several arguments to prove his client's freedom. He planned to argue that a man who had served a second cruise, and who was thereby as entitled to a share of the prize as any other hand, could not be libeled. He questioned why LaVille had not been brought before the court during his first stay in New York. Moreover, Scott reasoned, if the first captain had been so convinced of the freedom of the LaVilles that he promised to return them to Hispaniola, perhaps he should be brought in as a witness on their behalf.[52]

In the end, however, LaVille never had to make a case in front of the vice-admiralty courts. Before the case could be decided, McGillicuddy died in battle on the *Mars*, torn apart by a cannonball from a French ship that he was trying to capture.[53] The LaVilles nonetheless languished, presumably in the city jail, for another year, until McGillicuddy's widow Martha, as the executor of his estate, wrote a petition asking the court to drop the libel on the basis of the documentation of LaVille's freedom that the prisoners had obtained from a French official. At the same time LaVille obtained an affidavit from a Monsieur Laugardier, another wealthy French West Indian, who was in New York for his health, that LaVille and his nephew were born free. In September 1763 the vice-admiralty court dismissed the libel. The LaVilles, free at last, disappeared from the historical record.

British officials had never been dogmatically opposed to freeing prisoners of color. As early as 1688 the New York Common Council had ordered a number of "Spanish Indians" to be brought before them with a "view of liberating them."[54] These men were presumably prisoners of war, and at least one of them was owned by a privateer captain. Before members of the council would release the men, however, they wanted to be assured that the men could all recite the Lord's Prayer.[55] This seventeenth-century concern with conversion as the basis for freedom began to disintegrate by the 1700s. In 1706 the New York Assembly clarified that baptism of slaves did not guarantee them freedom in this life.[56] By the beginning of the eighteenth century, imprisoned sailors had to find other ways to convince their British captors to set them free.

For many men, the shift in status from slavery to imprisonment to freedom was very slow. In the middle of King George's War, Captain Thomas Grenell returned to New York with nine Afro-Spanish sailors. Two of them apparently were set free, but the vice-admiralty court sold the other seven into slavery. Three months later a Spanish governor sent affidavits of freedom for three of the seven men. The judge grudgingly agreed, but four of the men remained enslaved. At last the men— Anthony De Torres, Anthony Seymour, Fernando Bernal, and Manuel Servantes—all obtained affidavits and convinced the vice-admiralty court that they were freemen. Yet even this proof of their status was not enough to give them the freedom of the city. As they had already been sold (and in one case resold), the court claimed that it did not have the authority to free the men immediately. Instead, Judge Lewis Morris ordered the governor's council to find the four men "and secure them in the Gaol of the said city and county as Spanish prisoners of war until further order."[57]

The ultimately successful freedom suits of Jean-Baptiste LaVille and others demonstrate the many possibilities between complete slavery and complete freedom for black and mulatto Spaniards. The fact that many people disagreed whether Juan Miranda was an indentured servant or a slave also indicates how faint the line was that divided those two forms of labor. His owner's ability to shift between treating Miranda as a servant (whose freedom would come soon) and treating him as a slave (whose status was theoretically permanent) is equally telling. As Miranda pointed out in his petition, the widow Van Ranst had no bill of sale, no record that a court ever declared Miranda a slave, and no legal indications of his status. At the same time, however, the fact that she was able to convince Miranda to work for her for nearly twenty years (if not more) shows the support she must have had from her family and neighbors in keeping Miranda as a slave. Moreover, that Miranda could be held as a slave and then many years later still be able to contest that identification and argue for his freedom indicates that New Yorkers could see even slavery as temporary.[58]

From Slave to Prisoner of War

As much as these contingent and indeterminate ideas of servitude kept Juan Miranda from questioning his status too closely, the time came when he no longer felt like a young man. Having finished his apprenticeship, he referred to himself as a "sailmaker."[59] He had never forgotten his city and family and was no longer willing to accept his servitude and exile silently. It was, however, more than Miranda's own frustration with his situation that inspired him to go to Attorney General William Kempe. He decided to make his petition after he saw how other foreign sailors, some through the intervention of their home governments and others on their own, had gained their freedom through the courts. Although many of the sailors condemned by the vice-admiralty court or otherwise sold into slavery by privateers died in captivity, at least one-third, if not more, successfully protested their enslavement through official channels.

These marines of color were not enslaved through the African slave trade. When they were enslaved by Europeans, it was as prisoners of war, captured on the field or deck of battle. Africans who were captured and sold to slavers on the coast of Africa, and their still-enslaved descendants, had little hope of freedom in New York. These sailors, however, enslaved after they had lived as freemen in the African diaspora, had a different set of options.

Sailors turned to the same legal system that had enslaved them to try to find a way home. They did not argue that slavery was wrong or that they sought complete control over their lives and bodies. They did not even argue that they should simply be "freed." Instead, they tried to persuade British officials that they should be treated as prisoners of war rather than as slaves. Their goal was both more and less than to be released from bondage; they hoped to be exchanged with British prisoners on flag-of-truce ships. Their strategy, in other words, was to reverse the libel rulings that turned them from prisoners of war into slaves.

Although formal release from slavery was rare in New York and becoming increasingly harder to achieve over the course of the eighteenth century, a surprisingly high percentage of these Spanish sailors were able to convince courts that they should be treated as prisoners of war. The very confusion and multiplicity of the competing legal systems that held sway in the Atlantic world enabled men both to be enslaved after capture by a privateer and to be freed after petitioning the courts. Slavery was as much a legal as an economic status, and in this situation the conflicts between what was acceptable through international law on either side of the Atlantic created a situation whereby men could be both enslaved and redeemed. Legal chaos in the "outer Atlantic" was precisely what made privateering and piracy possible. These confusions led to war, which led to capture, which led in turn to a type of enslavement for black and mixed-race sailors that was quite different—at least at times, at least in their minds—from the chattel slavery around them.[60]

Some historians have argued that the key to understanding the legal victories of these sailors lies in the diplomatic relationships between England and Spain. Although private individuals such as privateer captains and investors were concerned for their own profits, New York officials had to make British imperial negotiations a priority; sailors achieved their freedom by exploiting this private/public disjunction for their own benefit.[61] It is true that when imperial officials such as Spanish governors became involved in the process, the New York vice-admiralty court was far more likely to free the Afro-Spaniards. However, looking to diplomatic issues alone does not entirely explain the stories of these prisoners of war. The imperial context for the sailors is not merely the polite letters exchanged between royal governors; it also includes the original commercial wars that conflated prisoners of war with libelable property.

Even before 1760 prisoner-of-war status was one of the possible outcomes for a libel suit, albeit one that rarely was granted without intervention on the part of the sailor. The designation of prisoner of war was more than a compromise position set out by the vice-admiralty court. Instead, it was the key to both freedom and the fluidity of racial status in New York City.

The colonial Spanish governments in particular tried hard to bring home their black and mixed-race subjects. In 1710 the lieutenant governor of Cartagena, captured en route to his new post, wrote to New York governor Robert Hunter from his prison in Boston demanding that his subjects be returned.[62] He promised in return to exchange English prisoners held in Cartagena for the Spanish prisoners who were being held as slaves in New York. The New York governor replied diplomatically but firmly that he would like nothing better than to free these men, but unfortunately, because he was "informed that it would be difficult to make their freedom appear [apparent?] he was rendered incapable of giving them their liberty."[63] Hunter later admitted to the Lords of Trade that he "secretly pittyed their condition but having no other evidence of what they asserted than their own words, I had it not in my power to releive [sic] them."[64]

This early exchange foreshadowed the future approaches that New York officials would take with Spanish sailors: they were willing to consider them prisoners equal to British men held in a Spanish prison, but only after their legal status was reversed in court. A list of subjects, even from so senior an official as the lieutenant governor, was not sufficient evidence of free status. Fortunately for this group of Spaniards, a privateer captain by the name of Russell had recently brought to New York a Spanish prisoner of war named Francis Fernandus. Fernandus gave a deposition to the governor and his council that he had known one of the men in question, Ambosia de Quever, whom Mr. Isaac Gouvernor held as a slave, and he assured the governor that de Quever was free-born. After he heard the deposition, Gouvernor told the court that he was convinced of de Quever's freedom and would send him back to the island of Palma. Perhaps influenced by Gouvernor's willingness to take Fernandus's word, the council decided to direct the attorney general to sue for the freedom of the other men taken in the war and held in New York as slaves.[65]

Not all the owners of sailors taken in Queen Anne's War were as trusting or as trustworthy as Gouvernor. De Quever, now free, deposed that another Spanish mulatto, John Marquess, was a freeman held as a slave by Captain Lewis, who planned to "run him off" and sell him elsewhere. The council called in Lewis and the owner of another reputedly free Spaniard. Despite the evidence of another witness that Marquess was free, neither the council nor Lewis was willing to admit to his free status or that of another sailor Lewis had captured. As a compromise, Lewis offered to take the two men on a trip with him to Jamaica, "where their freedom or slavery may more fully appear and if it shall there appear that they are free that there they shall freely discharge them." Perhaps suspicious of any course of action that would so thoroughly remove the captain and the colonel from oversight, the council recommended referring the entire matter to the common law and withheld judgment for the moment.[66]

This careful legality and emphasis on prisoner-of-war rather than slave status could work against the interests of sailors. Just as the governor could not set men free if the sailors had not been condemned by the vice-admiralty court, so its judge Lewis Morris refused to declare them free even if the proofs of their freedom were acceptable. Although Antonio Barcelona was on a list of free Spanish subjects sent by the governor of Havana in 1752, Morris refused to take official notice because Barcelona had been secretly sold without having been first libeled in court.[67] Other men were bounced from court to court for years.[68] Moreover, Morris's sympathy for privateers and penchant for condemning prizes made him far less willing, at least until the end of King George's War, to be moved by pity than the governor and his council were. Given that Morris received a fee for every prize he condemned, he had little personal interest in reversing judgments, much less refusing to libel sailors in the first place.[69]

Lewis Morris had a powerful position when it came to the determination of these men's status, regardless of the creativity of their legal strategy. His reluctance to overturn his previous decisions exceeded the patience of both prisoners and the governors who were agitating for their release. Governor Garcia de Solis of Cuba complained, for example, that while the Spanish usually accepted the word of fellow sailors as proof of their free status, the British court insisted on documentation that was difficult and time-consuming to produce.[70] Morris's obstreperousness reached a peak in the case of a mixed-race French sailor named John Reton. On July 4, 1745, Reton, having been successfully libeled despite his protests, was sold at public auction. Two years later, in May 1747, Reton succeeded in getting a certificate from the marquis de Vaudreuil, the deputy governor of Cap Français in Haiti attesting to his freedom. He also found two other white men, Peter Dejoncourt and Christopher Robert, to give affidavits that he was known as a freeman on the cape. The city recorder Daniel Horsmanden, speaking for the governor's council, ordered the attorney general to bring the case on Reton's behalf. Eight months later the vice-admiralty judge Lewis Morris gave his decision. Morris reasoned that despite the certificate and affidavits, the fact that Reton was born in Culdesac, 360 miles from the marquis's residence on the cape, invalidated the sworn testimony. Only evidence from the place of birth that a man was born free was sufficient. Morris would not overturn his earlier condemnation of Reton.

It was not unusual for the governor's council to refuse to hear a case. New York officials insisted that each case go through the court system in which it was originally heard, with the evidence appropriate to that court. In 1754, for example, three Spanish sailors sent petitions to the governor's council, along with all the proofs of their freedom that they could find. Like all these sailors, their argument was that as freemen, they could not be sold as Spanish property. They couched their strategy, however, as a reversal of the libel ruling. Unfortunately for them, the council decided that the only possible venue for these sailors was the court of chancery, "as the Papers on which the Proof of their freedom is founded, would not be admitted as Evidence in the Court of Common Law."[71] Clearly, some technical aspect of their papers, possibly a lack of seal or notarization, would not pass muster in the supreme court. As these men had been sold without ever being condemned in the vice-admiralty court, that court could not hear the case to reverse judgment.[72]

The obstacles that the vice-admiralty court put in sailors' way were only a part of the difficulty in obtaining freedom in New York. Cases often took years from the initial petition to the attorney general. In 1758, nearly ten years after Juan Miranda had begun his suit, his case was still before the courts. Putative owners often obstructed freedom attempts more directly. Cornelius Van Ranst imprisoned Miranda in the workhouse while his case was pending.[73] White New Yorkers often hid the men they had bought in the countryside around the city or in another colony so that they could not offer testimony to the courts.[74] Francis de Salas Cortilla was able to request his freedom only in 1761, eleven years after the governor of Havana had sent affidavits of his free status, because he had been "secreted" in Ulster County.[75] Alexander Joseph de la Torre, locked in his master's house to keep him from getting to the attorney general, pleaded in a letter, "God's sake sir do all that lays in your power to send me to my country."[76]

The drawn-out and difficult freedom trials, painful as they no doubt were to those seeking their freedom, did allow other enslaved New Yorkers, such as Juan Miranda, to watch the machinations of officials, courts, and prisoners. One particularly convoluted set of cases began even before King George's War had ended. In 1745 the governor of Havana complained to the governor of New York that several of his subjects "who were really freemen in their own country" were being held as slaves. In revenge, the Spanish governor seized twenty Rhode Islanders who had been involved in the capture of the sailors under question. The two governors agreed to a prisoner exchange, and three months later a Spanish flag-of-truce vessel sailed into New York's harbor with sixty-nine English prisoners.[77] Even with a Spanish envoy in town to oversee the release of the prisoners, however, the case dragged on for months. The attorney general did not enter a petition to the vice-admiralty courts to reconsider the slave condemnations until two months after the Spanish ship arrived, and even then he had to be prodded by the governor's council to complete his work.

Meanwhile, the cases of three of the men in question proved particularly contentious.[78] First their owners tried to hide the three men in the country. Judge Morris then decreed that although the documents brought by the envoy were sufficient to prove that the Spanish sailors were freeborn and he was forced to reverse his ruling, he did not feel that the men should go free until they had repaid the original purchase price. He reasoned that since "no evidence [had earlier] appeared [that these men were free] this court did therefore adjudge them to be slaves, and under that Decree they were sold at a Publick Vendue [auction], and therefore This Court thinks it would be extreamly hard for the severall Purchasers to lose their Purchase Money."[79]

The council disagreed with Morris's opinion and ordered the sailors to be sent back to Havana, telling the original purchasers to try to collect damages later. The purchasers, however, decided to take matters into their own hands. They seized the Spanish ship of truce, pulled off their former slaves, and demanded to be reimbursed for their purchase price by the Spanish envoy. Adding insult to injury, they asked Morris to condemn the ship as a prize.[80]

The story ended happily. The angry white men were put on trial, and the wrongly enslaved Spaniards were reconstituted as prisoners of war, exchanged for their English counterparts, and sent home as freemen.[81] Even so, the process had taken long enough for several men to die in slavery and others to spend almost two years in prison.

Eventually, however, the decisions of the vice-admiralty courts shifted to the sailors' benefit. Although as late as April 1745 the court continued to condemn sailors "for want of proof of their being free men," the momentum for overturning condemnations began to grow with the successful Spanish cases of 1746.[82] In 1747 four individual prisoners protested their enslavement to the governor's council, as did the governor of St. Augustine. The council asked the attorney general to look into the matter.[83] In 1750 the governor of Havana wrote to the governor of New York on behalf of eleven more subjects who had been wrongly enslaved, and in 1752 the governor of St. Augustine wrote about another forty-five black and mixed-race sailors. The governor of Havana wrote again about "certain Spaniards detained as prisoners."[84] Some individuals also managed to gain freedom if they could rally the support of a Crown official; Hilario Antonio, who had been captured before the war ended in 1748 and sent by his owner into the countryside, was finally able in 1756 to present a petition.[85]

Perhaps convinced by the large number of overturned condemnations, Morris stopped condemning soldiers after the end of King George's War in 1748. During the French and Indian War (1756–63) Morris made the privateers, not the prisoners, provide proof of imprisonment. After 1759 there were no more condemnations of black men. In a remarkable severance of race and status, the vice-admiralty courts of New York no longer assumed that a black sailor was or had to be a slave.[86]

Thus the success of Joseph, the black French sailor involved in the dispute over racial identity on board the *Prosperous Polly*, depended on a shift of historical momentum. Joseph had worried what his fate might be if his ship were taken by the British. He had therefore given written documentation of his freedom to a fellow sailor, a white Frenchman named John Baptiste Brown, while they were still in Porto Rico (later Puerto Rico). He asked Brown to be careful of it "because it contained certain proofs of his freedom which should they happen to be taken by the English might be of service to him in his captivity and might deliver him from slavery." However, in the rush of taking over the *Prosperous Polly*, Brown had left his sea chest, with the precious paper in it, on the French privateer.[87] Twenty years earlier Brown's carelessness might have resulted in Joseph's enslavement, but times had changed. Without a shred of documentary evidence, Justice Morris accepted Joseph's claim that he was a freeman.[88]

Using the same logic as the Spanish prisoners did, one particularly enterprising black sailor in the 1750s filed a petition for freedom with New York's attorney general William Kempe. In this petition Nero Corney did not argue that he had recently been a freeman; he openly admitted that he was currently a slave in New York under the legal ownership of one Captain Corney. His plea for freedom rested on the assertion of his identity as a British subject with strong patriotic feeling.

Nero had been "imported" (to use his term and the language of colonial commerce) from Guinea and had been a slave to "his Britannic Majesty's White Subjects" ever since. He had been sent to work as a mariner on one of his master's vessels out of New York on a cruise to Barbados. During the course of the voyage, Corney was taken prisoner by the French and brought to Martinique, where he was libeled and sold at auction to a Frenchman. Corney claimed that as a result of his identification with the British and not the French ("being willing and inclined to serve his Britannic Majesty's Subjects and not the French King's"), he managed to escape from Martinique and live as a freeman on the British island of St. Christopher. For some reason, however, Corney did not want to remain there, even with his freedom; perhaps he had a family in New York, although he did not say so. At any rate, claiming that he was "willing to pass the remainder of his Life Under his Majesty's Subjects," he chose to return to New York and to slavery.[89]

Once back in town, however, he found that Captain Corney, his previous master, would not allow him even the relative freedom he had enjoyed as an enslaved mariner; rather, Corney locked Nero up. Nero insisted that he had done nothing to deserve this treatment and that Captain Corney imprisoned him only because he feared that Nero would simply run away, or, as he put it, get his liberty "by regular methods." Nero Corney concluded his petition by begging Kempe that if he would only "see justice done to him who is and means to be subject of his Majesties without control," he would ever be a faithful subject of the king.[90] Following the reasoning of the Spanish sailors, Corney argued that a political subject could not be enslaved; voluntary political service ought to trump involuntary economic servitude.

Although Judge Morris of the vice-admiralty court stopped libeling Afro-Spanish and French sailors altogether by 1760, this legal shift, as we have seen, did not indicate that sailors were set free but only that they were to be treated as prisoners of war. Thus, in 1760 a mixed-race French sailor named John Roussel complained to the New York Common Council that he was being held as a slave by Captain Skinner, former privateer and commander of the *DeLancey*, a "private vessel of war" named after the famous New York family. Although in effect Roussel was enslaved, the official record, in a reversal of its earlier tendency to label such individuals as slaves, referred to him as a "French Prisoner of War in this City Claiming his Freedom." Although the captain was not immediately willing to release Roussel from servitude, he did agree that he would not sell Roussel or remove him from the city but rather would be willing to release him "upon any sufficient Proof appearing of his freedom.[91] In Roussel's case, New York officials were willing to consider him a priori a freeman; only the captain insisted that he was a slave.

The support that many sailors found in the Crown appointees to the governor's council and from the attorney general for their cases illustrates the "muted hostility" that metropolitan English law showed toward slavery through the eighteenth century.[92] Throughout the whole of this period, officials said again and again that it was wrong to enslave unjustly. Thus, in 1711 the governor's council considered the cases of two Spanish sailors, declaring that it went "hard against Law and Justice that if they were freemen at the time of their being taken they should be made slaves or being sold as such should continue so."[93]

Thirty-five years later an almost entirely different set of advisers suggested that the governor tell the governor of Havana that he would ask the vice-admiralty court to reconsider some libels "that justice may be done by a release of the Spanish prisoners condemned here as slaves."[94] Juan Miranda enjoyed the philosophical and rhetorical support of the attorney general; in his letter of support for Miranda's case, Kempe used the most ringing of declarations to dismiss Van Ranst's lawyer. Turning on its head Judge Morris's concern for the rights of property owners, Kempe proclaimed to Governor Charles Hardy that what the other lawyer "did for his fee, I [did] for the sake of Justice."[95]

In the end, we do not know what became of Juan Miranda. It is possible that the support of the attorney general and his affidavits were enough to set Miranda free in 1760. On one hand, the fining of Cornelius Van Ranst for unlawfully imprisoning the former sailor may indicate that Miranda had greater support among the judiciary than did the Van Ransts. On the other hand, New York manumission records reveal that a "John Moranda" was freed by John De Baan in 1795, thirty-five years after Miranda's freedom suit might finally have gone to trial. Three years after his own manumission, John had found the two hundred dollars needed to purchase his thirty-three-year-old wife Elizabeth and his four-year-old daughter Susan.[96] Was John Moranda Juan Miranda's son? If so, Miranda had clearly not won his freedom but had brought up a family in servitude. The records are silent on the outcome of Miranda's plea for freedom. The result would have mattered very much to Miranda, of course. However, knowing if Miranda died at home as a freeman and successful sailmaker is not necessary to understand the contingent nature of race in the eighteenth-century Atlantic world. Miranda's dark skin helped carry him to New York in the first place; it did not necessarily determine whether or not he stayed there.

Britain's eighteenth-century commercial culture often took the shape of a commercial war. The midcentury wars of trade led to the frequent enslavement of sailors, especially nonwhites, who suffered when their status shifted from prisoner of war to libelable property. Profiteering turned prisoners into slaves, and the legal code that enabled such a change in status was also used to turn slaves back not into freemen but into prisoners. Thus the move to prisoner-of-war status that formed the legal basis of these freedom suits makes sense only in the context of thinking about the commercial culture of war.

The sailors certainly did not see their suits in these strictly legal terms; these men were seeking their full freedom. Nor did the governor and his council relate the commercial context of the reversal of these judgments to the petitioners' prisoner-of-war status; clearly, they were responding to the diplomatic pressures brought by the Spanish Crown.[97] Even the vice-admiralty court judge Lewis Morris, concerned as he was with the pressures of individual profits and losses, did not emphasize the conflation of war and commerce when he reconsidered his libels of these sailors. However, the participants' limited perspectives do not obviate the presence of these larger forces. Their individual and self-interested interpretations were all encompassed by the problems and potential of the commercial war.

It is not surprising that when sailors of color felt they had been unjustly enslaved, they objected. Yet when sailors challenged their status as slaves, they used an imperial city's legal system to undermine protested easy relationship between skin color and slavery. For some, the decoupling of racial identity from legal status was persuasive. For others, particularly white captains who continued to try to libel some sailors, blackness still represented a possible profit. However, the very imperial system that led to their slavery also released them. Government officials such as William Kempe and Lewis Morris, charged with upholding the empire's laws, contributed to the city's racial fluidity. The sailors never challenged the institution of slavery itself, but members of the city's slaveholding class may have feared that these libel suits would do just that. Perhaps that is why in 1741, six years before he ordered the attorney general to bring a suit on behalf of an enslaved sailor, Daniel Horsmanden presided over one of the most extensive slave conspiracy trials in eighteenth-century British America.

Chapter Six

Status, Commerce, and Conspiracy

On the day after St. Patrick's Day in 1741, the tinderbox that was New York's concoction of status, race, and commerce literally went up in flames. On that day the roof of the New York governor's mansion caught fire. His house was completely destroyed, as were several other buildings adjoining it within Fort George. The next two weeks brought nine more fires. The fires, combined with a number of thefts, spurred a rumor among white New Yorkers that the city's slaves were planning an uprising to burn down the city, murder and rape its white inhabitants, and hand the city over to its Spanish enemies, with whom Britain was currently at war. The New York Supreme Court took up the challenge of finding a conspiracy and rooting out its ringleaders, although official opinion was split over whether its masterminds were white or black, British or Spanish. In an attempt to dig ever deeper into the conspiracy, city officials arrested 172 people for questioning, all but 20 of them black. With the help of an eager chief witness and an even more eager supreme court justice, 34 people had lost their lives by the end of the summer, and many more had been permanently deported from New York.[1]

Although executions moved quickly throughout the summer, by the end of the summer most New Yorkers seemed to feel that the danger had passed. As the trials unfolded, it became clear that this was less the tale of a racially based conspiracy than it was the story of an imperial port city. From their dramatic beginning to their feeble end, these trials rang with the echoes of the uncertain relationship between social standing and the marketplace. The broad themes of credibility, family networks, informal economies, commercialized gentility, and the racial products of imperial warfare together constitute the larger story of which these trials are only a part. The often unfulfilled desire for fixed social status and the city's fluid commercial culture created a perfect storm in the 1741 slave conspiracy trials. This failed attempt to violently reinscribe social order through courtroom drama exemplifies the enduring power of New York's economic culture over the simple ideology of white over black often associated with colonial America.

The New York winter of 1740–41 was a hard one. Near the end of

December one newspaper editor commented, "the Cold is so excessive, that while I am Writing in a Warm Room by a good Fire Side the Ink Freezes in the Pen."[2] Later that winter Christopher Wilson, an eighteen-year-old sailor from the warship *Flamborough*, went shopping with a shipmate. Wilson was friendly with some white servants who, with their masters, were boarding at a lodging house run by Robert and Rebecca Hogg. Their house was a respectable place to stay; Alexander Hamilton would make it his home during his 1744 trip to New York. The Hoggs' house was on the corner of Broad and Mill Streets, so close to the town synagogue that Wilson referred to Mill Street as "Jews' Alley." Wilson went to their house frequently, and Mrs. Hogg had seen him numerous times. From his many visits, he knew that she also ran a shop in which she sold cloth and clothing. On this expedition Wilson bought some checked linen, probably of the sort that sailors used for their blouses.[3] He bargained her down from the original price and then offered to pay with a Spanish silver piece, for which he would need change.

When Hogg opened up her cash drawer, Wilson got the idea of robbing her shop. Business had been brisk, and the drawer contained a good number of other milled Spanish pieces of eight. Hogg saw Wilson's gaze on her drawer and felt nervous. It would be better, she thought, not to have cash lying around where a young man of whom she knew little but who was around so often could get it. She pretended to send all the cash out of the shop to a neighbor's, in order to weigh it and be sure none of the precious metals from the coins had been clipped.[4] However, the money stayed in the shop, and Wilson planned his robbery. At a tavern on the west end of town, near the North (Hudson) River, he met three friends, all of them black slaves and experienced thieves. The owners of the tavern, John and Sarah Hughson, were happy to host the meeting; they did a brisk trade in receiving stolen goods.

The enslaved men—Prince, Cuffee, and Caesar, also known as John Gwin—were all accustomed to the Hughsons' tavern, since its owners felt no constraints about serving alcohol to slaves, even though this was formally forbidden by law. In addition, John Gwin boarded his mistress there. Peggy Kerry, whose other names included Margaret Sorubiero, Margaret Salingburgh, the "Newfoundland Irish beauty," and "Negro Peg" (for her relationship with Gwin), was a free Irish immigrant who helped the Hughsons pawn their stolen goods.

On Saturday night Prince and Cuffee broke into Rebecca Hogg's shop and stole money, linen, worked silver, and other valuable consumer goods. They even managed to grab the silver knee buckles that belonged to Rebecca's husband. Gwin hid the stolen goods in the yard of one of his neighbors, a shoemaker named John Romme, and returned to the Hughsons, where he climbed in through Kerry's window as usual. The next day he gave her part of the haul: snuffboxes, a child's whistle (perhaps for their child who had just been born), a ring, a pair of earrings, and a locket with diamonds in it. He also gave her money, a linen shirt, and other pieces of clothing, telling her that she should distribute them among the household, including the Hughsons' indentured servant. Gwin distributed the rest of the money among the Hughsons.

On Sunday morning Wilson, seemingly innocently, stopped by the Hoggs' house to visit. Rebecca Hogg complained to him that she "had lost all the goods out of the shop." Perhaps she had forgotten her earlier suspicions of Wilson but thought that perhaps some of his shipmates might have been involved or at least have some information. The shopkeeper described to him what was missing and asked for his help. Wilson, the instigator of the robbery, now betrayed his friends. He told Hogg that that very morning he had been at the Hughsons' house, where he had seen some of the money. A certain John Gwin had pulled out a knit cap full of silver, among which, said Wilson, were some of the distinctive coins she described.

The Hoggs assumed that John Gwin was a soldier, and Robert Hogg and one of the sheriffs went to the Hughsons' home to find him. When they inquired, however, they were told that no one named John Gwin had ever been there. Meanwhile, Gwin sat quietly next to the chimney and watched the search. It was not until Wilson later told the sheriff that Gwin also had the name Caesar that they arrested him and brought him to Wilson, who identified him. The city justices arrested both Gwin and Prince that afternoon. They also suspected that the Hughsons knew about the robbery, since Gwin had so openly displayed the booty there. They examined both John and Sarah Hughson and pressed them hard to reveal some knowledge of the stolen goods, but the couple remained silent, and the justices were forced to let them go. The sheriffs searched the Hughsons' house several times in the next couple of days but found nothing.

The sheriffs' break did not come until Tuesday night, when Mary Burton, the Hughsons' indentured servant, went to the home of one of the constables who had searched the house. The constable's wife, Anne Kannady, ran a shop from her house; while selling Burton some candles, she thought she would try her hand at getting someone in the Hughson household to crack the silence about the stolen goods. She offered Burton "motherly good advice": to tell her anything she could about the robbery. She threw in a sweetener: if Burton would tell what she knew, "she would get her freed from her master." The temptation for Burton was great, but she was too wily to give Kannady everything she wanted then. She told Kannady that she would tell her tomorrow about the stolen items, but she gave her a hint, "That her husband was not [a]cute enough, for that he had trod upon them." Burton thereupon made her exit.[5]

When the Hughsons and Kerry were brought in for questioning, they did their best to push the blame for the thefts onto their neighbors the Rommes. After a neighbor deposed that some of the Hoggs' stolen goods were now hidden in the Rommes' kitchen floor, the constables set off to arrest John Romme, but he had already skipped town. His wife, however, was still in the city.[6]

This robbery and others like it were central to eighteenth-century New York City's informal economy, and to the trials of 1741. The trial's third judge (and chief chronicler), Daniel Horsmanden, began his own account of the suspected slave conspiracy, which started with this robbery. In his opinion, "the inquiry concerning that, was the means of drawing out the first hint concerning the other; nay, this felony and such like, were actually ingredients of the conspiracy."[7] The robbery certainly drew the authorities' attention to the Hughsons, and not for the first time. They had been brought up on charges of serving slaves and running a disorderly house the year before. Horsmanden decided that the thefts were part and parcel of the conspiracy. In fact, it seems most likely, as contemporary observers later realized, that this and later thefts were themselves the conspiracy. In the 1770s William Smith, Jr., wrote in his *History of New York* that "when the ferments of that hour had subsided, an opinion prevailed that the conspiracy extended no further than to create alarms, for committing thefts with more ease."[8] Horsmanden was half right: minor acts of burglary were the beginning of the conspiracy, but they were also the end.

The second supreme court justice, Frederick Philipse, explicitly tied disorderly houses to the suspected conspiracy. At the opening of the trials in April 1741, in his first speech to the grand jury, the judge charged them

to find out and present all such persons who sell rum, and other strong liquor to negroes. It must be obvious to every one, that there are too many of them in this city; who, under pretence of selling what they call a penny dram to a negro, will sell to him as many quarts or gallons of rum, as he can steal money or goods to pay for. How this notion of its being lawful to sell a penny dram, or a penny-worth of rum to a slave, without the consent or direction of his master, has prevailed, I know not; but this I am sure of, that there is not only no such law, but that the doing of it is directly contrary to an act of assembly now in force, *for the better regulating of slaves.*[9]

As part of its attempt to enforce the slave code, the court indicted ten people for keeping disorderly houses as part of its investigation into the theft, and the governor called for more oversight of these taverns.[10] Once the fines were paid, however, the government dropped its attempt to tighten regulations over taverns. Indeed, the language, punishments, and fines for disorderly houses before and after 1741 remained remarkably similar.

Rebecca Hogg and Anne Kannady ran small and presumably reputable shops, but the places of exchange that Sarah Hughson, Elizabeth Romme, and other women maintained—with or without their husbands' knowledge or consent—were the linchpins of New York's informal economy. By robbing Rebecca Hogg's shop, Cuffee, Prince, and Gwin took their place on the illegal side of that informal economy. The economy's ability to upend status distinctions is most clearly shown in the relationship between John Gwin and Peggy Kerry. When he was arrested, Gwin admitted, to Horsmanden's horror, that he kept a free Irish woman as a mistress. He paid for her room and board, bought or brought her gifts, and had a child with her; in turn, she helped him fence stolen goods. It may seem amazing that a slave, himself someone else's property, could amass enough money to maintain a mistress. Through the resale of consumer goods, the informal economy allowed black men to have white women as dependents.

As an experienced shopkeeper, Rebecca Hogg knew when her suspicions were accurate. Although she had not been able to forestall the robbery of her shop, she was nonetheless a resourceful businesswoman. Not only was her husband Robert a successful merchant and trader; Hogg also was an active participant in New York's commercial economy: she took in boarders and ran a shop in which she sold her husband's imports. According to British law and custom, married women had no legal standing in the eighteenth century; they could not own property, much less run a business. The British legal fiction of coverture assumed that a married woman owned nothing, not even her own clothing. Christopher Wilson followed this convention, telling his accomplices that the money drawer "was at Hogg's house in the Broad street." Yet Wilson continued, "his wife kept a shop of goods, and sold candles, rum, molasses, etc."[11] In Wilson's mind, Robert Hogg owned the house but Rebecca Hogg had the store. Rebecca Hogg shared this view of the division of family property and labor. In her deposition to Horsmanden in the spring of 1742, she made clear that it was she, not her husband, who had been robbed. Her husband owned the property, but it was her business that suffered the theft.

In the middle of March, slightly more than two weeks after the theft of Rebecca Hogg's shop, Fort George, the garrison at the southern tip of Manhattan, which also included the governor's mansion, caught fire. The house, chapel, barracks, and governor's offices within the walls were all destroyed. Residents deployed the city's fire engines and a bucket brigade, but the fire still burned for a day and a half. Rumor first blamed the fire on a spark from a plumber who had been soldering a pipe on the roof. Then a rash of other fires throughout the city followed. Fires were common in eighteenth-century cities, and initially there seemed to be little cause for alarm. The particularly cold winter made for unusually soot-filled chimneys, which were always susceptible to catching fire. The pace of the fires accelerated over the following two weeks, however, until there were four in the first five days of April.

On April 6 alone four more fires broke out. Rumors of arson were floated, but no one could agree on the culprit or the purpose. Some New Yorkers wondered if the fires were part of an elaborate larceny plot, in which thieves would loot the homes of those who had gone to fight the fires. White New Yorkers began to look out for the usual suspects: slaves and foreigners.

It took only a few suspicious sights to stir New Yorkers' fears of a slave conspiracy. In 1712 roughly two dozen slaves had set fire to a building and ambushed the whites who arrived to extinguish the blaze. They managed to kill at least nine before the governor could lead the soldiers out from the garrison to put down the uprising. Thirty years later the association between unexplained fires and slave revolts spurred white residents to look suspiciously on slaves' behavior.

On April 5, as the pace of the fires increased, one woman claimed to hear three black men strolling down the street as one laughed, "Fire, Fire, Scorch, Scorch, A LITTLE, damn it, BY-AND-BY." Her neighbor told her that the man's name was Quack, and so she immediately informed the authorities, who arrested him. Cuffee, furthermore, who inexplicably had never been questioned about the Hogg burglary, was seen running away from one of the fires on April 6. A firefighter saw him and called out, "*A negro a negro.*" Others soon began to scream, "*the negroes [are] rising.*" Cuffee was dragged from his owner's house and thrown into jail with Quack. He could not come up with an explanation that would set him free. Quack, on the other hand, managed to convince his interlocutors that his comment was a response to the latest political news. The British navy, currently at war with Spain in the West Indies, had just captured Puerto Bello. Quack claimed that he was only talking about how much more devastation the British would still wreak on the Spanish. The magistrates believed him and set him free.

The political climate heightened still other fears. Two of the fires started in buildings that were almost next door to each other, at the Fly Market on the east end of town. The house that stood between the two torched buildings was the home of Captain Jacob Sarly, a successful privateer. He did not live there alone; among the members of his household was an enslaved man named Juan de la Sylva. "Wan," as he was known to many New Yorkers, had lived in New York for less than a year.

He was one of approximately 130 foreign sailors who had been taken prisoner during King George's War and brought to New York. Perhaps because of Wan's proximity to the two fires, and perhaps because of his Spanish origin, he was immediately suspected as the arsonist. Some New Yorkers cried, "*The Spanish negroes; the Spanish negroes; take up the Spanish negroes.*"[12] Two other Spanish sailors were already in jail, arrested after the third fire on April 1. Six more, including Wan, were arrested five days later.

Although these Spanish sailors were arrested early on in the investigation, they did not come to trial until the middle of June. By that point more than twenty suspects, including the Hughsons and Peggy Kerry, had been tried and convicted; thirteen people had already died, nine of them at the stake. In May 1741, two months after the first rash of fires in New York, the governor of Georgia, James Oglethorpe, sent a letter to New York in which he claimed to have uncovered a Spanish plot to burn the British cities of North America in order to impede the war effort.[13] Nine days after the date of the letter came the first testimony that Spanish blacks were indeed involved in the plot. The prosecution's chief slave witness, Sandy, testified that another slave, Jack, had told him about "the Spanish negroes who were concerned."[14] Less than a week after Sandy gave his testimony, the first two slaves to be burned at the stake implicated the Spanish prisoners. After that, testimonies that the Spanish blacks were leading the conspiracy came thick and fast.

One of the Spanish prisoners was among the first to be tried and burned at the stake; another, named Emanuel, may have indicated to the authorities that he would be willing to provide a confession and was not brought to trial for several weeks. On June 13, then, five Spanish sailors pleaded not guilty to charges of instigating a conspiracy. The Spaniards' initial defense was that they were not slaves and thus could not be accused by slaves. They insisted that as freeborn men, they never, either at home or in New York, even spent time with slaves. They claimed instead that they had been brought to New York after their ships were captured in the Caribbean by New York privateers. On arrival the sailors had not been treated as prisoners of war, as their white fellow seamen had been. Instead, the British vice-admiralty court had sold them as slaves.

One slave testified to Horsmanden that "he heard by captain Lush's house, about six of the Spaniards . . . say, that if the captain would not send them to their own country, they would ruin all the city; and the first house they would burn should be the captain's for they did not care what they did . . . they said '*d———n that son of a b———h, they would make a devil of him.*'"[15] These men had already seen that legal avenues were not effective. It is neither surprising nor improbable that the Spanish sailors had such animosity against John Lush (according to Mary Burton, common talk included planning to "tie Lush to a beam and roast him like a piece of beef"[16]). After all, Lush had claimed, when accused of torturing a Spanish captain, that he "had not realized you could use a Spaniard too cruel."[17]

The defendants had support for their argument that as freemen they could not be convicted on slave evidence. The owner of one of them admitted that he had been told that his servant was a freeman. The supreme court dismissed their arguments, however, on the basis that their status should have been properly adjudicated in the vice-admiralty courts. Given the complexities of reversing an improperly condemned prize, a process that often took years, the court's arguments must have further enraged the prisoners.

The prisoners then shifted their defense to argue that, unaccustomed to the cold winters of the Northeast, they all had frostbite and were lame the entire winter, and thus could not possibly have had a hand in the conspiracy. Although their owners and doctors also swore that the men had been confined to bed throughout the winter, and although one of the six was acquitted for lack of evidence, the remaining five were eventually found guilty. All of them were condemned to hang, but only Juan de la Sylva ended up on the gallows; the other four were eventually pardoned and ordered out of the colony.[18] One was transported to Newfoundland, which in its cold and isolation probably seemed a death sentence to him, but another was sent to Madeira, and the final two were sent to the Spanish West Indies. Were these in fact sentences, or were the men actually being sent home? The trial record that Justice Horsmanden published reveals little, but the rough notes of a governor's council meeting suggests that a deal with the survivors was struck after the public thirst to scapegoat the Spaniards had been slaked.[19]

Events now began to move rapidly. John and Sarah Hughson were brought back to jail. Daniel Horsmanden, one of the supreme court justices, was convinced that these fires were the leading edge of a grand conspiracy. With the support of the governor's ruling council, Horsmanden and the mayor of the city petitioned the governor to offer a reward for information about who had set the fires: one hundred pounds to a white person, twenty pounds and freedom to a slave (and twenty-five pounds to the slave's owner), and forty-five pounds to a free black or Indian. If informants had been involved in the arson, they would be pardoned. The day after the governor proclaimed the reward, the supreme court impaneled a grand jury. Their charge was threefold: to present for prosecution anyone who might have been involved in the arson, in thefts that occurred as a result of the fires, or in selling liquor to slaves. In the opinion of the court, all three illegal activities were closely related. The Hughsons' tavern, the theft of goods from Rebecca Hogg's shop, and the suspicious fires would all be prosecutable as one enormous conspiracy.

The grand jury immediately called Mary Burton to repeat her evidence about the stolen goods, but this time she refused to speak. After some time she agreed to tell the jury about the theft, but she claimed that she would not say a word about the fires. This tease was the first corroboration the court received in its belief that the thefts and the fires were related, and they pushed Burton hard to say more. When she began to tell more, her testimony confirmed their worst fears. She described meetings led by Cuffee, Prince, and Gwin but with another twenty or thirty slaves in attendance at her master's house, at which they plotted to reenact the 1712 uprising by burning the town and then killing the whites who came to put out the fires. Gwin, she said, had claimed that he would be the next governor, while Hughson would be the king. She also described caches of weapons in the tavern.

The grand jury questioned Peggy Kerry, who said that she knew nothing about the fires. Evidently assuming that they did not yet have enough evidence to indict on the charge of arson, the grand jury brought in charges against Prince and Gwin for theft and against the Hughsons and Kerry for receiving stolen goods. Less than two weeks later the slaves went to trial in front of the supreme court—not the special court that was sometimes convened for trying slaves—and were quickly convicted of theft. Both were sentenced to death by hanging.

Kerry, now faced with the approaching death of the father of her child, offered a confession in hopes of getting a pardon for herself. She told the grand jury that any plots concocted by whites and blacks in tandem for burning the city of New York had been hatched at the house of John and Elizabeth Romme, not at the Hughsons'. She also testified to seeing slaves bring quantities of stolen goods to the Rommes at night. John Romme was still at large, but the authorities found Elizabeth, who confessed to the stolen goods but asserted that although they might have occasionally allowed slaves to come drink in their house, there had never been any talk of a conspiracy. Elizabeth Romme was also jailed.

Two days later, on May 11, Gwin and Prince were executed at the gallows, and Gwin's dead body was left hanging to decompose. Although the two slaves had steadfastly refused to speak, others began to make accusations on all sides. Besides the names that Burton and Kerry began to give to the grand jury, one slave, perhaps hoping to exculpate himself, told his owner that a teenager recently sold out of the city to a purchaser in Albany knew plenty about the conspiracy. Cuffee, imprisoned now for over six weeks, also began to give names. Quack was the first to be arrested after the story of his suspicious "fire and scorch" speech was repeated to the grand jury. More arrests followed nearly every day. Detainees were pressured to confess by assurances that those who spoke frankly would receive pardons, while those who refused to help the prosecution would suffer.

On May 30 the extensive series of conspiracy trials began, with Quack and Cuffee as the first defendants. Seven whites, including Mary Burton, and two slaves gave evidence against them. Though Quack and Cuffee were allowed to call nine witnesses of their own (including their owners) to attest to their character and their actions on the days of the fires, that same day the jury quickly convicted them of a conspiracy to burn down the city of New York, and Justice Horsmanden sentenced them to death by burning at the stake.

As the wood was being piled around the two terrified men the next afternoon, officials tried to convince them to admit to the plot in return for a reprieved sentence. Not until each was told that the other had already confessed did they speak. Each named John Hughson as the ringleader and gave the names of nearly a dozen other men (and a few women) who knew about a plot to burn the city. The deputy secretary of the colony wanted to postpone the executions in the hopes of getting more names—each of the condemned said that there were at least forty or fifty slaves involved—but the eager crowd that had come to see the executions was so large that the sheriff told him there would be a riot if they delayed torching the wood. There was no delay.

After the deaths of Cuffee and Quack, the trials shifted from an examination into verifiable activities such as theft and arson to the more intangible question of the conspiracy. Magistrates immediately arrested those slaves named at the stake who were still at large and pressured them to give more names. Many of them did; by the end of June fifty-eight more slaves were in custody.

In addition to their previous indictments, the Hughsons and Peggy Kerry were arraigned for aiding and abetting a slave conspiracy. Since the evidence of blacks was not permissible against whites in the courtroom, Mary Burton's testimony was vital. She did not disappoint the prosecutors. On June 4 she described Hughson holding a Bible on which slaves swore oaths to uphold the conspiracy, and she elaborated on the collection of weaponry hidden in the house. She virtuously asserted that although both of the Hughsons often tried to bribe her with "silks and gold rings" to swear to join the conspiracy, she always held out against their blandishments.

Now charged with a far graver crime than simply receiving stolen goods, the Hughsons and Kerry had little chance of winning acquittals. The jury did not deliberate long before finding them guilty on all counts, singling out John as the ringleader of the conspiracy (although

Horsmanden later wondered whether Hughson had the brains to orga-
nize such an elaborate plot). All three were sentenced to death at the
gallows; John Hughson's body after death was to be left hanging next to
Gwin's. All three approached their executions with varying degrees of
visible emotion: John's ordinarily pale face burned red; Sarah stood, one
observer said, "like a lifeless trunk, with the rope around her neck, tied
up to the tree; she said not a word"; and Peggy was on the point of speaking when Sarah "gave her a shove with her hand." All died protesting
their innocence.[20]

In the days between the trial and the execution of these three, the
New York Supreme Court continued to examine and prosecute ever-
increasing numbers of slaves. Here the court depended on slave testimonies, including those taken at the stake from Cuffee and Quack, and
particularly on Mary Burton's seemingly never-flagging memory. As the
trials continued, Mary Burton became the prosecution's chief witness.
Without her evidence there would have been no trial, and as she repeatedly embellished her story, the investigation deepened. At the same
time, Horsmanden defended Burton's veracity against skeptics and
pressed for more trials. Meanwhile, some of the condemned slaves produced as many names as they could in the hopes of wringing pardons
from the governor. Those who refused to confess were killed. Nine more
men were burned at the stake over the course of eight days, and three
more were hanged. Including the executions of Gwin and Prince, the
court had now overseen nineteen executions, just as many as had died
in the Salem witchcraft trials.

The governor soon issued a proclamation that offered a pardon from
execution for any slave who testified to the plot, and the arrests grew
exponentially as each accused slave gave more names. After a while even
the constables began to see that the pressure to confess had produced
some false testimonies; at times they urged the court not to accept accusations that had been recanted. Other slaves offered such contradictory
stories that even the prosecutors could not believe them. Nonetheless,
the courts continued to find guilty almost every man who came to trial.
They executed fourteen more men, two by fire, in July.

In the middle of June the court next turned its attention to the Spanish prisoners awaiting trial. The shift highlighted the state's mounting
suspicion that it was uncovering more than a domestic uprising. As these
Spanish prisoners were both religious and national enemies, their
involvement seemed to imply a plot that would strike at the very heart
of a British city's Protestant identity. As New York governor George
Clarke wrote to his London supervisors on the Board of Trade,
"Whether or how far the hand of popery has been in this hellish con-

spiracy I cannot yet discover, but there is room to suspect it, by what two of the Negroes have confest."[21]

Burton offered the court vivid testimony of the bloodthirsty eagerness of the Spanish to murder Britons, and those slaves who had also agreed to give evidence supported her. The six Spanish prisoners all lost their cases, although five of them managed to secure pardons before they were hanged. Their insistence that they could not possibly speak enough English to communicate with slaves had some effect, however, because the magistrates began searching for a disguised Catholic priest who could have provided the leadership.

In June 1741, three and a half months after the trials began, the court was still not satisfied that it had reached the bottom of the plot. When Governor James Oglethorpe of Georgia sent the lieutenant governor of New York a letter reporting a rumor that Spain had sent out priests as spies, city officials scoured New York for any suspected Catholics.

As Horsmanden recounted, "Intimation having been given for some time past, that there had of late been Popish priests lurking about the town, diligent inquiry had been made for discovering them, but without effect; at length information was given that one Ury alias Jury, who had lately come into the city, and entered into partnership with Campbell, a school-master, pretending to teach Greek and Latin, was suspected to be one."[22] On April 14 Ury, "a little short man," had already been indicted as "a popish priest, for having come into the province of New York and there celebrated masses and granted absolutions."[23] He had been released, but on June 24 authorities picked up the itinerant schoolmaster and recommitted him to the city jail on suspicion of conspiracy.

The same day one of the judges brought Mary Burton to the prison to identify Ury. The next day Burton testified that she had seen him in her former master's house. She thought that he had first appeared the previous Christmas. Burton insisted that Ury had not been a casual visitor; from the first he "used to come there almost every night, and sometimes used to lie there."[24] The indentured servant could not quite recall when she had first met him, but she was quite sure that he used several different names, some of which might have been Ury, Jury, or Doyle. Burton insisted that there could be no question that Ury was deeply involved in the conspiracy. Whenever he came to the Hughsons' house, he "always went up stairs in the company of Hughson, his wife and daughter, and Peggy [Kerry], with whom the Negroes used to be at the same time consulting about the plot."[25] Burton's extensive testimony put Ury at the heart of the planning of the conspiracy.

Because there were no public schools in the British colonies, school teachers rarely settled for long periods in one place. Like dancing masters, painters, and other itinerants, schoolteachers made markets and dangers for themselves. When John Ury came to New York, he first made friends with John Croker, the landlord of the tavern in which he stayed. Croker then invited him to teach his son Latin. A few months later Ury made the acquaintance of John Webb, who not only asked Ury to instruct his two children but also recommended him to a Colonel Beekman. Beekman hired Ury to teach his daughter. Having then rounded up a number of pupils, Ury found another schoolteacher named John Campbell, and the two of them arranged to open a school together. The house they rented for their school was the very one in which the Hughsons had kept their tavern before their arrest. Ury and Mr. and Mrs. Campbell claimed that the first time Ury ever met a member of the Hughson household was the day when the three of them came to occupy the house. Making threats, uttering curses, and "swearing like a life guardman [that is, like a member of the cavalry]," Sarah Hughson, the teenage daughter of John and Sarah, refused to leave the house.[26] Two months later Ury had been arrested as the mastermind of an enormous international slave conspiracy.

Nearly as damning for Ury, moreover, were Burton's insinuations that he was a Catholic priest and no schoolmaster at all. She recounted several stories in which Ury assured her that he was capable of absolving her as well as any slaves from all possible sins. The New York court understood perfectly her implications that the absolution of sin was a hallmark of the Catholic priest. As William Smith, one of the attorneys for the prosecution, summarized, the power to forgive sins was one of the "notorious badges of popery."[27]

Burton's fellow accusers eventually followed her lead in naming Ury as the ringleader of the conspiracy; the judges helped the case by displaying Ury to all their witnesses. Although one of the soldiers who testified for the prosecution originally deposed that he had never met John Ury in his life, he later testified that he met Ury at the secret nighttime christening of a child, where Ury and two others "acted as priests."[28] He then claimed that he met him again at the Hughsons' tavern and that Ury had tried to "seduce" him into converting to Catholicism.

On one level, Ury's arrest is easily understandable in the context of 1740s New York City. The mere fact that he taught Latin put him in danger. Anti-Catholicism permeated the British Empire, often exacerbated by rumors of "popish plots" to overthrow a reigning Protestant king and replace him with a Catholic. New York's intimate connection with its first English ruler, the Catholic duke of York (later James I), provoked several generations of religious tension between the staunchly Protestant Dutch and James's Catholic governors, beginning with Leisler's Rebellion against James's absolutist government in 1689. After the Glorious

Revolution secured the Protestant succession for the monarchy, the New York government codified its restrictions against Catholics.

In August 1700 the assembly passed a law against "Jesuits and popish priests" that mandated life imprisonment for anyone who confessed to being a Catholic priest or anyone who might "otherwise appear to be such by preaching & teaching of others to say any popish prayers by Celebrating masses granting of absolutions or using any other of the Romish Ceremonies & Rites of worship." In New York it was as illegal to appear to be a Catholic priest as it was to be one. The law, intended to prosecute French Catholic missionaries who were working with Native Americans near the Canadian border, seems never to have been invoked until Ury's trial. Finding the "hand of popery" in a slave conspiracy made the uprising seem both more terrifying and more deplorable. Ury's refusal to acknowledge King George II as the head of the Anglican Church and his teaching of Latin, the language most closely associated with Catholicism, immediately marked him for suspicion among conformist New Yorkers.[29]

Yet anti-Catholicism does not entirely explain the scapegoating of Ury. The same week that Ury was arrested, the dancing master Henry Holt was accused of being in the plot. The slave who accused him explicitly drew forms of elite sociability such as drama and clubs into the plot, claiming in his deposition that Holt offered to burn down the theater when the time came. He also testified that Holt asked Hughson for the use of a room in the tavern for a freemasons' meeting.[30]

The prosecution began to hunt for still more dancing teachers. The judges shamelessly prompted their chief witness, Mary Burton, who replied that she had seen two other dancing masters whispering about the plot in the tavern. When asked for the name of one, Burton could only stammer out a "C," but she was sure that if she heard the name she would know it again. The court, later rationalizing its leading of the witness by arguing that there were no other dancing masters still in town, asked Burton whether the man's name was Corry. She "readily answered, that was his name."[31]

In total, three of the six white men implicated in the conspiracy of 1741 were dancing masters or tutors. More than tavern keepers, soldiers, or even sailors, the New York Supreme Court fingered dancing and school masters as the architects of an international slave conspiracy. As Horsmanden noted while unsuccessfully investigating yet another schoolmaster, "So that this is a fourth instance of suspicious school-masters infesting these parts, correspondent to general Oglethorpe's letter of advice. This man, Ury the priest, Holt a dancing-master, and John Corry an Irishman, a dancing-master and professed papist."[32]

The emphasis that elite men put on the important presence of dancing masters in the plot is clear from a letter that the New York governor sent to Governor Oglethorpe soon after Ury's trial. Confirming Oglethorpe's warning, Governor Clarke wrote, "it is now evident beyond a doubt that the hand of Popery is deep in the conspiracy." However, to Oglethorpe, Clarke went beyond the letter he wrote to the Board of Trade. He added, "we have a dancing master and many many other white men in prison," although he feared that they would not find the evidence to convict them. Clarke's suspicions focused sharply on the dancing master.[33]

Daniel Horsmanden himself found charges of itinerancy and poverty could overthrow even an established political elite. In September of 1747, the governor removed Daniel Horsmanden from his council. Although the governor was clear that he ejected Horsmanden because he felt the man was the leader of a cabal against him, in his explanation of the dismissal, Governor Clinton gave financial instability as the leading reason. The Governor accused the justice of having "no visible Estate in this Province, or anywhere else that is known; he left England deeply in Debt; has since contracted considerable Debts in this Province. . . ." Equally suspicious was his marriage to a rich widow.

Perhaps because he taught Latin, Ury was quickly identified as one of the priests "lurking" about the city, and he was arrested on the basis of that suspicion. Although he was originally indicted "for counseling, abetting, and procuring, etc. a Negro man slave called Quack, to set fire to the king's house in the fort," the indictment was soon changed to "being an ecclesiastical person, made by authority pretended from the See of Rome." Ury professed his innocence, but in vain. In his defense at his trial he insisted that he was in this situation only because of "some believing there can be no mischief in a country but a priest (if there be) must be in it[;] say they that in the chain of general woes the first and last link must be tied to the priest's girdle." Horsmanden believed and said exactly this, writing the next week to Cadwallader Colden that by the trials the "Old proverb has herein also been verifyed That there is Scarce a plot but a priest is at the Bottom of it." In his satisfaction at nabbing a priest, Horsmanden went so far as to turn Ury's own defense into a gruesome joke: "as the like per priest (Ury) said upon his Defence at his Trial (tho Sarcastically) 'according to the vogue of the World where there is a plot the first and last Link are usually fastened to the priests—"girdle;" but he must excuse us in this case, if the last Link be fastened to his Neck.' "[34] It took only fifteen minutes for the jury to find Ury guilty of aiding the conspiracy.[35]

On Saturday, August 29, 1741, John Ury was hanged. The *Pennsylvania Gazette* gave a full description of the execution: "He appeared at the gallows with a very composed countenance; he kneeled down and prayed very devoutly." In his prayer he laid the blame for his death on Mary Burton, entreating God "to cause some visible restraint against the Witnesses, to manifest to the World, that what they had witnessed against him was false." Then, having read his gallows speech and for the last time protested his innocence, "with the same steady and composed Countenance and Behavior, pull'd off his Wig and gave it to his Friend." Together, Ury and John Webb put the rope around his neck and covered his eyes, "Which done," the *Gazette* concluded simply, "the Cart drove away and he dyed."[36]

As the silver buckles from Rebecca Hogg's shop and the Spanish sailors threatening privateers made clear, New York in 1741 was as fully invested in the British commercial empire as at any point in its history. King George's War had just gotten under way when Christopher Wilson's warship, the *Flamborough*, docked in New York. Initially, the province supported the war enthusiastically, sending five hundred volunteers to help Admiral Edward Vernon take Puerto Bello from the Spanish. As the trials continued, however, the governor found it increasingly difficult to convince New Yorkers that they should join the armed forces; too many of them feared that battle had already come to New York.[37]

The reverberations of King George's War could be felt up and down the eastern seaboard. James Oglethorpe, the first governor of Georgia, was particularly vigilant where the Spanish were concerned. Oglethorpe repeatedly wrote to the governors of New York to warn them that the Spanish were planning an attack on the North American mainland and had focused their sights on New York in particular. No one took much notice of the first letter he sent in 1736. New Yorkers were happy to help the colony of Georgia succeed as a buffer against Spanish encroachments in North America, but they were less pleased at the idea of restricting their commerce with Spanish islands on the chance that their supplies would help Spain prepare for war.[38]

Five years later, in 1741, Oglethorpe sent another letter to the government of New York, and this one caused the death of John Ury. Oglethorpe claimed that some captured Spanish soldiers had informed him "of a villainous design of a very extraordinary nature"—that Spain had hired people to burn down all the magazines and major cities in English North America in order to keep the British from outfitting a fleet in the West Indies. Oglethorpe passed on the information that most of Spain's agents were priests, disguised as schoolteachers and dancing masters, who planned to infiltrate elite families and do their nefarious deeds. Even Oglethorpe admitted that the plot seemed a bit far-fetched, and he hesitated to believe it because "the thing was too horrid for any prince to order."[39]

As shocked as Oglethorpe was that a king would use such underhanded methods, he did not doubt the use of dancing masters as spies. Londoners frequently mocked their own dancing masters as effeminate yet seductive Frenchmen. Dancing masters were never sexualized in colonial New York; their role, both real and imagined, was quite different. Elite New York men sought gentility as a badge of masculine honor. Its meaning was refracted through New York's local and imperial politics. It was not sex that New Yorkers feared but spies, and Catholic spies at that. Thus, to use an anti-Catholic image from the eighteenth century, the harlot that seized the imaginations of men such as Daniel Horsmanden, Cadwallader Colden, and Governor George Clarke was the Scarlet Whore of Babylon.[40]

Oglethorpe's melodramatic story resonated perfectly with the slave conspiracy trials already under way. Before the letter arrived, the court had assumed that John Hughson, the alehouse keeper, was the ringleader of the plot. After Oglethorpe pointed to an organized imperial plot, however, the judges made a new effort to find someone else for that role. The connection of the suspected slave conspiracy to Britain's imperial foes fueled the mistrust of dancing masters. Other itinerant whites, such as sailors and soldiers, came under scrutiny too, but only teachers were suspected as the actual masterminds of the conspiracy. New York's lieutenant governor sent a copy of Oglethorpe's letter to the Lords of Trade on June 20; on June 24 John Ury was arrested.

In the person of Ury the court at last found the mastermind it had been seeking. An itinerant teacher with religious beliefs that were unorthodox (or, as his friend Joseph Webb testified, simply incomprehensible) came under automatic suspicion. His ability to read Latin, the language of the Catholic Church, made him yet more suspect. The arrest of Ury pulled on deeply woven strands of anti-Catholic fears in New York City.[41]

In the spring of 1741, the week after Mary Burton had given her first deposition to the New York Supreme Court hinting at an enormous slave conspiracy, Luke Barrington, another footloose young man passing himself off as a schoolteacher, was arrested in Ulster County, New York, for drinking a toast to King Philip of Spain. Barrington was thought to be not just a spy for the enemy but the enemy himself. Like John Ury, he was suspected of being a Catholic priest. Cadwallader Colden, in detailing the background of Barrington's arrest, explained to the lieutenant governor that "it is usual for the Romish Church to send forth young men into the Protestant countries in different Characters & for different purposes . . . they choose men of very different characters & some of very bad morals as best fitted for some purposes." Colden wrote that he understood that most of these men were not even told the entire plot in which they were involved; they just followed orders. Barrington, suggested Colden, was one of those. Barrington, on hearing these accusations, earnestly swore that he was "not Such a Person as you are pleas'd to have me Apprehended for, no Spy Sent in by the Pope or Spain."[42]

Daniel Horsmanden fully intended to examine Barrington and uncover the links among him, Ury, the king of Spain, and the pope. Colden, who had never been able to substantiate the rumor that Barrington was a priest, thought it unlikely that Horsmanden could ever find out the truth. The governor, however, clung to the hope that "if he [Barrington] has no other prospect than of remaining in Prison till next Summer, [he] may squeak." Unfortunately for Horsmanden, however, Barrington managed to escape from prison.[43]

Although Ury angrily rejected any claims that he had any sympathy with Africans, much less any desire to plot a rebellion with them, he admitted to holding political opinions much more germane to the issues of the British Empire than to the factional bickering of New York. Ury, as a nonjuring minister, insisted on his right to reject the monarch as the spiritual head of the Anglican Church. This was not merely a matter of doctrine. By the middle of the eighteenth century the influential British legal authority Sir William Blackstone thought that all who refused to swear oaths of loyalty should be considered papist dissenters. In the context of a war against a Catholic power, Ury's political beliefs suddenly mattered much more than his religious ones did. It was perhaps these unusual political beliefs that forced Ury to the gallows. The other dancing masters escaped execution—Holt had decamped for Jamaica in March, and John Corry had been dismissed when no one else testified against him.

Yet the rate of conviction in the trials was so high that it was almost inevitable that John Ury would die once he had been accused. The more significant question is not why he was executed, but why he was ever arrested. Less likely architects of a complex conspiracy than dancing masters and tutors would be hard to find. Ury's fatal flaw lay in his profession: itinerant teachers across British North America were suspicious characters. Ury, like so many other teachers, was caught between New York's shifting ideals of gentility and its heated factional and imperial politics.

The relentless progress of the executions in 1741 was entirely due to the work of two people: Justice Daniel Horsmanden and the indentured servant Mary Burton. Despite the increasingly contradictory evidence that Burton offered, Horsmanden's belief in her never wavered. In addition, the judge's support for his star witness persuaded the juries to continue to find both black and white prisoners guilty. Burton's and Horsmanden's credibility and success in convincing the judges and jury are part of a larger story in eighteenth-century New York about the connection between credibility and the city's commercial culture.

For ten years before Daniel Horsmanden sat in judgment on New York's suspected slave conspiracy, he struggled to find fame and fortune in that port city. When Horsmanden arrived in 1731, his life resembled the young con man William Ashburner's more than the well-established and successful Gerard Beekman's. He was in search of a life that would guarantee him a place in elite society, and he already understood the ways that imperial commerce and credit could undermine his claims to status. Horsmanden knew how to use names, connections, and clothing to reassure other New Yorkers that he deserved his genteel status. Like other confidence artists, his search for financial security and social status in New York's political arena shows how credibility—particularly fiscal credit—still underpinned status even for elite politicians.

Daniel Horsmanden immigrated to America after the failure of the South Sea Company's credit in 1720. It is unknown how much money he lost in England's first stock market crash, but he later admitted, "My Losses were such in the South Sea Year that I was Oblig'd to leave England."[44] In the late 1720s he sailed to Virginia, where his cousin William Byrd was one of the colony's largest and most important landholders. The son of one of his New York colleagues, William Smith, described Horsmanden as "a Gentleman by Birth . . . [who] wasting his fortune . . . fled from his Creditors to Virginia."[45] Leaving his unpaid bills behind him in England, Horsmanden needed to recoup his fortunes, and evidently even his wealthy Virginia cousins could not help him. He sailed north to New York.

Horsmanden was thirty-six years old on his arrival, and he had little private means that would support him in the manner of a gentleman. He had been trained as a lawyer in England and could use his profession to garner himself some notice. Perhaps with an eye to visually driving home his qualifications as a London-trained lawyer to the city's governor and judges, he wore the city's first known "barr gown" when he was sworn into practice on the supreme court.[46] It was a wise move on Horsmanden's part—people noticed—but the fees he could charge for practicing law would never be large enough to help him accumulate an independent fortune. For that sort of money he needed a political appointment that would give him both prestige and access to lucrative land grants. He used his elite connections in England to get a recommendation for a place on the governor's council in New York. After obtaining a position in this select circle of political appointees, he immediately began to look for ways to build his fortune.[47]

Soon after his arrival, Horsmanden's poverty provided political fodder for the city's factionalism. One councilman, looking for reasons to have

Governor William Cosby removed from office in 1733, noted that Cosby had appointed Horsmanden as "a Member of his Majties. Council here, who has no visible estate in this Government and [is] in necessitous circumstances."[48] Horsmanden complained to Cadwallader Colden that his political enemies "took indefatigable pains in Traducing and Villifying my Character in marking me out as a Person unsafe to Converse with, as if I were a Spy & Betrayer of Confidence."[49] Horsmanden was no spy, but he realized that his lack of financial credit endangered his social credibility.

His opponents had evidence from his creditors to prove his poverty, and the lack of a "visible Estate" advertised Horsmanden's dependence on others for his money and status. Horsmanden therefore spent a considerable amount of time fawning on New York's governor, and at last his efforts began to pay off. He was granted some land for development and resale, a permanent position as the secretary (or "recorder") of the council, and in 1737 a judgeship on the supreme court. Still, even though many New York lawyers and politicians turned to trade for their income, Horsmanden was wary of the potential pitfalls of commerce after his experience fleeing from creditors. Instead, he pinned his hopes on land speculation. As he wrote to another friend on the governor's council, "Lands are at Present the best View I have of making money."[50] He never managed to get as much land as he wanted, however, and in 1741 he still had the reputation of a man just scraping by.

The trials of 1741, then, need to be seen in part as one man's desperate attempt to wrest status from the city's political elite. Just as the defendants sought credibility from the jury, Horsmanden as the third justice played to the governor and his council for recognition as a respectable gentleman whose greatest concern was the protection of hierarchy. His description of Peggy Kerry, the white woman who boarded with the Hughsons, demonstrated his horror of racial mixing. He characterized her as a "person of infamous character, a notorious prostitute, and also of the worst sort, a prostitute to Negroes."[51]

The trials are also one woman's attempt to achieve freedom and wealth in a way that strikingly parallels Horsmanden's own quest. Mary Burton, the star witness, started the trials as a young indentured servant and ended them with her freedom and a fortune. Her testimony is a striking metaphor of the bill of exchange used by the men who brought her to the courtroom. In exchange for the imagined fiction she presented, the court, led by Horsmanden, first paid her credit and then paid her cash.

Over the course of ten weeks, one young woman's word put to death thirty people and exiled seventy-six others. Mary Burton, a sixteen-year-old orphan and indentured servant to a tavern keeper, was for a time one of the most powerful people in New York City. How did this happen? How did it come about that the word of a young woman without family or money had more credibility than that of free white men, including her own master? Burton had help, of course. The anti-Spanish fever, the fear of Catholicism, and the current war with Spain all contributed to giving her testimony the ring of truth. Burton said clearly what so many people already half-believed.

In April, after the initial rash of fires, the governor and the city council agreed to offer one hundred New York pounds to any white person who could name the guilty parties and offered a pardon if he or she had been involved in the arson.[52] The monetary amount was certainly enough to encourage people to come forward if they knew anything at all, and the thought of one hundred pounds seems to have tempted Mary Burton.

The Hughsons' indentured servant had already had a taste of the benefits her evidence might provide. Her conversation with Anne Kannady and her testimony at the trials of the Hughsons offered dramatic and damning evidence of her master's guilt. John Hughson tried to undercut Burton's credibility by asserting that she "was a vile, good-for-nothing girl" who had had a child by her former master, but he was unsuccessful in shaking the grand jury's belief in her testimony. Instead, Hughson confessed to receiving stolen goods. Flushed with her success at seeing her master caught, Burton then went much further.

On April 22, in front of a grand jury, after repeated refusals to give further information and repeated displays of nervous apprehension, Mary Burton delivered the goods. Under sworn deposition she laid out the narrative of the slave conspiracy and implicated her master and mistress as the ringleaders. Her testimony suggested that the Hughsons were not simply guilty of the misdemeanors of receiving stolen goods and serving alcohol to slaves; she had accused her master and mistress of the capital crime of aiding and abetting a slave revolt.

Of all the tricksters who passed through New York, Burton may have been the most successful. Like so many others, she found ways to gain the trust of her audience in that narrow gap between knowledge and belief. Her live performances in the courtroom allowed people to believe that they knew her, despite the fact that she had lived in New York for only a few months before the trials began. The very boldness of her story compelled trust by its own unverifiable nature. Like the forged bills of exchange that men found so tempting, Mary Burton's story was both dangerous and appealing.

That so many people listened to Burton reinforces the fact that class and gender were neither inevitable nor unchanging markers of power. Some people did, at times, mistrust Burton's testimony because she was a servant. When Chief Justice James DeLancey first heard her testimony at the beginning of July, he was openly suspicious and lectured her on the dangers of perjury. Her status, however, as Hughson's servant gave her credibility as an eyewitness. No one could have been better placed to know what happened in a dockside tavern.

Yet, despite the legal restrictions put on women, Burton's central role in the trials indicates that formal limitations did not necessarily translate into lived experience. Although many people suggested that Burton was falsifying her testimony, no one claimed that she was unbelievable because she was a woman. No one ever suggested that her physiology affected her rationality. Although the court marked her status in its condescending characterizations of her, it did not dismiss her testimony on those grounds. Mary Burton's story raised the fears of social upheaval and racial warfare. She claimed that the men agreed that once they had taken over the city, Gwin "should be governor, and Hughson, her master, should be king." Moreover, she added, one of the slaves argued quite explicitly for a redistribution of wealth: "Cuffee used to say, that a great many people had too much, and others too little; that his old master had a great deal of money, but that, in a short time, he should have less, and that he (Cuffee) should have more." This was not just the idle talk of a few malcontents, Burton assured the grand jury. At times, she said, she had seen "twenty or thirty negroes" at once in the Hughsons' house, all followers of the ringleaders. She had also seen guns and swords. The conspirators, both white and black, had threatened her with bodily harm if she told anyone about their plans. Additionally, Burton told the grand jury that no other whites were involved in the plot besides the Hughsons and Peggy Kerry. It was an incredible story, but the jury believed it because they feared it.[53]

Perhaps Horsmanden recognized a kindred spirit in Mary Burton. He described her examination in front of the grand jury in such a way as to give the impression that he strongly believed the truth of what he heard. "Her apprehensions," Horsmanden wrote, "gave suspicion that she knew something concerning the fires." When she refused to answer a question about the fires, her silence "increased the jealousy that she was privy to them." To convince her to talk, the proclamation of the reward "was read to her."[54] But one might inquire: who was it who was suspicious or jealous? Given Horsmanden's own determination to uncover the culprits behind the fires, he is most likely to have had these suspicions and jealousies himself.

Horsmanden's characterizations show his interest in bolstering Burton's credibility. Her coy demurral, he wrote, that she would say nothing about the fires, "as it were providentially, slipping from the evidence," implies that the mention of the fires was self-generated rather than the result of the grand jury's—and Horsmanden's—leading questions. Months later, as the trials were drawing to a close in August, Horsmanden wrote to a friend about those who had tried to "bring a discredit upon Mary Burton,"[55] and as he assembled his texts for publication in 1744, he reiterated the dangerous ignorance of those who did not credit his own interpretation of the fires and conspiracy. He therefore spent much of the conclusion of the *Journal* trying to prove that "Burton's testimony . . . was deserving of entire credit."[56]

By August, Burton's reputation certainly seemed in need of repair. With every new deposition, she implicated more people, both black and white, male and female. By the end of June she had testified that the Hughsons' younger daughter probably and their older daughter certainly were members of the conspiracy. She had also accused John Ury, the sort of Latin teacher whose involvement in an international plot had made even the governor of Georgia sense a certain implausibility. Yet, Horsmanden and the other judges still believed her, at least for a while.

The investigation came to an abrupt halt when Burton suggested that the conspiracy, rather than being limited to slaves, tavern keepers, and itinerants, also included members of the elite, whom she called "some people *in ruffles*." The grand jury pushed her for names, until at last "she mentioned several of known credit, fortunes and reputations."[57] With the exception of Horsmanden, for the first time the judges and jury refused to believe her. Burton's own credibility, as well as her desire for "fortune and reputation," struggled against those of "known credibility" and lost. Her bill, so to speak, was protested at the bank.

Even so, Horsmanden continued to believe her. Burton's indictment of gentlemen in ruffles marks the point at which the symbiotic relationship of Burton and Horsmanden diverges: Burton reached the limit of her credit, collected her winnings, and left; while Horsmanden, through his unflagging trust in the star witness, showed that his greatest desire was to stabilize his own status. Burton's last accusation failed because it attacked the hierarchy that supported New Yorkers' fears of a slave revolt. Elite New Yorkers could easily believe that slaves in New York would rise up against their masters just as they did in Antigua in 1736 and in South Carolina in 1739.[58] Yet these city residents could not believe that members of their own caste would destroy the city and upend the social hierarchy. Like a con artist, then, whose fabrications had finally caught up with her, Burton could no longer sustain the credit of her audience.

Horsmanden, however, needed Burton, because without her testimony there was no way to prosecute the conspiracy, and without prosecuting the conspiracy there was no way to gain social and financial prestige as a judge. Burton and Horsmanden used the trials to seek personal credibility and financial security, but only Burton obtained them. Once she got her money, Mary Burton disappeared from the historical record. In April 1742, just one year after the governor had first issued the proclamation, Burton collected the reward of one hundred pounds. Referring to Horsmanden and another supreme court justice, the council declared that "it was their Opinions that the said Mary Burton well deserved of the Publick for the great Service she has done in becoming the Chief Instrument in detecting great Numbers of the Confederates engaged in a Conspiracy for burning this City."[59] Burton's master was dead, but her indenture was not reassigned. Instead, the New York Common Council granted her request that George Joseph Moore, the council clerk, would become her guardian. At the age of sixteen Mary Burton had achieved more money and freedom than many New Yorkers would obtain in their lifetimes.

As most merchants knew, credit was both unstable and uncertain. Mary Burton and Daniel Horsmanden discovered this for themselves as the 1741 trials drew to a close. Ironically, Burton appears to have exploited the system even better than her more powerful supporter did. Burton was able to disappear with her money; Horsmanden was forced to defend his actions both in print and before the governor's council for another seven years.

Before the trials had ended, the judge had begun to hear grumbling. "Tho' the Town were well pleas'd with the first fruits of our Labours and inflicting the deserved punishment on the offenders," he fumed to Colden, "yet when it comes home to their own houses and is like to affect their own propertys in Negroes and Cosinship in others; then they are alarm'd and they cry out the Witness must needs be perjured."[60] Feeling beleaguered and disparaged, Horsmanden concluded that he needed to prove to white New Yorkers how close they had been to disaster. Only his efforts, he felt, had kept the city from total destruction. The recorder decided to prove to the rest of the city the errors of their ways by publishing the evidence from the trials.

Three years after the trials ended, some people were whispering that the entire set of trials and executions had been a useless sham. Horsmanden felt that there were altogether too many "wanton, wrongheaded persons amongst us, who took the liberty to arraign the justice of the proceedings, and set up their private opinions in superiority to the court and grand jury; though God knows (and all men of sense know) they could not be judges of such matters; but nevertheless, they declared with no small assurance (notwithstanding what we *saw* with our eyes, and *heard* with our ears, and everyone might have judge of by his intellects, that had any) *that there was no plot at all!*"[61]

In November 1741, nearly three months after John Ury's execution, Horsmanden agreed to arrange, index, and annotate an edition of the colony's laws. In return, the assembly offered to pay him £250.[62] Although Horsmanden was in desperate need of the money, he was far more concerned about the conspiracy than the legal code. He spent the money but never quite got around to preparing New York's laws for publication; bringing the *Journal* into print took all his time.[63]

However, Horsmanden's credibility among his peers was not a given. The problems with his reputation and financial standing that had dogged Horsmanden in the 1730s reappeared ten years later. When the judge's friendship with Governor George Clinton fell apart in 1747, six years after the trials, one of the reasons the governor gave the Board of Trade for ejecting Horsmanden from the council was his lack of any financial credit. According to Clinton, "Horsmanden came to New York a fugitive from the Sheriff of Essex, and at first lived as a person of some estate; but, his bills all coming back protested, he was reduced to the lowest necessity and lived on the hospitality of the gentlemen of the place."[64] Economic instability and shaky credit could turn out to be just as dangerous in their own way for a supreme court justice as for a con artist such as Tom Bell.

Although neither Burton nor Horsmanden was a confidence artist in the strict sense, both tried to use New York's commercial culture in similar ways for their own gain. The credibility of these two depended as much on New York juries' ideas about gender and class as it did on their words. As a servant and a young woman, Burton's stakes were lower. No one expected her to act like a gentleman; she had only to find the right balance between giving enough information to be credible while holding back enough to be desirable. Her winnings, in the end, released her from the most obvious bonds of gender and servitude. Horsmanden, as an aspiring gentleman, had a harder and less certain task. He needed the credibility offered by a successful prosecution of the suspected conspiracy to give his elite fellows confidence in him; at the same time, he could win guilty verdicts only by convincing his juries and fellow jurists that he was a trustworthy gentleman. Burton swindled Horsmanden out of his credit too.

In the month between Ury's trial and his execution, the rate of burnings and hangings slowed considerably. Only one man, one of the Spanish prisoners, died during this period. Faced with overcrowded jails and an enormous number of confessions, the court had begun to recommend pardons with transportation out of the British Empire for most of the defendants. Over seventy slaves, including the few enslaved women who had been implicated in the plot, were put on ships and sold in Madeira, the Spanish West Indies, or Haiti. Others were released to their owners under the condition that they be sold out of the British Empire immediately. A few were sent to Newfoundland. The white soldier most deeply implicated in the plot was reassigned to a unit in the front lines of battle in the West Indies.

Ury was hanged at the end of August. He had written a long speech declaring his innocence as well as his staunch Protestant beliefs. He magnanimously forgave those who had so falsely accused him. Benjamin Franklin, whose newspaper had been following the trials carefully, printed his gallows speech as a broadside.[65]

After Ury's execution, however, the trials petered out. The whites still awaiting trial were pardoned or the charges against them were dismissed. Seven months later one more slave was executed on charges of arson, but the paranoid Horsmanden could not convince the rest of the court that this was the start of another conspiracy. Hardly a year after the turmoil had begun, Mary Burton claimed her reward and disappeared from view. The trials disappeared from many white New Yorkers' consciousness almost as quickly. In fact, they appear to have had little effect on the city as a whole. For many New Yorkers, this episode had initially evoked memories of an earlier slave uprising in 1712. It also appeared to be part of a larger wave of slave revolts around the Atlantic world: in the West Indian island of Antigua in 1736 and in Stono, South Carolina, in 1739. As a result of those revolts, each community had instigated numerous changes to the slave code and instituted other legal and social restrictions.[66]

Yet in New York no new slave code was passed in the aftermath of the trials. The taverns and brothels in which the plot was said to have been hatched were never put under new regulations. Interracial sex never became an issue. The only piece of new legislation with an explicit connection to the suspected conspiracy was the establishment of a military watch. Six months later the assembly admitted that it could not find enough inhabitants to keep the watch, and it did not bother to renew the law.[67] The city's fluid social and commercial culture not only made a ghastly incident possible but also let it fade away with few lasting consequences.

Other historians have offered sensitive and thoughtful interpretations of this event, assessing the likelihood of an actual conspiracy or the contemporary meaning of the idea of a conspiracy altogether. Yet the push to interpret the trials of 1741 may have led to a fundamental misunderstanding of the world in which they took place. Despite the gruesome and extensive executions, these trials created almost no measurable aftermath in New York City. Although the trials centered on a possible slave uprising, they serve in the end to show us only that eighteenth-century New York was not a world overdetermined by race.

The events of 1741 touched on many of the concerns of eighteenth-century New York—race, gender, goods, war, commerce, strangers—and yet resolved none of them. Instead, the trials vividly and dramatically demonstrated the extent to which hierarchies and social orders were violently contested and rarely settled. The anxieties raised in the trials of 1741 did not afterward define New York's political or social cultures; they could not. The primacy of commerce in the British Empire, particularly within the context of a diverse and competitive Atlantic world, worked against any stiff adherence to an abstract social order.

In the end, the 1741 trials did matter, but not in the way that Horsmanden thought they did. To the individuals whom he sentenced to death or banished far from home, of course, they mattered very much indeed. The trials do offer a dramatic story, an engaging way to grab the reader's attention and bring the past to life. However, map is not territory, and to treat a set of trials as a piece of fiction is a travesty. As one legal theorist has wisely noted, "the words of court decisions have a force that differentiates them from most other utterances. However provocative and generative it may be to treat law as literature, we must never forget that law is not literature."[68] The struggle for order in imperial New York may have been perpetually unfinished, but it was fierce. The economies of this port city were more dangerous than Daniel Horsmanden could know.

Notes

Introduction

1. For the 1718 Burgis view, see I. N. Phelps Stokes, comp., *The Iconography of Manhattan Island, 1498–1909* (New York: Robert H. Dodd, 1915; reprinted Union, N.J.: Lawbook Exchange, 1998), 1:239–51; and John Hallam, "The Eighteenth-Century American Townscape and the Face of Colonialism," *Smithsonian Studies in American Art* 4 (1990): 144–62.

2. For some examples of coverage from Boston to South Carolina, see *American Weekly Mercury,* April 2, May 7, May 28, 1741; *New England Weekly Journal,* April 6, May 12, 1741; *Boston Weekly Newsletter,* July 30, 1741; *South Carolina Gazette,* April 9, July 23, 1741; *American Weekly Journal,* June 18, 1741; *Pennsylvania Gazette,* August 6, 1741; *Boston Evening Post,* May 11, 1741; *Boston Post-Boy,* May 11, 1741; and *Boston News-Letter,* May 11, 1741.

3. For eighteenth-century wars, see Ian Kenneth Steele, *Warpaths: Invasions of North America* (New York and Oxford: Oxford University Press, 1994); P. J. Marshall, ed., *The Eighteenth Century,* vol. 2 of *The Oxford History of the British Empire,* ed. William Roger Lewis (Oxford and New York: Oxford University Press, 1998); John Brewer, *Sinews of Power: War, Money, and the English State* (New York: Knopf, 1989); and Lawrence Stone, ed., *An Imperial State at War: Britain from 1689 to 1815* (London and New York: Routledge, 1994). For an enormously influential cultural study of the meaning of these wars, see Linda Colley, *Britons: Forging the Nation, 1707–1837* (New Haven, Conn.: Yale University Press, 1992).

4. For the fur trade, see Thomas Elliot Norton, *The Fur Trade in Colonial New York, 1686–1776* (Madison: University of Wisconsin Press, 1974); and Oliver Rink, *Holland on the Hudson: An Economic and Social History of Dutch New York* (Ithaca and London: Cornell University Press, 1986). For middling traders, see Cathy D. Matson, *Merchants and Empire: Trading in Colonial New York* (Baltimore: Johns Hopkins University Press, 1998). For elite traders, see Virginia D. Harrington, *The New York Merchant on the Eve of the Revolution* (New York and London: Columbia University Press, 1935). For female traders, see Patricia Cleary, "'She Merchants' of Colonial America: Women and Commerce on the Eve of the Revolution" (Ph.D. diss., Northwestern University, 1989); Patricia Cleary, "'She Will Be in the Shop': Women's Sphere of Trade in Eighteenth-Century Philadelphia and New York," *The Pennsylvania Magazine of History and Biography* 119 (1995): 181–202, and Jean P. Jordan, "Women Merchants in Colonial New York," *New York History* 43 (1977): 412–39. For ways in which commerce creates culture in other ports, see Christine Leigh Heyrman, *Commerce and Culture: The Maritime Communities of Colonial Massachusetts, 1690–1750* (New York and London: W. W. Norton, 1984).

5. For the consumer revolution, see T. H. Breen, *The Marketplace of Revolution:*

How Consumer Politics Shaped American Independence (New York: Oxford University Press, 2004). For gentility, see Cary Carson, "The Consumer Revolution in Colonial British America: Why Demand?," in *Of Consuming Interests: The Style of Life in the Eighteenth Century*, ed. Cary Carson, Ronald Hoffman, and Peter J. Albert (Charlottesville and London: University Press of Virginia for the United States Capital Historical Society, 1994); and Richard L. Bushman, *The Refinement of America: Persons, Houses, Cities* (New York: Random House, Vintage Books, 1992).

6. For overviews of colonial New York, see Michael Kammen, *Colonial New York: A History* (New York and Oxford: Oxford University Press, 1975); and Edwin G. Burrows and Mike Wallace, *Gotham: A History of New York City to 1898* (New York and Oxford: Oxford University Press, 1999), pts. 1 and 2. For immigration in New York, see Joyce Goodfriend, *Before the Melting Pot: Society and Culture in Colonial New York City, 1664–1730* (Princeton, N.J., and Oxford: Princeton University Press, 1991). For "warehousing" of immigrants, see Bernard Bailyn, *The Peopling of British North America: An Introduction* (New York: Vintage Books, 1986). For German and Irish immigration through New York, see Marianne S. Wokeck, *Trade in Strangers: The Beginnings of Mass Migration in North America* (University Park: Pennsylvania State University Press, 1999); and Nicholas Canny, ed., *Europeans on the Move: Studies on European Migration, 1500–1800* (Oxford: Clarendon Press, 1994). For population figures, see Thelma Wills Foote, "Black Life in Colonial Manhattan, 1664–1786" (Ph.D. diss., Harvard University, 1991), 78, table 4; and Gary B. Nash, *The Urban Crucible: Social Change, Political Consciousness, and the Origins of the American Revolution* (Cambridge and London: Harvard University Press, 1979), appendix. For gender balance, see David Narratt, *Inheritance and Family Life in Colonial New York City* (Ithaca, N.Y.: Cornell University Press, 1992), 238.

7. Ira Berlin, *Many Thousands Gone: The First Two Centuries of Slavery in North America* (Cambridge, Mass., and London: Harvard University Press, 1998), 178.

8. For slavery in New York, see Foote, "Black Life"; Graham Russell Hodges, *Root and Branch: African Americans in New York and East Jersey, 1613–1863* (Chapel Hill and London: University of North Carolina Press, 1999); and Edgar J. McManus, *A History of Negro Slavery in New York* (Syracuse, N.Y.: Syracuse University Press, 1966).

Chapter 1

1. Manuscript minutes of the New York Court of General Sessions, December 16, 1737, New York Municipal Archives. For Chalker, see Richard Webster, *A History of the Presbyterian Church in America from Its Origin until the Year 1760* (Philadelphia: J. M. Wilson, 1857), 432.

2. See Margot Finn, *The Character of Credit: Personal Debt in English Culture, 1740–1914* (Cambridge and New York: Cambridge University Press, 2003); and John Smail, "Credit, Risk, and Honor in Eighteenth-Century Commerce," *Journal of British Studies* 44, no. 3 (July 2005): 439–56.

3. Craig Muldrew, *The Economy of Obligation: The Culture of Credit and Social Relations in Early Modern England* (New York: St. Martin's Press, 1998), 148.

4. Michael Kammen, *Colonial New York: A History* (New York and Oxford: Oxford University Press, 1975), 71; Edwin G. Burrows and Mike Wallace, *Gotham: A History of New York City to 1898* (New York and Oxford: Oxford University Press, 1999), 72. For the argument that before the conquest New Netherland was on the same economic course as most British colonies, see Oliver Rink, *Hol-*

land on the Hudson: An Economic and Social History of Dutch New York (Ithaca, N.Y., and London: Cornell University Press, 1986). Population figures are from Gary B. Nash, *The Urban Crucible: Social Change, Political Consciousness, and the Origins of the American Revolution* (Cambridge, Mass., and London: Harvard University Press, 1979), appendix; and Thelma Wills Foote, "Black Life in Colonial Manhattan, 1664–1786" (PhD diss., Harvard University, 1991), 78, table 4. For comparisons of the three ports, see Nash, *Urban Crucible,* chapter 1; Cathy D. Matson, *Merchants and Empire: Trading in Colonial New York* (Baltimore: Johns Hopkins University Press, 1998), 3; and Jacob Price, "Economic Function and the Growth of the American Port Towns," *Perspectives in American History* 8 (1974), repr. in Jacob M. Price, *The Atlantic Frontier of the Thirteen American Colonies and States: Essays in Eighteenth Century Commercial and Social History* (Aldershot, Hampshire: Variorum, 1996). Price, "Economic Function," 145, suggests that New York and Philadelphia may have benefited directly from Boston's loss of leverage in the European market. For a more optimistic view of the New England economy in general, see Gloria L. Main and Jackson T. Main, "The Red Queen in New England?," *William and Mary Quarterly,* 3d ser., 56, no. 1 (January 1999): 121–50. Also see Cathy Matson, "'Damned Scoundrels' and 'Libertisme of Trade': Freedom and Regulation in Colonial New York's Fur and Grain Trades," *William and Mary Quarterly,* 3d ser., 51 (July 1994): 389–418; and John J. McCusker and Russell R. Menard, *The Economy of British America, 1607–1789* (Chapel Hill: Published for the Institute of Early American History and Culture by the University of North Carolina Press, 1985), 193.

5. In making a case for the study of New York's economy, Matson argues that even though the volume and value of Philadelphia's trade surpassed those of New York by the middle of the eighteenth century, "by then New York City dominated its own satellite regional economy in ways that replicated London's place at the hub of a great commercial wheel" (Matson, *Merchants and Empire,* 3). The uniqueness of New York's economy lies in the quality of its exchange, not the quantity.

6. For New York's status as "colonial mercantile capital," see McCusker and Menard, *Economy of British America,* 189. For its balance of trade, see ibid., 191; and Price, "Economic Function," 158. For its reshipments, see Price, "Economic Function," 159.

7. Matson, *Merchants and Empire,* 240–48. The city's positive balance of trade with the West Indies meant that merchants were likely to be paid in Spanish currency, which was then converted and sent to Great Britain to pay for finished goods. See Cadwallader Colden, "Account of the Trade of New York, 1723," in *Documents Relative to the Colonial History of the State of New York,* 15 vols., ed. John Romeyn Brodhead, E. B. O'Callaghan, and Berthold Fernow (Albany: Weed and Parsons, 1853–57), 5:686.

8. Virginia D. Harrington, *The New York Merchant on the Eve of the Revolution* (Gloucester, Mass.: Peter Smith, 1964), 105.

9. The economist Alexander Justice, writing in 1707, divided money into two sorts, "imaginary" and "real," quoted in John J. McCusker, *Money and Exchange in Europe and America, 1600–1775: A Handbook* (Chapel Hill: University of North Carolina Press, 1978), 3.

10. Charles Z. Lincoln, William H. Johnson, and A. Judd Northrup, eds., *Colonial Laws of New York,* 5 vols. (Albany, N.Y.: J. B. Lyon, State Printer, 1894), chapter 190, June 8, 1709, 1:666–68. (hereafter cited as *New York Colonial Laws*). See Leslie V. Brock, *The Currency of the American Colonies, 1700–1764: A Study in Colonial Finance and Imperial Relations* (New York: Arno Press, 1975), 67.

11. Harrington, *New York Merchant,* 109–11; quotation from Matson, *Merchants and Empire,* 245.

12. *New York Colonial Laws,* 1:668.

13. Matson, *Merchants and Empire,* 69.

14. This explanation is indebted to Bruce H. Mann, *Republic of Debtors: Bankruptcy in the Age of American Independence* (Cambridge, Mass.: Harvard University Press, 2002), 11–14.

15. Philip L. White, ed., *Beekman Mercantile Papers, 1746–1799* (New York: New-York Historical Society, 1956), 2:541.

16. McCusker, *Money and Exchange,* 22.

17. Cadwallader Colden to Mr. George Mifflin, Philadelphia, August 4, 1714, in *The Letters and Papers of Cadwallader Colden:* vol. VII, *Additional Letters and Papers, 1715–1748, Collections of the New-York Historical Society for the Year 1934,* The John Watts DePeyster Publication Fund Series, vol. 50 (New York: Printed for the New-York Historical Society, 1918), 20.

18. Henry Cruger to Peter Dubois, New York, February 20, 1753, F. A. DePeyster Papers, box 7, folder "Letters from Henry Cruger," New-York Historical Society.

19. James Steven Rogers, *The Early History of the Law of Bills and Notes: A Study of the Origins of Anglo-American Commercial Law* (Cambridge: Cambridge University Press, 1995); Curtis P. Nettles, *The Money Supply of the American Colonies before 1720* (Madison: University of Wisconsin Press, 1934; repr., 1964).

20. For female attorneys, see the work of Linda L. Sturtz, *Within Her Power: Propertied Women in Colonial Virginia* (New York: Routledge, 2002).

21. Gerard Beekman to Gamaliel Wallice, April 22, 1754, in White, ed., *Beekman Mercantile Papers,* p. 212.

22. Beekman to Peter Rutgers, April 22, 1754, in White, ed., *Beekman Mercantile Papers,* p. 213.

23. Beekman to Henry Lloyd, July 21, 1755, in White, ed., *Beekman Mercantile Papers,* p. 259.

24. *New-York Mercury,* August 25, 1755.

25. Gerard Beekman to William Beekman, October 26, 1763, in White, ed., *Beekman Mercantile Papers,* p. 449.

26. See, in particular, Kenneth Scott, *Counterfeiting in Colonial New York* (Glückstadt, Germany: J. J. Augustin for the American Numismatic Society, 1953); and Valerie Bohigian, "The Development of Counterfeiting Legislation in Colonial New York: The Relationship between Modernization and 'Thwart Law'" (Ph.D. diss., City University of New York, 1992). Also see Kenneth Scott, *Counterfeiting in Colonial America* (New York: Oxford University Press, 1957). For the numbers of coin clippers, see Bohigian, "Counterfeiting Legislation," fig. 1, 165.

27. Manuscript minutes of the New York Court of General Sessions, New York Municipal Archives, February 4, 1704; February 2, 1702, May 1, 1705.

28. Ibid., February 4, 1701/2.

29. Julius Goebel and T. Raymond Naughton, *Law Enforcement in Colonial New York: A Study in Criminal Procedure (1664–1776)* (New York: Commonwealth Fund, 1944), 95.

30. Manuscript minutes of the New York Court of General Sessions, February 2, 1702; August 7, 1710.

31. Manuscript minutes of the New York Court of Quarter Sessions, August 7, 1734; February 4, 1735; April 16, 1739.

32. Manuscript minutes of the New York Supreme Court, 1704–9, June 8, 1706, Division of Old Records, Office of the New York County Clerk.

33. Manuscript minutes of the New York Court of Quarter Sessions, March 3, 1736; *New-York Gazette*, March 8, 1736.

34. After a 1728 dramatic forgery case in London, English law made the counterfeiting of private bills of exchange a capital crime also, although that legislation does not seem to have had much influence in the colonies. See Randall McGowen, "From Pillory to Gallows: The Punishment of Forgery in the Age of the Financial Revolution," *Past & Present* 165 (November 1999): 107–40; and Chauncy Graham, *God Will Trouble the Troublers of His People* (New York: Hugh Gaine, 1759).

35. *New York Colonial Laws*, chapter 492, November 11, 1726, 2:345

36. Manuscript minutes of the New York Court of Quarter Sessions, November 2, 1720.

37. Ibid., *King v. Thomas Copley*, August 7, 1734. See also the case of William Fowler, May 1702, manuscript minutes of the New York Court of General Sessions.

38. *New-York Gazette*, January 18, 1731.

39. *New-York Gazette, or Weekly Post-Boy*, September 16, 1754. See also *New-York Gazette*, July 9, 1739; *New-York Weekly Post-Boy*, August 1, 1743; and *New-York Mercury*, January 28, 1754.

40. Bohigian, "Counterfeiting Legislation," table 9, 301.

41. Scott, *Counterfeiting in Colonial New York*, 196. Gerard Beekman's estimation "to live like a gentleman" is quoted in Burrows and Wallace, *Gotham*, 169. In England "middling" incomes ranged from £80 to £150 annually. See Margaret R. Hunt, *The Middling Sort: Commerce, Gender, and the Family in England, 1680–1780* (Berkeley and London: University of California Press, 1996), 15.

42. For foreign coins in the colonies, see McCusker, *Money and Exchange*, 3–12.

43. *Pennsylvania Gazette*, July 5, 1739; manuscript minutes of the New York Court of General Sessions, August 8, 1739.

44. *Pennsylvania Gazette*, June 26, 1740.

45. *New-York Gazette*, March 20, 1727; minutes of the Supreme Court of New York, October 22, 1727. See also Scott, *Counterfeiting in Colonial New York*, 26–30; and Goebel and Naughton, *Law Enforcement*, 515.

46. Manuscript minutes of the meeting of the mayor, the deputy mayor, and aldermen of New York City with the New York Court of Quarter Sessions, May 3, 1739.

47. For pleadings in New England, see John M. Murrin, "Magistrates, Sinners, and a Precarious Liberty: Trial by Jury in Seventeenth-Century New England," in *Saints and Revolutionaries: Essays on Early American History*, ed. David D. Hall, John M. Murrin, and Thad Tate (New York: Norton, 1984), 152–206.

48. Manuscript minutes of the meeting of the mayor, the deputy mayor, and aldermen of New York City with the New York Court of Quarter Sessions, May 3, 1739.

49. *New-York Gazette*, February 11, 1734; manuscript minutes of the New York Court of Quarter Sessions, May 4, 1734; manuscript minutes of the New York Supreme Court, April 19, 1734. Also see Scott, *Counterfeiting in Colonial New York*, 34–37.

50. Sir James Steuart, *An inquiry into the principles of political oeconomy: Being an essay on the science of domestic policy in free nations. In which are particularly considered population, agriculture, trade, industry, money, . . . By Sir James Steuart, . . . in two volumes* (London, 1767), vol. 2, bk. 4, chap. 1, p. 108.

51. Muldrew, *Economy of Obligation*, 7.

52. As Jean-Christophe Agnew, *Worlds Apart: The Market and the Theater in Anglo-American Thought, 1550–1750* (Cambridge and New York: Cambridge University Press, 1986), x, suggests, "the customer's will to believe was a stipulated or conditional act, a matter less of faith than of suspended disbelief. What bound the market and theater together, then as now, were the same peculiar experiential properties that set them apart from other kinds of exchange."

53. For the case, see manuscript minutes of the New York Court of Quarter Sessions, November 3, 1736. For some of Henry Row's voyages to the West Indies, see *American Weekly Mercury*, November 14, 1723, and March 29, 1732; and *New-York Weekly Journal*, July 8, 1734.

54. For examples of letters to ship captains instructing them to draw from an account held by a third party, see Gerard G. Beekman to Arthur Helms (Ship Captain), January 23, 1748, in White, ed., *Beekman Mercantile Papers*, 1:40.

55. McGowen, "From Pillory to Gallows," 118–19.

56. Gerard G. Beekman to Peleg Thuston, May 18, 1750, p. 107, and June 22, 1750, p. 109 in White, ed., *Beekman Mercantile Papers*. More than two years later Beekman was still waiting for Lord's payment and was clearly willing to salvage anything he could from the transaction. In August 1752 he asked a ship captain sailing to Halifax, "If by any means you Can git anything of John Lord so as to discount on his notes of hand, pray do and whatever it may be I will with Pleasure allow you one Quarter Part" (Beekman to Samuel Tingley, August 8, 1752, in White, ed., *Beekman Mercantile Papers*, p. 147).

57. White, *The Beekmans of New York in Politics and Commerce, 1647–1877* (New York: New-York Historical Society, 1956), 292.

58. For the changes that itinerancy brought, see also Cary Carson, "The Consumer Revolution in Colonial British America: Why Demand?," in *Of Consuming Interests: The Style of Life in the Eighteenth Century*, ed. Cary Carson, Ronald Hoffman, and Peter J. Albert (Charlottesville and London: University Press of Virginia for the United States Capital Historical Society, 1994), 483–697.

59. "Complaint of Abigail Cottrell against Philip Philipse et al with an Information of Mary Bush relating to the same," June 5, 1753, New York Supreme Court, parchment papers, 48-K-5. Division of Old Records, Office of the New York County Clerk.

60. Gerard G. Beekman to William Snell, September 29, 1750, in White, ed., *Beekman Mercantile Papers*, 122–23.

61. Testimony of Elizabeth Wright, April 1754, New York Supreme Court, parchment papers, K-673.

62. Sarah Pearsall, "'Not a Weak Womanish Affection': Creating Men of Credit for an Atlantic World, 1760–1815" (paper presented at the American Historical Association, Washington, D.C., January 2004); Toby L. Ditz, "Shipwrecked; or, Masculinity Imperiled: Mercantile Representations of Failure and the Gendered Self in Eighteenth-Century Philadelphia," *Journal of American History* 81, no. 1 (June 1994): 51–80.

63. *New-York Weekly Journal*, July 12, 1736.

64. Ibid., October 17, 1743. Vernon may have been the man's stage name.

65. *Pennsylvania Gazette*, October 7, 1736.

66. David Barclay and Sons to Mary Alexander, November 12, 1757, Alexander Papers, box 8, folder 1, New-York Historical Society.

67. *Pennsylvania Gazette*, December 29, 1747.

68. Manuscript minutes of the New York Court of Quarter Sessions, Novem-

ber 9 and February 6, 1738. For Bell generally, see Steven C. Bullock, "A Mumper among the Gentle: Tom Bell, Colonial Confidence Man," *William and Mary Quarterly*, 3d ser., 55 (April 1998): 231–58; and Carl Bridenbaugh, "'The Famous Infamous Vagrant' Tom Bell," in Bridenbaugh, *Early Americans* (New York and Oxford: Oxford University Press, 1981).

69. For Bell's confession, see *New-York Evening Post*, September 4, 1749. For warnings, see *New-York Weekly Journal*, February 14, 1742; *New-York Weekly Post-Boy*, July 18, 1743, November 5, 1744, and April 14, 1746; and *New-York Evening Post*, March 25, 1745.

70. *New-York Weekly Post-Boy*, July 11, 1743. The New York newspapers continued to report on Bell's activities in New York and Philadelphia until 1749.

71. On Beekman's web of business contacts, see Matson, *Merchants and Empire*, 151. For the company partnership, see the letter from Gerard Beekman to Seymour and Lloyd, August 17, 1754, signed also by William Ashburner, in White, ed., *Beekman Mercantile Papers*, 220. For the letter to Lloyd, see Beekman to William Lloyd, Jamaica, August 17, 1754, in White, ed., *Beekman Mercantile Papers*, 220–21. For merchants in Philadelphia assessing their local peers' credibility, see Doerflinger, *Vigorous Spirit of Enterprise*, 18.

72. Gerard G. Beekman to Abraham Rawlinson and William Preston, Lancaster, England, June 6, 1755, in White, ed., *Beekman Mercantile Papers*, 251–54.

73. Matson, *Merchants and Empire*, 154–55.

74. Gerard Beekman to Townsend White, Philadelphia, October 21, 1754, in White, ed., *Beekman Mercantile Papers*, 228–29. In fact, Beekman ended up paying only sixty pounds in damages on one of the bills because he had sold the rest conditionally on their acceptance; see Beekman to Seymour and Lloyd, Jamaica, October 21, 1754, in White, ed., *Beekman Mercantile Papers*, 229–230.

75. Gerard Beekman to Townsend White, Philadelphia, September 30, 1754, in White, ed., *Beekman Mercantile Papers*, 224–26.

76. Gerard G. Beekman to William Beekman, Liverpool, England, January 30, 1764, in White, ed., *Beekman Mercantile Papers*, 457–58.

Chapter 2

1. Cadwallader Colden to John Falconer, New York to London, May 4, 1724, in *The Letters and Papers of Cadwallader Colden*: vol. VII, *Additional Letters and Papers, 1715–1748, Collections of the New-York Historical Society for the Year 1934*, The John Watts DePeyster Publication Fund Series, vol. 50 (New York: Printed for the New-York Historical Society, 1918), 51–53 (hereafter *Colden Papers*),

2. Margaret Hunt's pathbreaking work on the relationship of the market to family life emphasizes the role of family and particularly husbands in restricting women's financial success; see Margaret R. Hunt, *The Middling Sort: Commerce, Gender, and the Family in England, 1680–1780* (Berkeley and London: University of California Press, 1996). For an excellent account of how "market transactions constructed social relationships and affective ties shaped economic transactions" in the early nineteenth century, see Ellen Hartigan-O'Connor, "'Abigail's Accounts: Economy and Affection in the Early Republic," *Journal of Women's History* 17, no. 3 (2005): 35.

3. "Empire of Virtue: The Imperial Project and Hanoverian Culture c. 1720–1785," in *An Imperial State at War: Britain from 1689–1815*, ed. Lawrence Stone (London: Routledge, 1994), 128–64.

4. See John Smail, "Credit, Risk, and Honor in Eighteenth-Century Commerce," *Journal of British Studies* 44, no. 3 (July 2005): 441; and Richard Grassby,

Kinship and Capitalism: Marriage, Family and Business in the English-Speaking World, 1580–1740 (New York: Cambridge University Press, 2001).

5. Susanah Shaw, "New Light from Old Sources: Finding Women in New Netherland's Courtrooms," *De Halve Maen* 74, no. 1 (Spring 2001): 9–14.

6. Sir William Blackstone, *Commentaries on the Laws of England, in Four Books,* Early American Imprints no. 11996 (Philadelphia, 1771–72), bk. 1, chap. 15, p. 442.

7. Edwin G. Burrows and Mike Wallace, *Gotham: A History of New York City to 1898* (New York and Oxford: Oxford University Press, 1999), 124–25; Michael Kammen, *Colonial New York: A History* (New York and Oxford: Oxford University Press, 1975), 91–94. On Dutch property law, see Linda Biemer, *Women and Property in Colonial New York: The Transition from Dutch to English Law, 1643–1727* (Ann Arbor: UMI Research Press, 1979). On inheritance and coverture in New York, see David Narratt, *Inheritance and Family Life in Colonial New York City* (Ithaca, N.Y.: Cornell University Press, 1992); and Marylynn Salmon, *Women and the Law of Property in Early America* (Chapel Hill: University of North Carolina Press, 1986). For the argument that there was little decline in women's economic power after the conquest, see Joan R. Gunderson and Gwen V. Gampel, "Married Women's Legal Status in Eighteenth-Century New York and Virginia," *William and Mary Quarterly,* 3d ser., 39 (January 1982): 114–34.

8. If a debtor happened to have assets in New York, a merchant might try to put those into the hands of a third party until a case could come to court or be settled. See Richard B. Morris, ed., *Select Cases of the Mayor's Court of New York City, 1674–1784* (Washington, D.C.: American Historical Association, 1935), 13–21; and Virginia D. Harrington, *The New York Merchant on the Eve of the Revolution* (New York and London: Columbia University Press, 1935), 116–23.

9. Morgan, *Bristol and the Atlantic Trade in the Eighteenth Century* (New York: Cambridge University Press, 1993), 110–18. The New York/Belfast firm of Greg & Cunningham, for example, told a Belfast merchant that it would keep the balance due to him on "credit with us, keeping you accountable to him [the New York merchant Waddell Cunningham] if any outstanding Debts on Sales should prove bad" (Thomas M. Truxes, ed., *Letterbook of Greg & Cunningham, 1756–57: Merchants of New York and Belfast* [Oxford: Oxford University Press, 2001], 300).

10. *Letter Book of John Watts,* 108, cited in Truxes, ed., *Letterbook of Greg & Cunningham,* 107n7; see also 106.

11. Truxes, ed., *Letterbook of Greg & Cunningham,* 209.

12. Catherine Ingrassia, *Authorship, Commerce, and Gender in Early Eighteenth-Century England: A Culture of Paper Credit* (New York: Cambridge University Press, 1998). See also Liz Bellamy, *Commerce, Morality and the Eighteenth-Century Novel* (Cambridge and New York: Cambridge University Press, 1998), 23.

13. Kathleen Wilson, "Empire, Gender, and Modernity in the Eighteenth Century," in *Gender and Empire,* ed. Phillippa Levine (Oxford: Oxford University Press, 2004), 14–45.

14. Wilson, "Empire, Gender, and Modernity," 18.

15. *Wallice v. Fairday* (1716), 208; *Renaudet v. Fairday* (1717), 213; *Swift v. Fairday* (1717), 215: these cases are all reproduced in Morris, ed., *Select Cases.* From the low numbers of women who appeared in suits for debt, one historian has concluded that women were increasingly closed out of the market economy in the eighteenth century. According to this thesis, the small numbers of women in the historical record who were explicitly acting on their own demonstrate how

marginal women were to the market. See Deborah Rosen, *Courts and Commerce: Gender and the Market Economy in Colonial New York* (Columbus: Ohio State University Press, 1997), chaps. 5 and 6. In the case for the Madeira debt, the creditor's witness claimed that the debtor knew that her then-suitor Warren was already married; he reported that she said "She Did not Care but if Warren had ninety nine wives She would make the Hundreth" (reproduced in Morris, *Select Cases,* 217ff.).

16. "Examination taken this 11th day of September before Jacobus van Cortland Esq. Mayor of the Citty of New York," in Ogden Goelet, comp., *Old New York, or, Reminiscences of the Past Sixty Years, by John W. Francis,* extra-illustrated, vol. 13, no. 69, BV Francis (Goelet), New-York Historical Society (hereafter Goelet's *Francis*)

17. Julius M. Bloch, ed., *An Account of Her Majesty's Revenue in the Province of New York, 1701–09: The Customs Records of Early Colonial New York* (Ridgewood, N.J.: Gregg Press, 1966), 94.

18. In *Abstracts of Wills on File in the Surrogate's Office, City of New York*: vol. I, *Collections of the New-York Historical Society for the Year 1892.* Publication Fund Series, vol. XXV (New York: Printed for the New-York Historical Society, 1893), 327 (hereafter cited as *Abstracts of Wills*).

19. When Francis's estate was inventoried in 1691, the total came to £1,131. Francis and Helena had also had a prenuptial agreement by which she received 4,000 guilders in cash, but the majority of the estate would be held in trust for their youngest daughter (*Abstracts of Wills*, I: 102–3; I:455).

20. Jean P. Jordan, "Women Merchants in Colonial New York," *New York History* 43 (1977): 412–39, 419–23.

21. Gertrude's uncle with whom she was in close contact was Herman Winkler (or Winclair), a naturalized New Yorker who held "several considerable posts in Surinam and Curacao." See Joyce Goodfriend, *Before the Melting Pot: Society and Culture in Colonial New York City, 1664–1730* (Princeton, N.J., and Oxford: Princeton University Press, 1991), 136. For relationship, see E. B. O'Callaghan, ed., *Calendar of British Historical Manuscripts in the Office of the Secretary of State, Albany, New York, 1664–1776* (Albany, N.Y.: Office of the Secretary of State, 1865; repr., Ridgewood, N.J.: Gregg Press, 1968), 662. For naturalization, see "An Act for Naturalizing Herman Winkler and other the [*sic*] persons therein Named." Charles Z. Lincoln, William H. Johnson, and A. Judd Northrup, eds., *Colonial Laws of New York*, 5 vols. (Albany, N.Y.: J. B. Lyon, State Printer, 1894), chap. 556, October 29, 1730, 2:665–66.

22. Christopher Bancker journal, 1740–50, BV Bancker, Christopher, New-York Historical Society. The transactions are from June 5, June 16, and September 15, 1749.

23. Hunt, *Middling Sort,* 128.

24. Minute books, New York Court of Special Sessions, July 15, 1735. Also see Patricia Cleary, "'She Merchants' of Colonial America: Women and Commerce on the Eve of the Revolution" (Ph.D. diss., Northwestern University, 1989).

25. Julius Goebel and T. Raymond Naughton, *Law Enforcement in Colonial New York: A Study in Criminal Procedure (1664–1776)* (New York: Commonwealth Fund, 1944), 42n203.

26. For a convincing refutation of the argument made by Elaine Crane that women's economic work was hidden from their contemporaries (Crane, *Ebb Tide in New England: Women, Seaports, and Social Change, 1630–1800* [Boston: Northeastern University Press, 1998]), see Ellen Louise Hartigan-O'Connor,

"The Measure of the Market: Women's Economic Lives in Charleston, South Carolina and Newport, Rhode Island, 1750–1820" (Ph.D. diss., University of Michigan, 2003).

27. For Mary Spratt's prenuptial agreement, see *Abstracts of Wills*, I:270–71. For biographical information about Mary Alexander, see *American National Biography*, s.v. Alexander, Mary; May Van King Rensselaer, *The Goede Vrouw of Manaha-ta at Home and in Society, 1609–1760* (New York: Arno Press, 1972); and Cleary, "She Merchants," chap. 6. For Cornelia DePeyster, see Cathy D. Matson, *Merchants and Empire: Trading in Colonial New York* (Baltimore: Johns Hopkins University Press, 1998), 137.

28. James Alexander Papers, box 8, New-York Historical Society. For James, see Henry Noble MacCracken, *Prologue to Independence: The Trials of James Alexander, American, 1715–1756* (New York: J. H. Heineman, 1964). James did want to leave a double share to his oldest son, in accordance with biblical tradition, and when Mary wrote her will, this was the only one of his suggested partitions that she did not follow. See Narratt, *Inheritance and Family Life*, 158–60.

29. Alexander Papers, box 8.

30. In 1741 a woman from Perth Amboy wrote to Alexander asking for more time on a small debt, pleading in a postscript, "Madam I beg you will not put me to charge" (Margaret Stele to Mary Alexander, Perth Amboy, March 30, 1741, Alexander Papers, box 8, folder "Letters, etc.").

31. "Estate of Mary Alexander with David Barclay and Sons," Alexander Papers, box 10, folder 11. Hunt, *Middling Sort*, 146, suggests that women may have begun investing more money in annuities rather than trade in order to avoid the risks of the market. Fifteen thousand pounds would have placed Alexander among the wealthiest 15 percent of Philadelphia traders. See Thomas M. Doerflinger, *A Vigorous Spirit of Enterprise: Mechanics and Economic Development in Revolutionary Philadelphia* (Chapel Hill and London: University of North Carolina Press for the Institute of Early American History and Culture, Williamsburg, Va., 1986).

32. Samuel Storke to Mary Alexander, Alexander Papers, box 11. Storke also credited fifteen barrels of rice marked "MA" to James's account.

33. James Alexander diary, Alexander Papers, box 4, folder 6.

34. *New-York Mercury*, April 21, 1760.

35. Account book of Ann Elizabeth Schuyler, "James Alexander account," New-York Historical Society. For a comparison of Schuyler's account with other merchant-shopkeepers', although without much consideration of gender, see Thomas David Beal, "Selling Gotham: The Retail Trade in New York City from the Public Market to Alexander T. Stewart's Marble Palace, 1625–1860" (Ph.D. diss., State University of New York—Stony Brook, 1998), chap. 4. For practices of diversification among "aspiring" traders, see Matson, *Merchants and Empire*, 150–52.

36. *New-York Gazette Revived in the Weekly Post-Boy*, December 18, 1752.

37. Account book of Ann Elizabeth Schuyler, 1737, New-York Historical Society; account of "Widow Margaret Vetch"; Henry Livingston to ——, October 11, 1742, reel 7, Livingston Papers, Pierpont-Morgan Library; Nicholas Bayard account book, August 23, 1743, New-York Historical Society; Bloch, ed., *Account of Her Majesty's Revenue;* Jordan, "Women Merchants," 422; Margaret Vetch to Peter Dubois, New York, July 5, 1753, F. A. Aston DePeyster Papers, box 7; Obadiah Wells, creditor's agreement, box 18, folder 2, Alexander Papers. For Vetch's biography, see Cynthia A. Kierner, *Traders and Gentlefolk: The Livingstons of New*

York, 1675–1790 (Ithaca, N.Y.: Cornell University Press, 1992); and George Macgregor Waller, *Samuel Vetch: Colonial Enterpriser* (Chapel Hill and London: University of North Carolina Press for the Institute of Early American History and Culture, 1960).

38. Margaret Vetch to Peter Dubois, February 17, 1753, FA DePeyster Papers, box 7.

39. Margaret Vetch to Peter Dubois, July 5, 1753, FA DePeyster Papers, box 7.

40. Doerflinger has isolated four "career paths" by which men in the second half of the eighteenth century in Philadelphia could become merchants. First, they could be born to wealthy merchants from whom they received considerable amounts of capital. Second, they could be wellborn with little capital. Third, they could come from other professions that led to trade, especially sailing and shop keeping. Fourth, they could have foreign contacts that they parlayed into capital or credit. See Doerflinger, *Vigorous Spirit of Enterprise*, chap. 1.

41. For the Livingstons, see Lawrence H. Leder, *Robert Livingston, 1654–1728, and the Politics of Colonial New York* (Chapel Hill and London: University of North Carolina Press for the Institute of Early American History and Culture, 1961); Kierner, *Traders and Gentlefolk;* and Linda Biemer, "Business Letters of Alida Schuyler Livingston, 1680–1726," *New York History* 63, no. 2 (1982): 183–207. For the education of the Livingston children, see Kierner, *Traders and Gentlefolk*, 49–53. For other examples, see Goodfriend, *Before the Melting Pot*, 173–74. For Samuel Vetch, see Waller, *Samuel Vetch*. For the Livingston men's trade apprenticeships, see Kierner, *Traders and Gentlefolk*, chap. 2.

42. Colden to Falconer, *Colden Papers*, 51–53.

43. Richard Morris, *John Jay: Making of a Revolutionary* (New York: Harper and Row, 1975).

44. Peter Jay account book and daybook, 1724–68, New-York Historical Society.

45. Jordan, "Women Merchants." For Elizabeth, see *New-York Weekly Journal*, May 4, 1741. For Crommelin and Son, see Matson, *Merchants and Empire*, 147. For the lack of trade with Italy, see David Hancock, *Citizens of the World*, 122. For a study of one female merchant in Boston, see Patricia Cleary, *Elizabeth Murray: A Woman's Pursuit of Independence in Eighteenth-Century America* (Amherst: University of Massachusetts Press, 2000), 71–72.

46. Bloch, *Account of Her Majesty's Revenue*, 161–62.

47. For Helena Cooper's imports, see ibid., 174, 182, 247, 265, 267.

48. See *New-York Weekly Journal*, May 13, 1734–March 22, 1735.

49. Advertisement, *New-York Weekly Journal*, November 28, 1744. For John Breese's will, in which he left his estate to his wife absolutely, see *Abstracts of Wills*, vol. 3 (1895), 407; Jordan, "Women Merchants," 425; and *New-York Mercury*, June 1, 1761. For Phenix, see *Calendar of British Historical Manuscripts*, 498; Nicholas Bayard account book, August 23, 1743; *New-York Post-Boy*, September 18, 1760; and Matson, *Merchants and Empire*, 435n138.

50. Ann Elizabeth Schuyler account book, New-York Historical Society.

51. Hunt, *Middling Sort*, chap. 5, argues that the structure of the early modern family explains the limitations of women's financial enterprises.

52. For the cost of widowhood, see Narratt, *Inheritance and Family Life*, 243; and Carole Shammas, "Inheritance and Social History," in *Women in the Age of the American Revolution*, ed. Ronald Hoffman and Peter J. Albert (Charlottesville: University Press of Virginia, 1989), 59–63. For data that "refute the widely held assumption that middling women could not respectably live on their own and

be self-supporting," see Hunt, *Middling Sort*, 134. For Vetch's fur trade, see Henry Douglas to Philip Livingston, December 27, 1709, reel 6, Livingston Papers, Pierpont-Morgan Library.

53. For the bills of exchange, see Philip L. White, ed., *The Beekman Mercantile Papers, 1746–1799* (New York: New-York Historical Society, 1956), 1:336. For other Beekman accounts with women, see ibid., 2:528–29 and 1:56, 269, 157.

54. Ibid., 1:353.

55. *Francis and Anne Judkin v. John Delap*, October 19, 1723, New York Mayor's Court minutes; "Examination taken this 11th day of September 1710 [or 1719; the handwriting is unclear] before Jacobus van Cortland Esq. Mayor of the Citty of New York," in Goelet's *Francis*, vol. 13, no. 31; and *William Osborn [illeg] v. Mary Webb*, November 23, 1726, New York Mayor's Court minutes, New York County Clerk's Office, Division of Old Records, New York.

56. Mary Beth Norton, "Gender and Defamation in Seventeenth-Century Maryland," *William and Mary Quarterly*, 3d ser., 44, no. 1 (January 1987): 3–39; Cornelia Hughes Dayton, *Women before the Bar: Gender, Law, and Society in Connecticut, 1639–1789* (Chapel Hill and London: University of North Carolina Press for the Institute of Early American History and Culture, Williamsburg, Va., 1995), chap. 6. For the household's reputation, see Hunt, *Middling Sort*, 137.

57. *Mary Schamp v. Alexander Phenix*, New York Mayor's Court papers, July 26, 1720.

58. *Roger Groves v. Anne Elderton*, New York Mayor's Court papers, August 21, 1724.

59. *New-York Weekly Journal*, November 26, 1750.

60. "Examination taken" in Goelet's *Francis*, vol. 13, no. 69

61. Hunt, *Middling Sort*, 157; William Livingston, *Independent Reflector* (New York: 1752–53). For a programmatic statement of the *Reflector*'s purpose, see the November 30, 1752, issue. For widows and orphans on road repair, see ibid., December 14, 1752, and January 11, 1752. Eighteen years earlier, on September 2, 1734, the *New-York Weekly Journal* printed the same complaint on widows, orphans, and road repair. For widows and orphans in the chancery court, see *Independent Reflector*, June 7, 1753.

62. *New-York Weekly Journal*, January 21, 1733/34.

63. Jane F. Gardner, *Women in Roman Law and Society* (Bloomington and Indianapolis: Indiana University Press, 1986), 20–22.

64. Young maids: *New York Weekly Journal*, January 28, 1733/34; Roman tutors: *New-York Weekly Journal*, September 8, 1740; Lyttleton poem: *New-York Weekly Journal*, September 30, 1734. Examples of other articles about "husband lotteries," lotteries for "superannuated virgins," and women's petitions for husbands are *New-York Weekly Post Boy*, February 26, 1746/47; and *New-York Evening Post*, April 10, 1749, and April 3, 1749.

65. *New-York Weekly Journal*, July 12, 1736. Defoe's famous phrase is "a Tradesman's credit, and a virgin's virtue, ought to be equally sacred from the tongues of men" (Daniel Defoe, *The complete English tradesman, in familiar letters; directing him in all the several parts and progressions of trade. . . .* [London, 1726 (1725)], 228).

66. Deposition of John Hamilton, Alexander Papers, folder "Memorandum and Certificates." Other sources related to this letter include deposition of Elizabeth Hamilton and Anne DePeyster, Alexander Papers, folder "Memorandum and Certificates"; *The Report of the Committee of His Majesty's Council, to whom it was referred, to examine and make enquiry, touching a Letter found in the House of Mr. Alex-*

ander in New-York, on Friday the First Day of February, 1733/4. In Order to Make the fullest Discovery *concerning the Author of the same* (New York: William Bradford, printer, 1734); *New York Gazette,* February 25 and March 4, 1733; and Berthold Fernow, comp., *Calendar of Council Minutes 1668–1783* (Harrison, N.Y. : Harbor Hill Books, 1987), February 15, 1733, 320.

67. In 1733 James Alexander, William Smith, and Lewis Morris had established the *New-York Weekly Journal,* with John Peter Zenger as printer, in order to publish opposition to Governor William Cosby's administration. The governor ordered the *Journal* burned by the public hangman and Zenger arrested for libel. Andrew Hamilton of Philadelphia eventually obtained a triumphant acquittal for the printer. See Stanley Nidur Katz, *A Brief Narrative of the Case and Trial of John Peter Zenger, Printer of the New York Weekly Journal* (Cambridge, Mass.: Belknap Press of Harvard University, 1963); Charles E. Clark, *The Public Prints: The Newspaper in Anglo-American Culture, 1665–1740* (New York: Oxford University Press, 1994), 178–84; and Michael Warner, *The Letters of the Republic: Publication and the Public Sphere in Eighteenth-Century America* (Cambridge, Mass., and London: Harvard University Press, 1990), 49–58.

68. In 1734 and 1735 New Yorkers claimed that only one or two ships were being built each year. See Gary B. Nash, *The Urban Crucible: Social Change, Political Consciousness, and the Origins of the American Revolution* (Cambridge, Mass., and London: Harvard University Press, 1979), 123–24; and Matson, *Merchants and Empire,* 130.

69. For the "free Commerce" granted to the West Indian sugar planters by the Molasses Act of 1733, see Matson, *Merchants and Empire,* 194–96.

70. See Raphael E. Solomon, "Foreign Specie Coins in the American Colonies," in *Studies on Money in Early America,* ed. Eric P. Newman and Richard G. Doty (New York: American Numismatic Society, 1976), 25–42.

71. Toby L. Ditz, "Shipwrecked; or, Masculinity Imperiled: Mercantile Representations of Failure and the Gendered Self in Eighteenth-Century Philadelphia," *Journal of American History* 81, no. 1 (June 1994): 66.

72. William Smith, *History of the Province of New York,* 2 vols., ed. Michael Kammen (Cambridge, Mass: Belknap Press of Harvard University Press, 1972), 2:8. The pamphlet explains explicitly that a "villainous demand had been made of the Wife of the Honorable James Alexander, Esq."

73. See also Eben Moglen, "Considering *Zenger*: Partisan Politics and the Legal Profession in Provincial New York," *Columbia Law Review* 94 (June 1994): 1495–1524; Vincent Buranelli, "Governor Cosby's Hatchet-Man," *New York History* 37 (1956): 26–39; and Herbert L. Osgood, *The American Colonies in the Eighteenth Century* (New York: Columbia University Press, 1924), 2:455–56.

74. See Patricia Bonomi, *The Lord Cornbury Scandal: The Politics of Reputation in British America* (Chapel Hill: Published for the Omohundro Institute of Early American History & Culture, Williamsburg, Virginia, by the University of North Carolina Press, 1998).

75. *Report of the Committee of His Majesty's Council.*

76. Likewise, when Robert Gilbert Livingston, one of the most successful traders of his generation, received a similar threat in 1752, the governor proclaimed a one-hundred-pound reward and a pardon to any accomplices who turned in the writer (*New-York Gazette, Revived in the Weekly Post-Boy,* January 13, 1752).

77. Deposition of Robert Lurting, in *Report of the Committee of His Majesty's Council,* 61.

Chapter 3

1. In records from 1691 to 1776 Douglas Greenberg has found 193 accusations in the New York Court of General Sessions for keeping disorderly houses; the number increases noticeably after 1750. See Douglas Greenberg, *Crime and Law Enforcement in the Colony of New York, 1691–1776* (Ithaca, N.Y.: Cornell University Press, 1976), table 12, 88. For the period 1700–1739 and 1750–65 (the minute books for the years 1740–50 are no longer extant), I have found another 18 accusations in the New York Supreme Court records and other papers. Daniel Horsmanden recorded another ten tavern keepers pleading guilty to the same accusation before the New York Supreme Court in 1741. See Daniel Horsmanden, *A Journal of the Proceedings in the Detection of the Conspiracy Formed by Some White People, in Conjunction with Negro and Other Slaves, for Burning the City of New-York in America, and Murdering the Inhabitants. . . .* (New York: Printed by James Parker, 1744), 150–51.

2. New York Supreme Court, H.R. pleadings, Pl.K. 662.

3. Manuel Castells and Alejandro Portes, "World Underneath: The Origins, Dynamics, and Effects of the Informal Economy," in *The Informal Economy: Studies in Advanced and Less Developed Countries,* ed. Alejandro Portes, Manuel Castells, and Lauren A. Benton (Baltimore and London: Johns Hopkins University Press, 1989), 11–37, 12. For a definition of the informal economy that includes "any economic activity," see M. Estellie Smith, "The Informal Economy," in *Economic Anthropology,* ed. Stuart Plattner (Stanford, Calif.: Stanford University Press, 1989), 292–317. For one example of British consumers often thought to be on the social margins, see, on the Mohawks of New York, Timothy Shannon, "Dressing for Success on the Mohawk Frontier: Hendrick, William Johnson, and the Indian Fashion," *William and Mary Quarterly* 53, no. 1 (1996): 13–42.

4. For tavern keeping, see Peter Clark, *The English Alehouse: A Social History, 1200–1830* (London and New York: Longman, 1983). For trade, see Merry Wiesner Wood, "Paltry Peddlers or Essential Merchants? Women in the Distributive Trades in Early Modern Nuremberg," *Sixteenth Century Journal* 12 (1981): 3–13.

5. For the "economy of makeshifts," see Olwen Hufton, *The Poor of Eighteenth Century France, 1750–1789* (Oxford: Clarendon Press, 1974), 109; and Penelope Lane, "Work on the Margins: Poor Women and the Informal Economy of Eighteenth and Early Nineteenth-Century Leicestershire," *Midland History* 22 (1997): 85–99.

6. Cornelia Hughes Dayton, *Women Before the Bar: Gender, Law, and Society in Connecticut, 1639–1789* (Chapel Hill and London: University of North Carolina Press for the Institute of Early American History and Culture, Williamsburg, Va., 1995); Peter C. Hoffer and N. E. H. Hull, *Murdering Mothers: Infanticide in England and New England, 1558–1803* (New York: New York University Press, 1981).

7. For the county of Surry, J. M. Beattie finds that property offenses made up 58.6 percent of accusations against women and 50.2 percent of accusations against men. These crimes against property made up 52 percent of the total number of accusations against both men and women. Similar to the numbers for New York, women made up a total of 23.9 percent of the total accusations of property offenses. See J. M. Beattie, "The Criminality of Women in Eighteenth-Century England," *Journal of Social History* 8 (summer 1975): 80–116, 81.

8. New York Supreme Court pleadings, November 9, 1759, PL.K 954.

9. Julius Goebel and T. Raymond Naughton, *Law Enforcement in Colonial New York: A Study in Criminal Procedure (1664–1776)* (Montclair, N.J.: Patterson Smith, 1944; repr., 1970), 442.

10. Manuscript minute book, New York Court of General Sessions, November 4, 1718, New York Municipal Archives; John Tabor Kempe Papers, unsorted lawsuits, box M–O, unmarked folder, October 1760, New-York Historical Society.

11. Manuscript minute book, New York Court of General Sessions, November 4, 1718.

12. Ibid., August 6, 1718.

13. *New-York Weekly Post-Boy*, January 28, 1744.

14. Manuscript minute book, New York Court of General Sessions, November 4, 1729.

15. Manuscript minute book, New York Supreme Court, October 22, 1751.

16. New York Supreme Court pleadings, K-359, July 1755.

17. "Special Sessions of the Mayor and Aldermen," manuscript minute book, New York Court of General Sessions, February 10, 1737, and August 1, 1738.

18. Greenberg, *Crime and Law Enforcement*, 79. Men also were acquitted of theft at a slightly higher rate than for other crimes: 20.7 percent of men accused of theft were acquitted, although men's acquittal rate in New York was closer to 18.1 percent overall. Statistics based on the New York court records cannot be absolute since no final judgment was recorded for roughly 36 percent of the cases. Nonetheless, the numbers are suggestive. For Mary Cullen, see "Special Sessions of the Mayor and Aldermen," manuscript minute book, New York Court of General Sessions, November 11, 1740. Also see the trial of Sarah Whaling, a "loose woman" accused of picking pockets; the jury both acquitted and banished her (*New-York Weekly Post-Boy*, August 13, 1750).

19. New York Court of General Sessions, August 7, 1728.

20. Greenberg, Crime and Law Enforcement, 80.

21. In the minutes of the New York Court of General Sessions for 1700–1765, only two women were indicted for prostitution or bastardy (Mary Lawrence and Bridget Williams, May 4, 1738). One man (Henry Cordus, February 7, 1710) was indicted for "a luxurious irregular and rioting manner of living against the law of modesty honesty and a virtuous cause of life" for living openly with another man's wife. For New England, see Dayton, *Women Before the Bar*, chap. 4.

22. Goebel and Naughton, *Law Enforcement*, 100.

23. Bruce Wilkenfield, "New York City Neighborhoods, 1730," *New York History* 57 (April 1976): 165–82; Nan Rothschild, *New York City Neighborhoods: The Eighteenth Century* (San Diego: Academic Press, 1990).

24. New York Mayor's Office, "Tavern Keeper's License Book, 1757–66," New-York Historical Society; Sharon V. Salinger, *Taverns and Drinking in Early America* (London and Baltimore: Johns Hopkins University Press, 2002), 163.

25. New York Supreme Court, H.R. pleadings, Pl.K. 999; manuscript minute book, New York Court of General Sessions, February 6, 1754 (Peter), and May 6, 1754 (Anne).

26. New York Supreme Court, H.R. pleadings, Pl.K. 1094.

27. Ibid., Pl.K. 1015.

28. Ibid., Pl.K. 1058.

29. Manuscript minute book, New York Court of General Sessions, August 1, 1710; Salinger, *Taverns and Drinking*, 130–36.

30. For Elizabeth Ranger, see manuscript minute book, New York Court of General Sessions, November 6, 1711.

31. Manuscript minute book, New York Court of General Sessions, February 6, 1704.

32. Ibid., August 1, 1710.

33. Greenberg, *Crime and Law Enforcement*, 52; *New-York Weekly Journal*, June 29, 1741.

34. New York Court of General Sessions, minute books, February 3, 1712/13.

35. *John Webb et ux. v. Abigail Cogan*, minutes of the New York Mayor's Court, 1710–15, ff. 215–19, August 5, 1712, repr. in Richard B. Morris, *Select Cases of the Mayor's Court of New York City, 1674–1784* (Washington, D.C.: American Historical Association, 1935), 327.

36. New York Court of General Sessions, minute books, May 6, 1713.

37. For the standard works on the consumer revolution, see "Introduction" in this book.

38. This theory is most explicitly set out by Richard L. Bushman, *The Refinement of America: Persons, Houses, Cities* (New York: Random House, Vintage Books, 1992). For the production of "populuxe" goods in France for a lower-class market that seems to have paralleled the middle-class market, see Cissie Fairchilds, "The Production and Marketing of Populuxe Goods in Eighteenth-Century Paris," in *Consumption and the World of Goods*, ed. John Brewer and Roy Porter (London and New York: Routledge, 1993), 228–48. For the argument against emulation of social superiors as a cause for the consumer revolution, see Cary Carson, "The Consumer Revolution in Colonial British America: Why Demand?," in *Of Consuming Interests: The Style of Life in the Eighteenth Century*, ed. Cary Carson, Ronald Hoffman, and Peter J. Albert (Charlottesville and London: University Press of Virginia for the United States Capital Historical Society, 1994); and Beverly Lemire, "Second-hand Beaux and 'Red-armed Belles': Conflict and the Creation of Fashions in England, c. 1660–1800," *Continuity and Change* 15, no. 3 (2000): 391–417. For later arguments that the fashions of working-class women drove middle-class fashion, see Christine Stansell, *City of Women: Sex and Class in New York, 1789–1860* (New York: Knopf, 1986); and Kathy Peiss, *Cheap Amusements: Working Women and Leisure in Turn-of-the-Century New York* (Philadelphia: Temple University Press, 1986). See also John Styles, "Involuntary Consumers? Servants and Their Clothes in Eighteenth-Century England," *Textile History* 33, no. 1 (2002): 9–21.

39. E.g., a runaway ad for a "Mulatto Fellow named Isaac . . . Had on when he went away, a very good Head of Hair," *New York Gazette, Revived in the Weekly Post-Boy*, September 25, 1749. See also David Waldstreicher, "Reading the Runaways: Self-Fashioning, Print Culture, and Confidence in Slavery in the Eighteenth-Century Mid-Atlantic," *William and Mary Quarterly*, 3d. ser., 56 (April 1999): 243–72.

40. Horsmanden, *A Journal of the Proceedings*, 10.

41. T. H. Breen, "'Baubles of Britain': The American Consumer Revolutions of the Eighteenth Century," *Past & Present* 119 (May 1988): 73–104.

42. T. H. Breen, *The Marketplace of Revolution: How Consumer Politics Shaped American Independence* (New York: Oxford University Press, 2004), chap. 2.

43. *Pennsylvania Gazette*, March 4, 1735.

44. *An Account of the Robberies Committed by John Morrison*, 1750/1 (Philadelphia, 1750/51).

45. "Special Sessions of the Mayor and Aldermen," manuscript minute book, New York Court of General Sessions, August 24, 1738, and September 13, 1738.

46. Beverly Lemire, *Dress, Culture and Commerce: The English Clothing Trade before the Factory, 1660–1800* (New York: St. Martin's Press, 1997), 97.

47. Ibid.

48. These numbers are gleaned from my own studies of the extant newspapers and minute books of the New York Court of General Sessions and of the New York Supreme Court, 1700–1760.

49. Manuscript minute books, New York Court of General Sessions, February 27, 1700, and June 24, 1701.

50. For osnaburg, see "Special Sessions of the Mayor and Aldermen," manuscript minute book, New York Court of General Sessions, October 21, 1735. For the coat, see *New-York Post-Boy*, February 27, 1758.

51. J. M. Beattie, *Crime and the Courts in England, 1660–1800* (Oxford: Oxford University Press, 1986), table 4.9, 186; Garthine Walker, "Women, Theft and the World of Stolen Goods," in *Women, Crime, and the Courts in Early Modern England*, ed. Jennifer Kermode and Garthine Walker (Chapel Hill and London: University of North Carolina Press, 1994), table 4.3, 88.

52. Beattie, *Crime and the Courts*, 243.

53. Greenberg, *Crime and Law Enforcement*, 61.

54. "Special Sessions of the Mayor and Aldermen," manuscript minute book, New York Court of General Sessions, January 16, 1737.

55. For James Thomas, see manuscript minute book, New York Court of General Sessions, February 2, 1725. For Isaac Moore, see ibid., August 5, 1730.

56. Presentation of Michael McNamarra, Kempe Papers, unsorted lawsuits, box M–O, unmarked folder, December 30, 1740.

57. New York Supreme Court, H.R. pleadings, Pl.K. 177.

58. *New-York Mercury*, February 20, 1758.

59. "Special Sessions of the Mayor and Aldermen," manuscript minute book, New York Court of General Sessions, September 18, 1741.

60. Charles Z. Lincoln, William H. Johnson, and A. Judd Northrup, eds., *Colonial Laws of New York*, 5 vols. (Albany, N.Y.: J. B. Lyon, State Printer, 1894), chap. 651, December 16, 1737, 2: 952 (hereafter cited as *New York Colonial Laws*).

61. Ibid., 953.

62. Deborah Rosen, *Courts and Commerce: Gender, Law, and the Market Economy in Colonial New York* (Columbus: Ohio State University Press, 1997). For other examples of marginal economic agents in the marketplace, see the discussion of enslaved women in Philip D. Morgan, "Black Life in Eighteenth-Century Charlestown," *Perspectives in American History* 1 (1984): 187–232.

63. Herbert L. Osgood et al., eds., *Minutes of the Common Council of the City of New York, 1675–1776*, 8 vols. (New York: Dodd, Mead, 1905), 4:448 (hereafter, *Minutes of the Common Council*).

64. New York City Common Council Papers, Municipal Archives, box 4, folder 204, petitions, 1750.

65. E. B. O'Callaghan, ed., *Calendar of British Historical Manuscripts in the Office of the Secretary of State, Albany, New York, 1664–1776* (Albany, N.Y.: Office of the Secretary of State, 1865; repr., Ridgewood, N.J.: Gregg Press, 1968), 523; Obadiah Wells creditor agreement, 1752, Alexander Papers, box 18, folder 2, New-York Historical Society.

66. *New York Colonial Laws*, chap. 543, July 12, 1720, 2:571–75.

67. Osgood et al., eds., *Minutes of the Common Council*, April 24, 1691, 1:222,

68. Ibid., May 25, 1704, 2:264,.

69. Ibid., December 22, 1704, 2:277–78.

70. Examination of Mary Lawrence, Alexander Papers, box 45, "Court of General Quarter Sessions," New-York Historical Society.

71. *New-York Mercury*, May 4, 1772; Eugene P. McParland, "Colonial Taverns and Tavern Keepers of British New York City," *New York Genealogical and Biographical Record* 103–7 (1972–76): 103.

72. *Minutes of the Common Council*, May 25, 1715, 3:91. For the granting of free licenses to poor widows in Boston, see David W. Conroy, *In Public Houses: Drink and the Revolution of Authority in Colonial Massachusetts* (Chapel Hill and London: University of North Carolina Press for the Institute of Early American History and Culture, Williamsburg, Va., 1995), 112–13; "Tavern Keeper's License Book, 1757–66," New-York Historical Society.

73. I. N. Phelps Stokes, *The Iconography of Manhattan Island* (New York: Robert H. Dodd, 1922; repr., Union, N.J.: Lawbook Exchange, 1998), 4:487; quote from *Minutes of the Common Council*, 4, 314.

74. In *Abstracts of Wills on File in the Surrogate's Office, City of New York*: vol. I, *Collections of the New-York Historical Society for the Year 1892*. Publication Fund Series, vol. XXV (New York: Printed for the New-York Historical Society, 1893), 317.

75. Morris, *Select Cases of the Mayor's Court*, 240–44.

76. *New York Colonial Laws*, "An Act for Regulating of Slaves," November 27, 1702, chap. 123, I:519.

77. Ibid., December 10, 1712, chap. 250, I:761 (this act is continued, unrevised, in 1726); ibid., June 17, 1726, chap. 483, II:310.

78. Ibid., October 29, 1730, chap. 560, II:679.

79. Ibid., November 7, 1741, chap. 713, III:166. Compare New York's slave laws with those in the southern colonies that had as their goals the codification of slaves as property; see A. Leon Higginbotham, *In the Matter of Color: Race and the American Legal Process* (New York: Oxford University Press, 1978) and Kathleen M. Brown, *Good Wives, Nasty Wenches, and Anxious Patriarchs: Gender, Race, and Power in Colonial Virginia* (Chapel Hill and London: University of North Carolina Press for the Institute of Early American History and Culture, Williamsburg, Va., 1996).

80. *New-York Weekly Journal*, June 29, 1741.

81. Clark, *English Alehouse*, 229.

82. "Special Sessions of the Mayor and Aldermen," manuscript minute book, New York Court of General Sessions, April 19, 1742.

83. "Ann Elizabeth Schuyler Account Book, 1737–69," sale to Samuel Goodness, blacksmith, February 22 and March 1, 1738, New-York Historical Society.

84. Lemire, *Dress, Culture, and Commerce*, 95–120.

85. *New-York Gazette Revived in the Weekly Post-Boy*, April 1, 1751.

86. Lemire, *Dress, Culture, and Commerce*, 104–12.

87. Alexander Papers, box 49, folder 4.

88. Goebel and Naughton, *Law Enforcement*, 108, 675.

89. Lynn MacKay, "Why They Stole: Women in the Old Bailey, 1779–1798," *Journal of Social History* 32 (Spring 1999): 623–39.

90. Lemire, *Dress, Culture, and Commerce*, 140.

91. Manuscript minute book, New York Court of General Sessions, February 1, 1708.

92. New York Supreme Court pleadings, Pl. K. 1022, July 24, 1754.

93. *New-York Weekly Post-Boy*, August 19, 1754. The *New-York Mercury* on the same day also reported the whipping.

94. The narrative is taken from William Kempe's legal brief for the case against Lawrence, Arding, and Livingston; see H.R. pleadings, Pl.K. 501, repr. in Goebel and Naughton, *Law Enforcement*, 786–91.

95. Kempe Papers, "unsorted letters."
96. *New York Colonial Laws*, ch. 578, October 14, 1732, 2, 745. Also see Goebel and Naughton, *Law Enforcement*, 115.
97. H.R. pleadings, Pl.K. 501, repr. in Goebel and Naughton, *Law Enforcement*, 786–91.
98. *New-York Mercury*, August 19, 1754.
99. New York Supreme Court Minute Books, October 24, 1754.
100. Sharon Block, "Coerced Sex in British North America, 1700–1820" (Ph.D. diss., Princeton University, 1995), 72. Also see Sharon Block, *Rape and Sexual Power in Early America* (Chapel Hill: University of North Carolina Press, 2006); and Dayton, *Women Before the Bar*, chap. 5.

Chapter 4

1. *New-York Gazette*, June 21, 1731.
2. Ibid., June 28, 1731.
3. Lawrence E. Klein, "Politeness and the Interpretation of the British Eighteenth Century," *Historical Journal* (Great Britain) 45, no. 4 (2002): 869–98, esp. 876. Also see H. R. French, " 'Ingenious & learned gentlemen': Social Perceptions and Self-Fashioning among Parish Elites in Essex, 1680–1740," *Social History* 25, no. 1 (2000): 44–66.
4. For the argument that the rise of early modern commerce drove a shift from "aristocratic" to "bourgeois" manners, see G. J. Barker-Benfield, *The Culture of Sensibility: Sex and Society in Eighteenth-Century Britain* (Chicago: University of Chicago Press, 1992), 77–98.
5. Alan Tully, *Forming American Politics: Ideals, Interests, and Institutions in Colonial New York and Pennsylvania* (Baltimore: Johns Hopkins University Press, 1994), 249. For the most complete discussion of New York's factional politics, see Patricia Bonomi, *A Factious People: Politics and Society in Colonial New York* (New York: Columbia University Press, 1971).
6. *New-York Weekly Journal*, November 26 and December 10, 1733. See Alison Gilbert, "The Zenger Case Revisited: Satire, Sedition, and Political Debate in Eighteenth Century America," *Early American Literature* 35, no. 3 (2000): 223–45.
7. *New-York Weekly Journal*, March 15, 1735, 2.
8. For the effects of migration, see Cary Carson, "The Consumer Revolution in Colonial British America: Why Demand?," in Cary Carson, Ronald Hoffman, and Peter J. Albert, eds., *Of Consuming Interests: The Style of Life in the Eighteenth Century* (Charlottesville and London: University Press of Virginia for the United States Capital Historical Society, 1994), 523–24. For consumption more generally, see Carson, "Consumer Revolution"; Richard L. Bushman, *The Refinement of America: Persons, Houses, Cities* (New York: Random House, Vintage Books, 1992); and T. H. Breen, *The Marketplace of Revolution* (New York: Oxford University Press, 2004), pt. 1. For the meanings ascribed to the "proper" use of consumer goods, see T. H. Breen, "The Meaning of Things: Interpreting the Consumer Economy in the Eighteenth Century," in John Brewer and Roy Porter, eds., *Consumption and the World of Goods* (London and New York: Routledge, 1993), 249–60. Sir Joshua Reynolds was amazed to learn that the stiff posture of a gentleman was not the natural way to hold the body (cited in Karin Calvert, "The Function of Fashion in Eighteenth-Century America," in *Of Consuming Interests*, ed. Carson, Hoffman, and Albert, 273–74).
9. *New-York Weekly Journal*, July 4, 1737. See Arthur Benson, "The Itinerant

Dancing and Music Masters of Eighteenth-Century America" (Ph.D. diss., University of Minnesota, 1963). Some of Benson's biographical information about Holt is incorrect; he never became the owner of the Fraunces Tavern. For advertising, see Richard L. Bushman, "Shopping and Advertising in Colonial America," in *Of Consuming Interests*, ed. Carson, Hoffman, and Albert, 241–42.

10. *Pennsylvania Gazette*, July 3, 1732. For the personal and financial difficulties of another dancing master, see Judith Cobau, "The Precarious Life of Thomas Pike, a Colonial Dancing Master in Charleston and Philadelphia," *Dance Chronicle* 17, no. 3 (1994): 229–62.

11. I. N. Phelps Stokes, comp., *The Iconography of Manhattan Island, 1498–1909* (New York: Robert H. Dodd, 1915; repr., New York: Arno Press, 1967), 4:341.

12. Cynthia Adams Hoover, "Music and Theater in the Lives of Eighteenth-Century Americans," in *Of Consuming Interests*, ed. Carson, Hoffman, and Albert, 310; *New-York Gazette*, April 21, 1729. For Brownell, see *New-York Gazette*, June 14, 1731; Carl Bridenbaugh, *Cities in the Wilderness: The First Century of Urban Life in America, 1625–1742* (New York: Alfred A. Knopf, 1955), 277, 282–83; and Benson, "Itinerant Dancing and Music Masters," 287–309. Kate Van Winkle Keller finds that in England, "the first decade of the eighteenth century was one of unprecedented growth of public interest in dance education"; see Van Winkle Keller, "The Eighteenth-Century Ballroom: A Mirror of Social Change," in Peter Benes, ed., *New England Music: The Public Sphere, 1600–1900, The Dublin Seminar for New England Folklife Annual Proceedings, 1996* (Boston: Boston University, 1998), 16–29. For Franks, see Abigail Franks to Naphtali Franks, May 7, 1733, in Leo Hershkowitz and Isidore S. Meyer, eds., *Letters of the Franks Family (1733–1748)* (Waltham, Mass.: American Jewish Historical Society, 1968). For Colden children, see Mrs. (Alice) Colden to Mrs. John Hall, September 8, 1732, in *The Letters and Papers of Cadwallader Colden: Vol. VIII, Additional Letters and Papers, 1715–1748*, vol. 67, *Collections of the New-York Historical Society for the Year 1934*, The John Watts DePeyster Publication Fund Series (New York: Printed for the New-York Historical Society, 1937), 200–202 (hereafter *Colden Papers*).

13. George Whitefield was probably the most successful individual in the eighteenth century at exploiting the elastic potential of both print and market cultures. See Frank Lambert, *Peddler in Divinity: George Whitefield and the Transatlantic Revivals, 1737–1770* (Princeton, N.J.: Princeton University Press, 1994). C. J. Rawson explains that the "obsessional frequency with which [English] writers of the period keep mentioning dancing-masters" is best explained by their uncomfortable understanding that "the gentleman had to learn from a laboured specialist the graceful ease which was supposed to be his birth-right"; see Rawson, *Henry Fielding and the Augustan Ideal under Stress* (London and Boston: Routledge & Kegan Paul, 1972), 28.

14. [James Burgh], *Britain's Remembrancer: Being Some Thoughts on the Proper Improvement of the Present Juncture*, 6th ed. (New-York: Reprinted and sold by James Parker, at the new printing-office in Beaver-Street, 1748). For the impact of Burgh in the American colonies, see J. C. D. Clark, *The Language of Liberty 1660–1832: Political Discourse and Social Dynamics in the Anglo-American World* (Cambridge: Cambridge University Press, 1994), 30–32. For the classic discussion of radical Whig ideology, see Bernard Bailyn, *The Ideological Origins of the American Revolution* (Cambridge, Mass.: Belknap Press for Harvard University Press, 1967).

15. *Boston Gazette*, November 20, 1732. For a discussion of this debate, see Charles E. Clark, *The Public Prints: The Newspaper in Anglo-American Culture, 1665–*

1740 (New York: Oxford University Press, 1994), 186–87. For the fear of dancing as potentially destructive, see Richard Leppert, *Music and Image: Domesticity, Ideology, and Socio-Cultural Formation in Eighteenth-Century England* (Cambridge and New York: Cambridge University Press, 1988), 72–75.

16. *New-York Gazette*, December 18, 1732.

17. Ibid.

18. "The courtier, the trader, and the scholar should all have an equal pretension to the denomination of a gentleman. . . . The appellation of gentleman is never to be affixed to a man's circumstances, but his behaviour in them" (Richard Steele, *Tatler*, no. 207, August 5, 1710).

19. *New-York Gazette*, December 18, 1732.

20. Ibid. For the seventeenth-century order of family and society in which men had authority over women, and masters and mistresses had authority over servants and apprentices, see Susan Dwyer Amussen, *An Ordered Society: Gender and Class in Early Modern England* (New York: B. Blackwell, 1988).

21. *New-York Gazette*, December 18, 1732.

22. Ibid.

23. For sexual difference, see David S. Shields, *Civil Tongues and Polite Letters in British America* (Chapel Hill and London: University of North Carolina Press for the Institute of Early American History and Culture, Williamsburg, Va., 1997), xx; and Carson, "Consumer Revolution," 591. For refinement, see Kathleen Wilson, "Citizenship, Empire, and Modernity in the English Provinces, c. 1720–1790," *Eighteenth-Century Studies* 29 (1996): 69–96, esp. 76. See also Barker-Benfield, *Culture of Sensibility*, xxvi; and Lawrence Klein, "Gender, Conversation and the Public Sphere," in *Textuality and Sexuality*, ed. Judith Still and Michael Worton (Manchester: Manchester University Press, 1993), 100–115. Shields, *Civil Tongues*, 148, has insightfully explained the ways that balls in Philadelphia and the West Indies acted as sites for competition among men in which men served as arbiters. In New York, however, polite sociability was not simply the object of social competition; it was also the form in which political competition was expressed.

24. James Forester, *The Polite Philosopher*, 15th ed. (New York: J. Parker and W. Weyman, 1758), 35.

25. For Charles Love, see *New-York Mercury*, January 21, 1754. For assemblies, see *New-York Gazette*, December 11, 1732; *New-York Gazette and Weekly Post-Boy*, March 20, 1758; and *New-York Gazette* (Weyman's), October 11, 1762.

26. *New-York Mercury*, October 23, 1758.

27. *New-York Gazette*, October 24, 1763.

28. *New-York Gazette and Weekly Post-Boy*, December 5, 1757.

29. *New-York Weekly Mercury*, April 26, 1762.

30. David Cressy, *Bonfires and Bells: National Memory and the Protestant Calendar in Elizabethan and Stuart England* (Berkeley and Los Angeles: University of California Press, 1989), 22.

31. Berthold Fernow, comp., *Calendar of Council Minutes 1668–1783* (Harrison, N.Y.: Harbor Hill Books, 1987), July 1, 1704.

32. Bushman, *Refinement of America*, 186, has pointed out that "This elevation of ordinary, even suspect activities into the regions of refinement was the characteristic project of genteel culture."

33. John Fitzhugh Millar, *Country Dances of Colonial America* (Williamsburg, Va.: Thirteen Colonies Press, 1990), 1–8.

34. Leppert, *Music and Image*, 89–90.

35. Shields, *Civil Tongues*, 147; Calvert, "Function of Fashion," 272–73. Also see Bushman, *Refinement of America*, 55–56; and Rhys Isaac, *The Transformation of Virginia, 1740–1790* (Chapel Hill and London: University of North Carolina Press for the Institute of Early American History and Culture, Williamsburg, Va., 1982; New York: W. W. Norton, 1988), 81–87.

36. *New-York Gazette & Weekly Post-Boy*, September 13, 1764.

37. Shields, *Civil Tongues*, 145. For new dances, see *New-York Weekly Journal*, January 26, 1736.

38. *New-York Mercury*, October 27, 1760.

39. Kate Van Winkle Keller and George A. Fogg, *Country Dances from Colonial New York: James Alexander's Notebook, 1730* (Boston: Country Dance Society, Boston Centre, 2000), 8.

40. Calvert, "Function of Fashion," 273; Shields, *Civil Tongues*, 38. Bushman, *Refinement of America*, 68, describes at length the polite body and notes that "the services of a dancing master [were] a necessity for young ladies and gentlemen."

41. Abigail Franks to Naphtali Franks, May 7, 1733, in Edith Belle Gelles, ed., *The Letters of Abigaill Levy Franks, 1733–1748* (New Haven, Conn.: Yale University Press, 2004), 4.

42. Mrs. (Alice) Colden to Mrs. John Hall, September 8, 1732, in *Colden Papers*, 201.

43. For children, see *New-York Gazette & Weekly Post-Boy*, August 13, 1761, and *New-York Journal and General Advertiser*, November 6, 1766; for Turner, see *New-York Gazette & Weekly Post-Boy*, September 13, 1764; for Riveirs, see *New-York Gazette or Weekly Post-Boy*, November 14, 1757; for Trotter, see *New-York Mercury*, December 5, 1768; for Hulett, see *New-York Gazette & Weekly Post-Boy*, January 19, 1764; and for adults still learning, see *New-York Journal*, September 8, 1768.

44. *New-York Gazette*, November 11, 1734.

45. *American Weekly Mercury*, November 6, 1735.

46. *New-York Gazette*, March 3, 1735.

47. Ibid., November 11, 1734.

48. Shields, *Civil Tongues*, 145n3, has speculated that balls commemorating the sovereign's birthday may have been created in the English provinces and supported by the government as an "attempt to build a monarchal mystique around Charles II." There is no evidence of balls in the North American colonies before 1700.

49. Because New York did not establish a newspaper until 1725, this account was printed in the *Philadelphia American Mercury* on June 3, 1723.

50. See other accounts of royal birthdays, e.g., *New-York Gazette*, November 11, 1734: "Between the hours of eleven and twelve in the fore-noon, his Excellency our Governour was attended at his House in Fort George by the Council, Assembly, Merchants, and other Principal Gentlemen and Inhabitants of this and adjacent Places. The Independent Companies posted here being under Arms, and the Cannon round the Ramparts firing while his Majesty's the Queens, the Prince's and the Royal Families and their Royal Highnesses the Prince and Princess of Oranges' Healths were drank; and then followed the Healths of his Grace the Duke of New Castle, of the Duke of Gratin, of the Right Honorable Sir Robert Walpole, and many other Royal Healths."

51. Leppert, *Music and Image*, 75, points out that the English considered dancing an antidote to perceived English "rusticity."

52. Herbert L. Osgood et al., eds., *Minutes of the Common Council of the City of New York, 1675–1776*, 8 vols. (New York: Dodd, Mead, 1905), 3:41–42; *Boston*

News-Letter, August 24, 1713. By including "another" in its headline, the article implies that New York's celebration in August 1713 was not the first ball for peace; it may have been preceded by an earlier celebration in Boston.

53. In England the ringing of church bells was also a constant component of state festivals; there is no evidence of ringing bells in New York City as a part of festivals. See Cressy, *Bonfires and Bells*, 67. For coronation and royal birthday balls in the British provinces, see Peter Borsay, *The Urban Renaissance: Culture and Society in the Provincial Town 1660–1770* (Oxford: Oxford University Press, 1989), 155–56. The date of the first example Borsay cites is 1738.

54. *New-England Weekly Journal*, February 19, 1733.

55. *New-York Post-Boy*, October 3, 1748.

56. Peter Thompson, "'The Friendly Glass': Drink and Gentility in Colonial Philadelphia," *Pennsylvania Magazine of History and Biography* 113, no. 4 (1989): 549–74; *New-York Gazette*, November 7, 1737.

57. For the Cosby-Morris dispute, see Bonomi, *Factious People*, esp. chap. 4.

58. Archibald Kennedy to Cadwallader Colden, January 17, 1736, in *Colden Papers*, vol. 51 (1918), 145–46.

59. *New-York Weekly Journal*, January 26, 1736. Euphemia Norris was the daughter of Lewis Morris. She married Captain Matthew Norris about 1734. See Eugene R. Sheridan, *Lewis Morris 1671–1746: A Study in Early American Politics* (Syracuse, N.Y.: Syracuse University Press, 1981).

60. For the opposition ball, see *New-York Evening Post*, November 7, 1748; and Elaine Chalus, "'That Epidemical Madness': Women and Electoral Politics in the Late Eighteenth Century," in Hannah Barker and Elaine Chalus, eds., *Gender in Eighteenth-Century England: Roles, Representations, and Responsibilities* (London and New-York: Longman, 1997), 168.

61. "From the Third Volume of Dean Swift's Miscellanies," *New-York Weekly Journal*, January 2, 1748.

62. *New-York Mercury*, June 3, 1754.

63. *Boston Gazette*, January 27, 1735. See also the *Spectator*, no. 68, May 17, 1711: "It is the proper Business of a Dancing-Master to regulate these Matters [of bodily carriage]; tho' I take it to be a just Observation, that unless you add something of your own to what these fine Gentlemen teach you, and which they are wholly ignorant of themselves, you will much sooner get the Character of an Affected Fop, than of a Well-bred Man."

64. Steven C. Bullock, *Revolutionary Brotherhood: Freemasonry and the Transformation of the Social Order, 1730–1840* (Chapel Hill and London: University of North Carolina Press for the Institute of Early American History and Culture, Williamsburg, Va., 1996), quote on p. 65.

65. Ibid., 68–69.

66. *Pennsylvania Gazette*, February 21, 1738.

67. *New-York Journal*, September 8, 1768.

68. Quoted in Jane Landers, "Black-Indian Interactions in Spanish Florida," *Colonial Latin American Historical Review* 2 (1993): 141–62, 156. See also Jane Landers, *Black Society in Spanish Florida* (Urbana: University of Illinois Press, 1999), 33.

69. *New-York Weekly Post-Boy*, June 26, 1746; *Pennsylvania Gazette*, February 8, 1746. For the Moravians, see E. B. O'Callaghan, ed., *Calendar of British Historical Manuscripts in the Office of the Secretary of State, Albany, New York, 1664–1776* (Albany, N.Y.: Office of the Secretary of State, 1865; repr., Ridgewood, N.J.: Gregg Press, 1968), February 16 and March 18, 1745, 571; and Fernow, comp., *Calendar of Council Minutes*, March 29, 1745, 347.

182   Notes to Pages 104–108

70. John Romeyn Brodhead, E. B. O'Callaghan, and Berthold Fernow, eds., *Documents Relative to the Colonial History of the State of New York*, 15 vols. (Albany: Weed and Parsons, 1853–57), May 16, 1741, 6:199.
71. Keller, "Eighteenth-Century Ballroom, 20–22."
72. Leppert, *Music and Image*, 71–106.
73. Fernow, *Calendar of Council Minutes*, April 6 and April 26, 1755, 415.
74. *New-York Gazette & Weekly Post-Boy*, January 20, 1755.
75. Philip Carter, *Men and the Emergence of Polite Society, Britain, 1660–1800* (Harlow, England and New York: Pearson Education, 2001), 209.

Chapter 5

1. Daniel Parish Jr., slavery transcripts, Box "New York," folder 158, 1, New-York Historical Society; Berthold Fernow, comp., *Calendar of Council Minutes, 1668–1783* (Harrison, N.Y.: Harbor Hill Books, 1987) (hereafter cited as *CCM*), 253, September 18, 1713. Charles Pinkethman was honored with the "freedom of the city" in 1715 for his privateering contributions. See Herbert L. Osgood et al., eds., *Minutes of the Common Council of the City of New York, 1675–1776*, 8 vols. (New York: Dodd, Mead, 1905), January 15, 1714/15, 3:84; and Howard M. Chapman, *Privateer Ships and Sailors: The First Century of American Colonial Privateering, 1625–1725* (Toulon: G. Mouton, 1926), 229–31.
2. For the slave trade in New York, see James G. Lydon, "New York and the Slave Trade, 1700–1774," *William and Mary Quarterly*, 3d ser., 35 (1978): 375–94. For the philosophical debate over who could be justifiably enslaved, see David Brion Davis, *The Problem of Slavery in Western Culture* (Ithaca, N.Y.: Cornell University Press, 1966); David Eltis, *The Rise of African Slavery in the Americas* (Cambridge and New York: Cambridge University Press, 2000); and Robin Blackburn, *The Making of New World Slavery: From the Baroque to the Modern, 1492–1800* (London and New York: Verso, 1997). For maritime slavery, see W. Jeffrey Bolster, *Black Jacks: African American Seamen in the Age of Sail* (Cambridge, Mass.: Harvard University Press, 1997); Michael J. Jarvis, "Maritime Masters and Seafaring Slaves in Bermuda, 1680–1783," *William and Mary Quarterly*, 3d ser., 59, no. 3 (July 2002): 585–622; Marcus Rediker and Peter Linebaugh, *The Many-Headed Hydra: Sailors, Slaves, Commoners, and the Hidden History of the Revolutionary Atlantic* (Boston: Beacon Press, 2000), chaps. 3 and 4; and Marcus Rediker, *Between the Devil and the Deep Blue Sea: Merchant Seamen, Pirates, and the Anglo-American Maritime World, 1700–1750* (Cambridge and New York: Cambridge University Press, 1987). Also see Philip D Morgan, "British Encounters with Africans and African-Americans, circa 1600 to 1780," in Bernard Bailyn and Philip D. Morgan, eds., *Strangers in the Realm: Cultural Margins of the First British Empire* (Chapel Hill: University of North Carolina Press for the Institute of Early American History and Culture, 1991), 157–219, 194–95.
3. Five hundred of these were volunteers; see Lieutenant Governor George Clarke to the Duke of Newcastle, September 22, 1740, in John Romeyn Brodhead, E.B. O'Callaghan, and Berthold Fernow, eds., *Documents Relative to the Colonial History of the State of New York*, 15 vols. (Albany: Weed and Parsons, 1853–57).
4. Kathleen Wilson, "Empire, Trade and Popular Politics in Mid-Hanoverian Britain: The Case of Admiral Vernon," *Past & Present* 121 (1988): 74–109.
5. Petition of Juan Miranda to James DeLancey, [n.d.], John Tabor Kempe Papers, Box 3, folder "Juan Miranda," New-York Historical Society (hereafter cited as "Juan Miranda" folder).

6. Richard Pares, *War and Trade in the West Indies, 1739–1763* (London: F. Cass, 1936, repr., 1963), 14–18.

7. For Axon's privateering career, see the *Pennsylvania Gazette*, March 27, 1740; April 7, 1743; August 30, 1744; and March 12, 1745.

8. Carl E. Swanson, *Predators and Prizes: American Privateering and Imperial Warfare, 1739–1748* (Columbia: University of South Carolina Press, 1991).

9. David J. Starkey, "Eighteenth-Century Privateering Enterprise," *International Journal of Maritime History* 2 (1989): 279–86. Also see James G. Lydon, *Pirates, Privateers, and Profits* (Upper Saddle River, N.J.: Gregg Press, 1970).

10. Before 1744 British customs officials in New York insisted that prize goods become British goods at the moment of capture, not when they were condemned by a vice-admiralty court. Therefore, prizes should be treated as foreign goods and were liable to import taxes. Governor Clinton eventually convinced the duke of Newcastle to persuade the customs collectors to drop their claims. See Lydon, *Pirates*, 91–93.

11. Swanson, *Predators and Prizes*, 34–35.

12. David Armitage, *The Ideological Origins of the British Empire* (Cambridge, Mass.: Harvard University Press, 2000); Patrick K. O'Brien, "Inseparable Connections: Trade, Economy, Fiscal State, and the Expansion of Empire, 1688–1815," in William Roger Lewis, ed., *The Oxford History of the British Empire* (Oxford and New York: Oxford University Press, 1998), 2:28–52; Daniel A. Baugh, "Maritime Strength and Atlantic Commerce: The Uses of 'a Grand Maritime Empire,'" in L. Stone, ed., *An Imperial State at War* (London and New York: Routledge, 1994), 185–223; John Brewer, *The Sinews of Power: War, Money, and the English State, 1688–1783* (New York: Alfred A. Knopf, 1989). Of course, as Kathleen Wilson notes, plenty of people, particularly Africans, Native Americans, and Celts, would have disagreed with the idea that "Britain did not possess a 'territorial' empire before the 1760s"; see Wilson, *A New Imperial History: Culture, Identity and Modernity in Britain and the Empire, 1660–1850* (Cambridge: Cambridge University Press, 2004), 11.

13. *New-York Gazette*, October 3, 1757.

14. Lydon, *Pirates*, 85, 92; Swanson, *Predators and Prizes*, ch. 3.

15. *New-York Weekly Journal*, November 26, 1739.

16. *New-York Gazette*, November 26, 1739.

17. *New-York Weekly Journal*, April 28, 1740; Daniel Horsmanden, *A Journal of the Proceedings in the Detection of the Conspiracy Formed by Some White People, in Conjunction with Negro and Other Slaves, for Burning the City of New-York in America, and Murdering the Inhabitants. . . .* (New York: Printed by James Parker, 1744), 80.

18. For prizes brought into Newport, Rhode Island, see *New-York Weekly Journal*, January 14, 1739, and March 21, 1742; for prizes brought to Boston and England, see *New-York Weekly Journal*, March 31, 1740; and for Charleston, see *New-York Weekly Journal*, July 12, 1742.

19. *New-York Weekly Journal*, May 19, 1740.

20. Cathy D. Matson, *Merchants and Empire: Trading in Colonial New York* (Baltimore: Johns Hopkins University Press, 1998).

21. *New-York Weekly Journal*, January 23, 1748.

22. Petition of Juan Miranda to James DeLancey and notes on the case of Juan Miranda, "Juan Miranda" folder.

23. Carl Bridenbaugh, ed., *Gentleman's Progress: The Itinerarium of Dr. Alexander Hamilton, 1744* (Chapel Hill: University of North Carolina Press, 1948), 151.

24. Carl E. Swanson, "American Privateering and Imperial Warfare, 1739–

1748," *William and Mary Quarterly*, 3d ser., 42 (July 1985): 357–82, 362, 364. Also see Swanson, *Predators and Prizes*, 118.

25. For Morris's vice-admiralty court, see Michael Watson, "Judge Lewis Morris, the New York Vice-Admiralty Court, and Colonial Privateering, 1739–1762," *New York History* 78, no. 2 (April 1997): 116–46.

26. Carl Ubbelohde, *The Vice-Admiralty Courts and the American Revolution* (Chapel Hill and London: University of North Carolina Press for the Institute of Early American History and Culture, Williamsburg, Va., 1960).

27. Vice-admiralty court records for New York in the National Archives, Northeast Division, New York City. Selected cases are published in Charles Merrill Hough, *Reports of Cases in the Vice Admiralty of the Province of New York and in the Court of Admiralty of the State of New York, 1715–1788* (New Haven, Conn.: Yale University Press, 1925); and J. Franklin Jameson, *Privateering and Piracy in the Colonial Period: Illustrative Documents* (New York: Macmillan Company, 1923). For a complete discussion of the legal authority and procedures of the colonial vice-admiralty courts, see the introduction by Charles M. Andrews in Dorothy S. Towle, ed., *The Records of the Vice-Admiralty Court of Rhode Island, 1716–1752* (Washington, D.C.: Plimpton Press for the American Historical Association, 1936), 1–80.

28. Petition of Juan Miranda to Gov. DeLancey, "Juan Miranda" folder.

29. Eltis, *Rise of African Slavery*, 51, 76.

30. Hugo Grotius, *Of the Rights of War and Peace, in Three Volumes* (London, 1715), vol. 3, chap. 7, sec. 9.

31. "Europeans and the Rise and Fall of African Slavery in the Americas: An Interpretation," *The American Historical Review*, vol. 98, no. 5 (Dec., 1993), pp. 1399–1423.

32. Quoted in Jane Landers, *Black Society in Spanish Florida* (Urbana: University of Illinois Press, 1999), 44–45.

33. Governor Robert Hunter to the Lords of Trade, June 23, 1712, in *Docs. Rel.*, 5:342.

34. "The Case of Jean-Baptiste and Pierre LaVille" in the Records of the Vice-Admiralty and Admiralty Court of New York, National Archives, Northeast Region, New York City. The file papers are in *Prize Cases*, 1757–63, box 2, folder "John-Baptiste LaVille." (hereafter cited as "John-Baptiste LaVille" folder).

35. For the difference in general between the treatment of white and black sailors, see Bolster, *Black Jacks*, chap. 1.

36. "Captain Elford has to subsist the prisoners taken by him in prizes," in *CCM*, September 20, 1712.

37. Lydon, *Pirates*, 104.

38. "John Baptiste LaVille" folder.

39. See the deposition of Anthony Deas, in which all of Deas's white colleagues leaped ashore and got away; only Deas, a mixed-race Spaniard, was caught. See "John-Baptiste LaVille" folder.

40. Charles Z. Lincoln, ed., *Messages from the Governors: Comprising Executive Communications to the Legislature and Other Papers Relating to Legislation from the Organization of the First Colonial Assembly in 1683 to and including the Year 1906* (Albany, N.Y.: J. B. Lyon Co., 1909), 1:327.

41. For prisoner-of-war exchange as an attempt to craft British naval supremacy, see Olive Anderson, "The Establishment of British Supremacy at Sea and the Exchange of Naval Prisoners of War, 1689–1783," *English Historical Review* 75 (1960): 77–89. For prisoner-of-war exchanges as an attempt to subvert British

naval power, see Alain Cabantous, "Gens de Mer, Guerre et Prison: La Captivité des Gens de Mer au XVIIIe Siècle," *Revue d'Histoire Moderne et Contemporaine* 28 (1981): 246–67.

42. For one example of many, see the vice-admiralty minute books for November 27, 1741, in which the case was recorded as "Capt. Ephraim Brasier and company of the Sloop *Hummingbird* agt. Two Baggs and one Basket of Silver, one bagg of Gold and two pairs of Silver Knee buckles, one pair of Silver Shoe Buckles, and 45 of Tortoise Shell 2 Negro and one Molatto Slave and 36 pieces of eight." The next day the two "negroes" were libeled, but the "molatto" was declared a freeman. See New York Vice-Admiralty Court minute books, National Archives, Northeast Division.

43. Depositions of William Dumbar, James Lomasney, and John Baptist Brown, *Prize Cases*, folder *Orleans vs. Prosperous Polly*.

44. Council minutes, October 1, 1746, Parish transcripts, box "New York", folder 162.

45. M. de la Jonquière to M. de Rouillé, July 16, 1750, in *Docs. Rel.*, 10:209–11.

46. Council minutes, April 24, 1711, Parish transcripts, box "New York," folder 157, 18d–19. For the apprenticing of free black children in Virginia, for whom indenture could be either a guarantee of eventual freedom or a step toward slavery, see Kathleen M. Brown, *Good Wives, Nasty Wenches, and Anxious Patriarchs: Gender, Race, and Power in Colonial Virginia* (Chapel Hill and London: University of North Carolina Press for the Institute of Early American History and Culture, Williamsburg, Va., 1996), 230–35.

47. Affidavits of Mary Pinhorne and Jacobus Kiersted, [n.d.], "Juan Miranda" folder.

48. For the low number of free blacks in New York, see Graham Russell Hodges, *Root and Branch: African Americans in New York and East Jersey, 1613–1863* (Chapel Hill and London: University of North Carolina Press, 1999), 69–72; and Leslie Harris, *In the Shadow of Slavery* (Chicago: University of Chicago Press, 2003), 39.

49. Copy of indenture of Francisco Gosé, 1753, Kempe Papers, box 5, unmarked folder.

50. Eric Foner, *The Story of American Freedom* (New York and London: W. W. Norton, 1998), 10.

51. The difference between servitude and slavery was still unclear in early nineteenth-century New York, even after the beginning of gradual emancipation. See Shane White, *Somewhat More Independent: The End of Slavery in New York City, 1770–1810* (Athens and London: University of Georgia Press, 1991), chap. 2.

52. *Prize Cases*, 1757–63, box 2, "John Baptiste LaVille" folder.

53. *Pennsylvania Gazette*, October 7, 1762.

54. Spanish "Indians" seems to refer to any dark-skinned Spaniard. See Governor Hunter to the Lords of Trade, June 23, 1712, in *Docs. Rel.*, 5:342.

55. *CCM*, July 30, 1688.

56. Charles Z. Lincoln, William H. Johnson, and A. Judd Northrup, eds., *Colonial Laws of New York* (Albany, N.Y.: J. B. Lyon, State Printer, 1894), 1:597–98. Also see Hodges, *Root and Branch*, 58–60.

57. October 1, 1746, Parish transcripts, Box "New York," folder 162.

58. It is clear that Miranda had convinced the attorney general, William Kempe, of his freedom. Moreover, the fact that Kempe managed to impose bail of one hundred pounds on Cornelius Van Ranst (Sarah's son) for threatening

to remove Miranda from New York shows that Miranda had also acquired the sympathy of the city's magistrates. See brief of *Juan Miranda v. Cornelius Van Ranst* [n.d.], "Juan Miranda" folder. Also, for the role of the public in maintaining slavery, see John Wood Sweet, *Bodies Politic: Negotiating Race in the American North, 1730–1830* (Baltimore: Johns Hopkins University Press, 2003), chap. 3.

59. Petition of Juan Miranda to John Chambers, October 10, 1758, "Juan Miranda" folder, in which Miranda refers to himself as "a free Man a Subject of the King of Spain, but late of the City of New York, Sailmaker."

60. Christopher Tomlins and Bruce H. Mann, eds., *The Many Legalities of Early America* (Chapel Hill, Published for the Omohundro Institute of Early American History and Culture by the University of North Carolina Press 2001); Eliga H. Gould, "Zones of Law, Zones of Violence: The Legal Geography of the British Atlantic, circa 1772," *William and Mary Quarterly* (July 2003), http://www.history-cooperative.org/journals/wm/60.3/gould.html (accessed July 24, 2007).

61. Hodges, *Root and Branch*, 129–30. For other discussions of these Spanish sailors that consider the individuals more than the underlying cultural-political structure, see Charles R. Foy, "Seeking Freedom in the Atlantic World, 1713–1783," *Early American Studies* 4, no. 1 (2006): 46–77; and Richard E. Bond, "Ebb and Flow: Free Blacks and Urban Slavery in Eighteenth-Century New York" (Ph.D. diss., Johns Hopkins University, 2005), chap. 5.

62. *CCM*, October 21, 1710

63. Council minutes, September 15, 1712, Parish transcripts, Box "New York," folder 157, 27d.

64. Governor Hunter to the Lords of Trade, June 23, 1712, in *Docs. Rel.*, 5:342.

65. Council minutes, September 15, 1712, Parish transcripts, Box "New York," folder 157, 27d.

66. Ibid., June 30, 1713, Box "New York," folder 157, 32.

67. Report of a letter from Lewis Morris to Governor Crosby, August 21, 1752, Parish transcripts, folder 160, 5d.

68. See the cases of Joseph Antonio Fiallo and Miguel Joseph Fuentes, "Order of Council," September 29, 1753, Parish transcripts, Box "New York," folder 160, 9.

69. Watson, "Judge Lewis Morris," 116–46.

70. Cited in Landers, *Black Society*, 45.

71. Council minutes, March 1, 1754, Parish transcripts, folder 160.

72. Report of the governor, June 13, 1753, Parish transcripts, folder 160.

73. Petition of Juan Miranda to John Chambers, October 10, 1758, "Juan Miranda" folder.

74. For the cases of selling men who had not been libeled that came to light, see the cases of Antonio Varcelona, August 21, 1752, and Francisco Isquena, June 13, 1753, Parish transcripts, folder 162. Also see Hosea Antonio, June 26, 1752, in E. B. O'Callaghan, ed., *Calendar of British Historical Manuscripts in the Office of the Secretary of State, Albany, New York, 1664–1776* (Albany, N.Y.: Office of the Secretary of State, 1865–66; repr., Ridgewood, N.J.: Gregg Press, 1968), 662. See also the case of Paul Mesquia, sent away "in irons to Albany" on December 22, 1752, Parish transcripts, folder 162, August 21, 1752.

75. Petition of Francis de Salas Cortilla to Gov. Cadwallader Colden [n.d.] and council minutes, February 4, 1761, Kempe Papers, box 5, unmarked folder; letter and affidavits from the governor of Havana, Parish transcripts, folder 160, 3d.

76. Petition of de la Torre, [n.d.], Kempe Papers, box 4, Davenport-Flood folder.

77. Council minutes, May 3, July 19, and July 29, 1746, Parish transcripts, folder 162. The historical record does not preserve the total number of Spanish sailors involved in this case. Some of the Spanish sailors had also been brought into Newport on the *Defiance*, where they too had been sold into slavery. See Howard M. Chapin, *Rhode Island Privateers in King George's War, 1739–1748* (Providence: Rhode Island Historical Society, 1926), 152–53.

78. Council minutes, August 20 and September 20, 1746, Parish transcripts, folder 162.

79. Hough, *Reports of Cases*, 29–31.

80. Council minutes, October 1 and October 15, 1746; examinations of John Easom and Michael Beazley, November 6, 1746, Parish transcripts, folder 162.

81. *CCM*, November 6 and December 16, 1746.

82. Hough, *Reports of Cases*, 29.

83. Deposition of Juan Francisco de la Cruz, Manuel Anthonia de los Reyes, Joseph Francisco, and Juan Domingo Rodriges, in *CCM*, April 15, 1747; letter from governor of St. Augustine, August 25, 1747, Parish transcripts, folder 162.

84. For the governor of Havanah, see communication of Governor George Clinton to Executive Council, April 5, 1750, re: letter "dated the 30th November last respecting eleven Spanish Negroes and Mulattos now slaves in this Province," Parish transcripts, Box "New York," folder 160; For the governor of St. Augustine, see communication of Governor George Clinton to Executive Council, May 25, 1752, re: letter from Don Melchor De Navarette, "claiming forty five Spanish Mulattos or Negroes taken and brought into this Province during the late War and Condemned here as slaves by Decree of the Court of Vice Admiralty." Parish transcripts, Box "New York," folder 160.

85. Petition of Hilario Antonio, May 15, 1756, Parish Papers, folder 160.

86. Hough, *Reports of Cases*, 201n1; Lydon, *Pirates*, 114–15.

87. Deposition of John Baptiste Brown, *Prize Papers*, folder *Orleans vs. Prosperous Polly*.

88. Hough, *Reports of Cases*, 201.

89. Petition of Nero Corney, in "New York Miscellaneous Manuscripts," box 7, no. 25, New-York Historical Society.

90. The petition is not clear about the threat to run away: "Your Honor's Petitioner (being much afflicted by his latter Master Captain Corney by being but in Irons etc. without any view of his, or dishonor of my own, than that he has a notion of my getting my liberty by regular methods (which he can't help thinking Prachable)"; see ibid.

91. Colonial Office Papers 5/1200: minutes of council from March 3, 1755, to December 31, 1760 (Public Record Office, London).

92. Gould, "Zones of Law," paragraph 35.

93. Council minutes, April 24, 1711, Parish transcripts, folder 157.

94. Council minutes, May 3, 1746, Parish transcripts, folder 162.

95. Letter to Governor Charles Hardy from Kempe [1757] re *Juan Miranda vs. the Widow Van Ranst*, "Juan Miranda" folder.

96. Harry B. Yoshpe, "Record of Slave Manumissions in New York during the Colonial and Early National Periods," *Journal of Negro History* 26 (January 1941): 78–107, 81, 84, 85.

97. Hodges, *Root and Branch*, 129–30.

Chapter 6

1. For information on the fires, see Lieutenant-Governor George Clarke to the Lords of Trade, April 22, 1741, reprinted in E. B. O'Callaghan, ed., *Documents Relative to the Colonial History of the State of New York* (Albany, N.Y.: Weed, Parsons and Company, Printers, 1853–87), 6:184–86; and Daniel Horsmanden, *A Journal of the Proceedings in the Detection of the Conspiracy Formed by Some White People, in Conjunction with Negro and Other Slaves, for Burning the City of New-York in America, and Murdering the Inhabitants* (New York: James Parker, 1744), 6 (hereafter cited as *New York Conspiracy*). The 1741 trials have long been a source of fascination for historians. Much excellent work has been written about the suspected conspiracy. Graham Russell Hodges, *Root and Branch: African Americans in New York and East Jersey 1613–1863* (Chapel Hill: University of North Carolina Press, 1999), 91–98, argues that New York's slaves did plan an uprising in 1741. Peter Linebaugh and Marcus Rediker, *The Many-Headed Hydra: Sailors, Slaves, Commoners, and the Hidden History of the Revolutionary Atlantic* (Boston: Beacon Press, 2000), 174–210, agree that there was a violent uprising in the works that was part of a larger wave of eighteenth-century Atlantic rebellions. In the first monograph on the event, T. J. Davis, *A Rumor of Revolt: The "Great Negro Plot" in Colonial New York* (New York: Free Press, 1985), argues that even the talk of conspiring among slaves constituted a rebellion. Peter Hoffer's thoughtful legal history, *The Great New York Conspiracy of 1741: Slavery, Crime, and Colonial Law* (Lawrence: University Press of Kansas, 2003), concurs with this narrow definition of revolt. An early but persuasive article by Ferenc M. Szasz, "The New York Slave Revolt of 1741: A Reexamination," *New York History* 48 (1967): 215–30, argues that the authorities uncovered a biracial conspiracy to commit thefts. Other historians have moved away from the question of whether or not there was a conspiracy to consider issues of context. Andy Dolan, "Reading and Writing Terror: The New York Conspiracy Trials of 1741," *American Literary History* 16, no. 3 (2004): 377–406, considers the geopolitical context of the War of Jenkins' Ear. Eric Plagg, "New York's 1741 Slave Conspiracy in a Climate of Fear and Anxiety," *New York History* 84 (2003): 275–99, likewise considers the myriad anxieties that beset colonial New York City. Richard Bond, "Shaping a Conspiracy: Black Testimony in the 1741 New York Plot," *Early American Studies: An Interdisciplinary Journal* 5, no. 1 (2007): 63–94, reads the trials for evidence of black agency, while Rebecca Hall, "Not Killing Me Softly: African American Women, Slave Revolts, and Historical Constructions of Racialized Gender" (Ph.D. diss., University of California–Santa Cruz, 2004), creatively uses them to extend our understanding of African American women's history. Thelma Wills Foote, *Black and White Manhattan: The History of Racial Formation in Colonial New York City* (New York: Oxford University Press, 2004); and Jill Lepore, *New York Burning: Liberty, Slavery, and Conspiracy in Eighteenth-Century Manhattan* (New York: Alfred A. Knopf, 2005), consider the trials in light of New York's political factionalism.

2. *New-York Weekly Journal,* December 22, 1740. At the end of the century William Smith recorded, "The winter which ushered in this year (ever since called the hard winter,) was distinguished by the sharpest frost, and the greatest quantity of snow, within the memory of the oldest inhabitant. The weather was intensely severe from the middle of November to the latter end of March." William Smith, *History of the Province of New York,* ed. Michael Kammen, 2 vols. (Cambridge, Mass.: Belknap Press of Harvard University Press, 1972), 2:49.

3. Florence M. Montgomery, *Textiles in America, 1650–1870: A Dictionary Based*

on Original Documents, Prints and Paintings, Commercial Records, American Merchants' Papers, Shopkeepers' Advertisements, and Pattern Books with Original Swatches of Cloth (New York: W. W. Norton, 1984), 197.

4. This account comes from Rebecca Hogg's deposition and Horsmanden's narrative introduction; see Horsmanden, *New York Conspiracy*, 1–3, Appendix 2–3.

5. Horsmanden, *New York Conspiracy*, 3; deposition of Anne Kannady, in ibid., Appendix 1–2.

6. Horsmanden, *New York Conspiracy*, 4–5.

7. Ibid., 1.

8. Smith, *History of New York*, 2:53. Szasz, "New York Slave Revolt of 1741," 215–30, has argued that the conspiracy was a larceny ring headed by John Hughson.

9. Horsmanden, *New York Conspiracy*, 11.

10. Ibid., 281. For the governor's proclamation, see *New-York Weekly Journal*, June 29, 1741.

11. Horsmanden, *New York Conspiracy*, 1.

12. Ibid., 7.

13. Reprinted in ibid., 161. The dateline of the letter was May 16, 1741.

14. Ibid., 35. The testimony was given on May 25, 1741.

15. Ibid., 49.

16. Ibid., 79.

17. James G. Lydon, *Pirates, Privateers, and Profits* (Upper Saddle River, N.J.: Gregg Press, 1970), 88. Quote is from Richard Pares, *Colonial Blockade and Neutral Rights* (Oxford: Oxford University Press, 1938), 54.

18. Berthold Fernow, comp., *Calendar of Council Minutes, 1668–1783* (Harrison, N.Y.: Harbor Hill Books, 1987), August 10, 1741.

19. "His Honour required the advice of the Council concerning five Spanish Negroes brought into this City by Captain John Lush Commander of a Privateer and sold as slaves here but pretending themselves free been some time since convicted in the supreme court for being concerned in the late conspiracy, who advised his Honor to grant his Majesties most gracious Pardon to four of them In order for Transportation to Newfoundland Madeira or Lisbon and to order Juan als Wan a Negro belonging to Capt. Sarley for Execution" (Executive Council meeting minutes, August 10, 1741, Daniel Parish slavery transcripts, Jr., Box "New York," folder 160, New-York Historical Society).

20. Horsmanden, *New York Conspiracy*, 72.

21. O'Callaghan, ed., *Documents*, 6:197–98.

22. Horsmanden, *New York Conspiracy* 94.

23. Indictment against John Ury, April 1741, in E. B. O'Callaghan, ed., *Calendar of British Historical Manuscripts in the Office of the Secretary of State, Albany, New York, 1664–1776* (Albany, N.Y.: Office of the Secretary of State, 1865–66; repr., Ridgewood, N.J.: Gregg Press, 1968), 553. Ury's description is given by a slave testifying for the prosecution. See Horsmanden, *New York Conspiracy*, 207.

24. Horsmanden, *New York Conspiracy*, 95.

25. Ibid.

26. Ibid., 162, 165.

27. Ibid., 374. For anti-Catholic prejudice in the colonies, see Joseph J. Casino, "Anti-Popery in Colonial Pennsylvania," *Pennsylvania Magazine of History and Biography* 105 (July 1981): 279–310. For anti-Catholicism in New York during Leisler's Rebellion, see Randall Balmer, "Traitors and Papists: The Religious

Dimensions of Leisler's Rebellion," *New York History* 70 (October 1989): 341–72; and John Murrin, "The Menacing Shadow of Louis XIV and the Rage of Jacob Leisler: The Constitutional Ordeal of Seventeenth-Century New York," in Stephen L. Schechter and Richard B. Bernstein, eds., *New York and the Union* (Albany: New York State Commission on the Bicentennial of the United States Constitution, 1990), 29–71.

28. Horsmanden, *New York Conspiracy*, 125–27.

29. Linda Colley, *Britons: Forging the Nation, 1707–1837* (New Haven, Conn.: Yale University Press, 1992); Adrian Howe, "The Bayard Treason Trial: Dramatizing Anglo-Dutch Politics in Early Eighteenth-Century New York City," *William and Mary Quarterly*, 3d ser., 47, no. 1 (1990): 57–89; Charles Z. Lincoln, William H. Johnson, and A. Judd Northrup, eds., *The Colonial Laws of New York from the Year 1664 to the Revolution* (Albany, N.Y.: J. B. Lyon, State Printer, 1894), 1:84, August 9, 1700 (hereafter *New York Colonial Laws*); John Gilmary Shea, "Negro Plot of 1741," a paper read before the New-York Historical Society, May 6, 1862, in Joseph Shannon, comp., *Manual of the Corporation of the City of New York* (New York: Printed by order of the Common Council, 1870), 764–71.

30. Horsmanden, *New York Conspiracy*, 107–8.

31. Ibid., 278.

32. Ibid., 323.

33. Lieutenant Governor George Clarke to General James Oglethorpe, August 5, 1741. This letter is filed with a document indicating that the letter was intercepted when a corsair seized an English ship; see Santo Domingo 2658, Archivo General de India, Seville. My thanks to Jane Landers for this reference.

34. Horsmanden, *New York Conspiracy*, 286–87, 299, 325; Daniel Horsmanden to Cadwallader Colden, August 7, 1741, *New-York Historical Society Collections* 51 (1918): 224–28.

35. Horsmanden, *New York Conspiracy*, 343.

36. *Pennsylvania Gazette*, September 3, 1741.

37. For the commercial pressures to war, see Paul Langford, *A Polite and Commercial People: England, 1727–1783* (Oxford: Oxford University Press, 1989), 50–53; and Lieutenant Governor Clarke to the Lords of Trade, June 20, 1741, in O'Callaghan, ed., *Documents*, 6:197–98.

38. *New-York Gazette*, March 1, 1736; Lieutenant Governor George Clarke to the Duke of Newcastle, June 18, 1736, in O'Callaghan, ed., *Documents*, 6:70–71.

39. General Oglethorpe to Lieutenant Governor Clarke, May 16, 1741, repr. in Horsmanden, *New York Conspiracy*, 329–30.

40. Richard Leppert, *Music and Image: Domesticity, Ideology, and Socio-Cultural Formation in Eighteenth-Century England* (Cambridge and New York: Cambridge University Press, 1988), 71–88.

41. See, for example, a poem scarifying Catholics and entitled "A humble Address to that most venerable and ancient Punk the Whore of Babylon: Translated from a French Original by a zealous Protestant; reprinted from the Maryland Gazette," *New-York Evening Post*, April 13, 1747.

42. Colden to Clarke, August 24, 1742, *New-York Historical Society Collections* 51 (1918): 265; affidavit of Villars Roche, ibid., 269.

43. Colden to Clarke, August 24, 1742, 265; Clarke to Colden, September 14, 1742, *New-York Historical Society Collections* 51 (1918): 270.

44. Daniel Horsmanden to Charles Cotton, New York, July 2, 1756, Horsmanden Papers, addendum no. 31, New-York Historical Society, cited in Mary P. McManus, "Daniel Horsmanden: Eighteenth-Century New Yorker" (Ph.D. diss., Fordham University, 1960), 4n4.

45. Smith, *History of New York*, 39, cited in McManus, "Daniel Horsmanden," 4.

46. James Alexander to Cadwallader Colden, New York, March 23, 1732, *New-York Historical Society Collections* 51 (1918): 59; Smith, *History of New York*, 39.

47. Jessica Kross, "Power Most Ardently Sought: The New York Council, 1675–1775," in Bruce C. Daniels, ed., *Power and Status: Officeholding in Early America* (Middletown, Conn.: Wesleyan University Press, 1986), 205–31, 208.

48. O'Callaghan, ed., *Documents*, 5:976.

49. Daniel Horsmanden to Cadwallader Colden, November 11, 1734, in *The Letters and Papers of Cadwallader Colden*, vol. VIII, *Additional Letters and Papers, 1715–1748*, Collections of the New-York Historical Society for the Year 1935, The John Watts DePeyster Publication Fund Series, vol. 51 (New York: Printed for the New-York Historical Society, 1918), 117 (hereafter *Colden Papers*).

50. For lawyers in trade, see Ellen Maria Russell, "James Alexander, 1691–1756" (Ph.D. diss., Fordham University, 1995); and Horsmanden to Colden, New York, July 23, 1736, in *Colden Papers*, vol. 51 (1918), 153.

51. Horsmanden, *New York Conspiracy*, 2.

52. Ibid., 9.

53. Ibid., 13.

54. Ibid., 12.

55. Horsmanden to Colden, August 7, 1741, in *Colden Papers*, vol. 51 (1918), 224–28.

56. Horsmanden, *New York Conspiracy*, 202.

57. Ibid., 205.

58. For coverage of Antigua in New York, see the *New-York Weekly Journal*, February 7, 1736; and the five-part series in the *New-York Weekly Journal* beginning March 28, 1737. For coverage of the South Carolina Stono Rebellion in the New York papers, see *New-York Weekly Journal*, May 22, 1740. For New Jersey rebellions in the 1730s, see Hodges, *Root and Branch*, 89–91.

59. New York City Common Council papers, 1670–1831, box 4, folder 171. New York Municipal Archives.

60. Horsmanden to Colden, August 7, 1741, in Colden Papers, vol. 67 (1934), 288–89.

61. Horsmanden, *New York Conspiracy*, v.

62. *New York Colonial Laws*, November 27, 1741, 3: 719.

63. In July 1745 the assembly established a committee to investigate why Horsmanden had not yet prepared the laws; see I. N. Phelps Stokes, comp., *The Iconography of Manhattan Island, 1498–1909* (New York: Robert H. Dodd, 1915; repr., New York: Arno Press, 1967), 4:590. William Smith, Jr., and William Livingston agreed to take over the project in 1750, and the laws appeared in 1752; *New York Colonial Laws*, November 24, 1750, 3:907, Horsmanden kept the money.

64. George Clinton to the president of the Board of Trade, October 30, 1748, in *Acts of the Privy Council of England, Colonial Series*, 6 vols. (Hereford: For His Majesty's Stationary Office, 1908–12), 6:271, quoted in McManus, "Daniel Horsmanden," 130.

65. John Ury, *The defence of John Ury, made before the Supream Court in New-York, at his tryal for being concerned in the late Negro-conspiracy* (Philadelphia: Printed by Benjamin Franklin, 1741).

66. For Antigua, see David Barry Gaspar, *Bondmen and Rebels: A Study of Master-Slave Relations in Antigua with Implications for Colonial British America* (Baltimore: Johns Hopkins University Press, 1985), pt. 1. For Stono, see Mark M. Smith, ed.,

Stono: Documenting and Interpreting a Southern Slave Revolt (Columbia: University of South Carolina Press, 2005).

67. "An Act for the more Equal and Orderly Keeping a Sufficient night Watch in the City," November 7, 1741, chap. 711, in *New York Colonial Laws,* 3:158. An act revived at the same time and entitled "to Restrain Tavern Keepers and Innholders from Selling Strong Liquors to Servants and Apprentices and from giving Large Credit to Others" (in ibid., November 7, 1741 chap. 713, 3:166) nowhere mentions slaves. Also see Oscar R. Williams, "The Regimentation of Blacks on the Urban Frontier in Colonial Albany, New York City and Philadelphia," *Journal of Negro History* 63, no. 4. (October 1978): 329–38; and Edwin Olson, "The Slave Code in Colonial New York," *Journal of Negro History* 29, no. 2 (April 1944): 147–65.

68. Peter Brooks and Paul Gewirtz, eds., *Law's Stories: Narrative and Rhetoric in the Law* (New Haven, Conn.: Yale University Press, 1996), 5.

Bibliography

Archival Sources

Archivo General de India, Seville
  Santo Domingo 2658
National Archives, Northeast Region
  Prize Cases Papers
  Vice-Admiralty Minute Books
New York County Clerk's Office, Division of Old Records
  Manuscript Minutes of the New York Supreme Court
  Mayor's Court papers
  Supreme Court Parchment Papers
New-York Historical Society
  Alexander Papers
  Nicholas Bayard Receipt Books
  F. A. Aston DePeyster Papers
  Francis Goelet Common-place book
  Peter Jay Account Book and Daybook
  John Tabor Kempe Papers
  New York Mayor's Office, Tavern Keeper's License Book
  New York Miscellaneous Manuscripts
  Parish Transcripts
  Account book of Ann Elizabeth Schuyler
New York Municipal Archives
  Manuscript Minute Book, Court of General Sessions (also known as Court of
    Quarter Sessions)
  Minute Books, Court of Special Sessions
  New York City Common Council, Common Council Papers, 1670–1831
Pierpont-Morgan Library
  Livingston Papers
Public Record Office, London
  Colonial Office Papers

Published Primary Sources

An Account of the Robberies Committed by John Morrison, 1750/1 (Philadelphia, 1750/
  51).
American Weekly Journal
American Weekly Mercury
Blackstone, William. *Commentaries on the laws of England. In four books.* Philadel-
  phia, 1771–72. Early American Imprints no. 11996.

Bloch, Julius M., ed. *An Account of Her Majesty's Revenue in the Province of New York, 1701–09: The Customs Records of Early Colonial New York* (Ridgewood, N.J.: Gregg Press, 1966).

Boston Evening-Post

Boston Gazette

Boston News-Letter

Boston Post-Boy

Boston Weekly Newsletter

[Burgh, James], *Britain's Remembrancer: Being Some Thoughts on the Proper Improvement of the Present Juncture.* 6th ed. [New York] London: printed; New-York: Reprinted and sold by James Parker, at the new printing-office in Beaver-Street, 1748.

"Colden Letter Books." New-York Historical Society, *Collections* (2 vols., 1877, 1878).

"Letters and Papers of Cadwallader Colden," New-York Historical Society, *Collections* 50–51 (10 vols., 1917–23, 1931–35).

Fernow, Berthold, comp. *Calendar of Council Minutes 1668–1783.* Harrison, N.Y.: Harbor Hill Books, 1987.

Gelles, Edith Belle. *The Letters of Abigail Levy Franks, 1733–1748.* New Haven, Conn.: Yale University Press, 2004.

Horsmanden, Daniel. *A Journal Of The Proceedings In The Detection Of The Conspiracy Formed By Some White People, In Conjunction With Negro And Other Slaves, For Burning The City Of New-York In America, And Murdering The Inhabitants.* New York: James Parker, 1744.

Lincoln, Charles Z., ed. *Messages from the Governors: Comprising Executive Communications to the Legislature and Other Papers Relating to Legislation from the Organization of the First Colonial Assembly in 1683 to and including the Year 1906.* Vol. 1. Albany, N.Y.: J. B. Lyon Co., 1909.

Lincoln, Charles Z., William H. Johnson, and A. Judd Northrup, eds. *The Colonial Laws of New York from the year 1664 to the Revolution.* Albany, N.Y.: J. B. Lyon, State Printer, 1894.

New-England Weekly Journal

New-York Evening Post

New-York Gazette

New-York Gazette (Weyman's)

New-York Gazette, or Weekly Post Boy

New-York Journal

New-York Journal and General Advertiser

New-York Mercury

New-York Post-Boy

New-York Weekly Mercury

New-York Weekly Post-Boy

New-England Weekly Journal

O'Callaghan, E. B., ed. *Calendar of British Historical Manuscripts in the Office of the Secretary of State, Albany, New York, 1664–1776.* Albany, N.Y.: Office of the Secretary of State, 1865–66; reprint, Ridgewood, N.J.: Gregg Press, 1968.

O'Callaghan, E. B., ed. *Documents Relative to the Colonial History of the State of New York: procured in Holland, England, and France by John Romeyn Brodhead, Agent.* Vols. 1–13. Albany, N.Y.: Weed, Parsons, 1853–81.

Pennsylvania Gazette

The report of the committee of His Majesty's Council, to whom it was referred, to examine and make enquiry, touching a Letter found in the House of Mr. Alexander in New-York, on Friday the First Day of February, 1733/4. In Order to Make the fullest Discovery concerning the Author of the same. New York: William Bradford, printer, 1734.

South Carolina Gazette

Spectator

Steuart, Sir James. *An inquiry into the principles of political oeconomy: being an essay on the science of domestic policy in free nations. In which are particularly considered population, agriculture, trade, industry, money, . . . By Sir James Steuart, . . . In two volumes. . . .* Vol. 2. London, 1767.

The Tatler

The trial of John Ury for being an ecclesiastical person, made by authority pretended from the See of Rome, and coming into and abiding in the province of New York, and with being one of the conspirators in the Negro plot to burn the city of New York, 1741: Abridged from The New York conspiracy, or, A history of the Negro plot, with the Journal of the Proceedings against the conspirators, at New York, in the years 1741–2. By Daniel Horsmanden. 2d ed. *1810.* Philadelphia: Martin I. J. Griffin, 1899.

Towle, Dorothy S., ed. *The Records of the Vice-Admiralty Court of Rhode Island, 1716–1752.* Washington: The Plimpton Press for the American Historical Association, 1936), 1–80.

Truxes, Thomas M., ed. *Letterbook of Greg & Cunningham, 1756–57: Merchants of New York and Belfast.* Oxford: Oxford University Press, 2001.

Ury, John. *The defence of John Ury, made before the Supream [sic] Court in New-York, at his tryal [sic] for being concerned in the late Negro-conspiracy.* Philadelphia: Printed by Benjamin Franklin, 1741.

White, Philip L., ed. *The Beekman Mercantile Papers, 1746–1799.* New York: New-York Historical Society, 1956.

Index

Page numbers in italics indicate figures.

Alexander, James, 40, 52, 54, 61, 93, 171
Alexander, Mary Spratt Provoost (trader), 27, 39–41, 43–44, 46, 52–55, 61
Allman, Thomas (con artist), 26
American Weekly Mercury, 95
The Analysis of Beauty, plate II: *The Country Dance* (William Hogarth), 92
Anderson, Elizabeth (shopkeeper), 57, 75–80
anonymity: in social environment, 24; in trading practices, 14–16
anti-Catholicism: and conspiracy trials of 1741, 142–49; and imperial wars, 103–4; and the press, 112–13
Ashburner, William (con artist), 28–31, 150
Atlantic slavery vs. plantation slavery, 107–8, 123, 176n79
Axon, William (privateer), and Miranda case, 109, 113, 115

balls: *American Weekly Mercury* on, 95; *Boston Gazette* on, 87; William Bradford's defense of, 87–90; heterosociability of, 89–90, 97–98, 100; and imperial politics, 90, 95–100, 180n48; and New York's image, 90–91; sponsors of, 90; and status, 89–92, 96
Bayard, Samuel (privateer), 111–12
Beattie, J. M., 68, 171n7
Beekman, Gerard G. (trader), 15–16, 24–25, 28–30, 47
Beekman, James (trader), 13, 47
Bell, Tom (con artist), 27–28
bills of credit: counterfeiting penalties, 12, 18–19; as counterfeit target, 19–22; as state-financed, 11–12, 22
bills of exchange: Burton's testimony as metaphor of, 151–52, 154; and con art-

ists, 22–30; and the "culture of credit," 14–16, 22–25; and personal interactions, 13–16, 22–25
black sailors: considered slaves, 111, 113, 115–18; contingent status of, 106–7, 113–14, 117–22, 130; forms of servitude, 115, 119–20, 122; as prisoners of war, 8, 107, 113, 123–31, 138; privateer capture of, 8, 107, 111, 113, 117; and Spanish colonial governments, 124–25, 128
Blackstone, William: on coverture, 34; on loyalty oaths, 149
Boston, 11
Boston Gazette, 87
Bradford, William, 87–90, 99
British Empire: currency requirements of, 11–14; rivalry with France and Spain, 4–5; role of port cities in, 3, *4. See also* imperial politics; imperial wars
Brownell, George (dancing master), 86
Burgis, William (*A South Prospect of ye Flourishing City of New York*), 2
Burton, Mary: credibility of, 152–54; and Hogg robbery, 134–35; rewarded, 155; testimony of, 138–39, 141–45, 152–53

circulating systems of exchange, 11, 13–15
Clarke, George (governor of New York), 139, 142–43, 146
Clinton, George (governor of New York): and ball dispute, 99, 100; dismissal of Daniel Horsmanden, 146, 156; on white prisoners of war, 117
cloth and clothing: as currency, 68–70; pawning of, 75; secondhand market in, 67–70, 75, 78; as status marker, 8, 68–69
coin clipping, 16–17
coin counterfeiting, 17–18

Colden, Cadwallader: on bills of exchange, 14; on Catholic plots, 148–49; and children playing merchant, 32; and children's dance lessons, 93; as Horsmanden correspondent, 151, 155; support of aunt's trade, 45

commerce: entrapment through, 77, 79; and gender ideology, 7, 32–36, 48, 51, 53–56; and issues of dependence, 35–36, 46–48; personal and impersonal interactions in, 14–16, 22–26, 28, 31; range of participants, 5–6, 32; regulation of women's activities in, 70–75; and slave code, 72–73; and status, 7, 9–11, 28, 31, 158; and war, 110–12, 114–15, 131. *See also* female traders; informal economy

con artists: and bills of credit, 18–22; and bills of exchange, 22–30; and counterfeit coins, 17–18; and credibility, 7, 10–11, 22–31; examples of, 10, 23–24, 26–30, 152; reliance on personal interactions, 22–23, 26, 28; and social fluidity, 11, 23–25

conspiracy trials of 1741: and anti-Catholicism, 142–49; and arson, 136–37, 141; criticism of, 155; cultural context, 1, 3, 8–9, 132; and the "disorderly house," 135–36, 144; and Daniel Horsmanden, 9, 139, 141–46, 149–51, 153–54, 156; impact of, 156–58; schoolmasters' and dancing masters' convictions, 143–49; slave convictions, 140–43; Spanish prisoner convictions, 137–39, 142–43; and theft, 133–35; and winter weather, 132–33, 137, 188 n.2

consumer goods: as currency, 68–70, 80; as status markers, 6, 8, 58–59, 65–66, 80–82

"consumer revolution": cultural implications of, 6, 8; and informal economy, 58–59, 65–69

Cosby, William (governor), 99, 151, 171n67

counterfeit bills of credit, 19–22

counterfeiting: as capital offense, 12, 18–19, 163n34; examples of, 17–18, 20–22; as misdemeanor, 17–18

country dances vs. court dances, 91, 93

court dances vs. country dances, 91, 93

court records: informal economy expressed in, 57–60, 70, 172n1; and

prize cases, 114–15; women's representation in, 48–50

coverture: and female traders, 7, 34–38, 40–41, 51, 55–56, 136; historical interpretation of, 39; under common law, 32–34

credibility: and bills of credit, 12; and bills of exchange, 13–16, 22–25; and con artists, 7, 10–11, 22–31; and credit, 7, 10–11, 150–51, 156; and dancing masters, 85–86, 103–5; expansion of, 22; and gender, 7, 25–26, 31, 152–53, 156; and itinerancy, 22–25, 85–86, 103–5; and status, 10, 25–31, 83–84, 150–53, 156. *See also* reputation

credit: and bills of credit, 11–12; and bills of exchange, 13–16, 22–25; and credibility, 7, 10–11, 150–51, 156; emergence of, 11–16; meaning of, 31; and on webs of dependence, 35–36; and trust, 12–16; and women, 7, 33, 47–51, 55

crime: and "disorderly house" charges, 62–65; and theft charges, 60–62, 68

Cruger, Henry, 14, 41

Cuffee (slave), 133, 137, 140–41

"culture of credit": as con artist opportunity, 16, 22; and genteel masculinity, 26; and ideas of status, 31; as mix of personal and impersonal, 14–16, 22–26, 28, 31

currency: consumer goods as, 68–70, 80; types of, 11–14

"currency of reputation," 31

customhouse records, 37–38

dancing: court vs. country, 91, 93; and dancing masters, 91–93; as political allegory, 98

dancing assemblies. *See* balls

dancing masters: ambiguity of status, 101–5; attitude toward, 85–87, 103–5; and conspiracy trials of 1741, 145–49; curriculum of, 93; as essential, 91–93; as peddlers of gentility, 8, 82–87, 105, 178 n.13; satire of, 100–102

dancing schools, 93–94

dark-skinned sailors. *See* black sailors

debt collection: and international traders, 34–35; and power of attorney, 14–16

defamation suits: and economic reputa-

tion, 48–50; and sexual probity, 48; and threats of bodily harm, 49–50
Defoe, Daniel, 51, 64, 170n65
DeLancey, James (chief justice): and ball dispute, 100; and Mary Burton, 153
dependence, female, 33, 35–36, 46–51, 53–54
"disorderly house": and conspiracy trials of 1741, 135–36, 144; and informal economy, 62–65, 172n1

elite: and balls, 89–90, 96; Mary Burton's testimony against, 154; and dancing masters, 8, 82–85, 100–102; and poor people's consumerism, 65–66, 81–82

factional politics: and balls, 89–90, 179n23; and gentility, 84, 98–100
Fairday, Elizabeth, use of coverture, 37
family networks: and coverture, 35–36, 55–56; and female traders, 33, 37–47; and women's dependent status, 46
female dependence, 33, 35–36, 46–51, 53–54
female traders: business ventures, 45–47; and court records, 48–50; and coverture, 7, 34–38, 40–41, 51, 136; and customhouse records, 37–38; examples of, 37–46; and family networks, 33, 37–47; goods exchanged by, 5–6; and historical records, 37–39; and international market, 35–37, 46–48; and, 7–8, 52–56; widows as, 5–6, 46. See also commerce; informal economy
fencing, 61, 66
Fielding, Henry, 64
financial fraud: coin clipping, 16–17; counterfeiting, 12, 17–22; forgery, 22–27; and gender, 16–17; and gentility, 25–31
foreign black sailors. See black sailors
Forester, James, 89
forgery, 26–30
Fort George: balls at, 95, 97; fire at, 132, 136–37, 146
France, 4–5, 103–5
Franklin, Benjamin, 157
fraud. See financial fraud
freedom suits: and British officials, 130; Stephen Domingo case, 106; and imperial wars, 124–25; LaVille case, 116, 120–21; Miranda case, 108–9, 113, 115, 119–20, 122–23, 126–27, 130–31,

185n58; and prisoner of war status, 123–24, 129, 131; and prosecution, 125–27; and slavery justification, 107–8; success of, 123, 128–31. See also prize cases
Freemasonry, and social status, 102
French and Indian War, 4, 5, 104, 128
French dances, 91, 104

gender: and balls, 89–90; and capitalism, 47, 51, 55; and credibility, 7, 25–26, 31, 152–53, 156; and financial fraud, 16–17
gender ideology and commerce, 7, 32–36, 48, 51, 53–56
gentility: as behavior, 8, 83–84, 87–88, 179n18; commodification of, 8, 82–87, 105, 178n13; and consumer goods, 8, 81–82; and credibility, 25–31, 83–84; and dancing masters, 8, 82–87, 91–93; and factional politics, 84, 98–100; and heterosociability, 89–90, 97–98; and imperial politics, 89–90, 95–100; and masculinity, 105, 148. See also status
Grotius, Hugo, 115–16
Gwin, John (slave): and Mary Burton's testimony, 140, 153; convicted of theft, 140; and Hogg robbery, 133–34, 136

Hamilton, Alexander, 6, 114, 133
heterosociability: of balls, 89–90, 97–98, 100; and gentility, 89–90, 97–98; of political celebrations, 97–98
Hill, Elizabeth (trader), 45, 46
History of New York (William Smith, Jr.): on Mary Alexander, 54; on conspiracy's beginning, 135
Hogarth, William (The Analysis of Beauty, plate II: The Country Dance), 92
Hogg, Rebecca (trader), 133–36, 140–47
Hogg, Robert, 133
Holt, Henry (dancing master): accused as conspirator, 145; as Freemason, 102; career, 85
Horsmanden, Daniel (justice): appointment to Governor's Council, 30, 146, 150–51, 156; belief in conspiracy, 139, 155; and Mary Burton's testimony, 141–46, 149, 153–54; credibility of, 150, 156; on freedom suits, 126, 131; on Hogg robbery, 135; Journal, 9, 154–56; struggle for status, 150–51, 154–56
Hughson, John, 133–35, 139–42, 152
Hughson, Sarah, 139–41, 133–35

ideology, gender and commerce, 7, 32–36, 48, 51, 53–56
"imaginary money" vs. "real money," 12, 161n9. *See also* bills of credit; bills of exchange
imperial politics: and balls, 90, 95–100, 180n48; and dancing masters, 101, 103–5. *See also* British Empire
imperial wars: and freedom suits, 124–25; and New York, 5; and privateering, 109–13. *See also* British Empire
impersonal interactions, and the "culture of credit," 14–16, 22–26, 28, 31
indenture, 115, 119–20, 122
informal economy: centrality of clothing in, 67–70, 78; and the "consumer revolution," 58–59, 65–66; in court records, 57–60, 70; dangers of, 75–80; defined, 58; and the "disorderly house," 62–65; goods exchanged in, 65–70; interracial collaboration in, 61–65; legal ambiguities in, 58, 75, 77; reflected in Hogg robbery, 135–36; status undermined by, 8, 59, 65–66, 68–69, 80, 81–82, 136; ties to formal economy, 59, 63, 66; types of exchange, 58–59; women as linchpins, 59–60. *See also* commerce; female traders
international market: and coverture, 34–35; and female traders, 35–37, 46–48
international vs. local trade practices, 14–16, 22–26, 28, 31
interracial collaboration, 61–65; and "disorderly house" charge, 64–65
itinerancy: and conspiracy trials of 1741, 143–46; and credibility, 22–25, 85–86, 103–5; and dancing masters, 85–87, 103–4; odium of, 85, 103, 146; as population characteristic, 6, 24; and schoolmasters, 143–44; and social fluidity, 6–7, 24

Jay, Judith (trader), 45

Kannady, Anne (shopkeeper), 134, 152
Kempe, William (attorney general): and Elizabeth Anderson case, 77, 79; and Nero Corney case, 129; and the Miranda case, 123, 130, 185n58
Kerry, Peggy, 133, 136, 141–42, 151

King George's War, 5, 98, 108, 111, 112, 114, 117, 118, 122, 125, 128, 138, 147

larceny. *See* theft
LaVille, Jean-Baptiste (black sailor), 116, 120–21
libeled goods, defined, 109. *See also* prize cases
libel suits. *See* freedom suits
licensing regulations, 70–73
liquor laws, 69–70
Livingston, Alida, 44–45
Livingston, Robert, 44–45
local knowledge. *See* personal interactions
local vs. international trade practices, 14–16, 22–26, 28, 31
Lush, John (privateer), 111, 138–39
Lyttelton, George, 51

manners: commodification of, 8, 82–85, 105; *New York Gazette* on, 81–82, 87–90; *New-York Weekly Journal* on, 84; as status marker, 8, 81–84
marketplace. *See* commerce
McGillicuddy, Dennis (privateer), 116, 120–21
minuet, 91, 104
Miranda, Juan (black sailor), 108–9, 113, 115, 119–20, 122–23, 126–27, 130–31, 185n58
mobility. *See* social fluidity
Morris, Lewis, Jr. (judge): and ball dispute, 99–100; and freedom suits, 125–26, 128, 129, 131; and privateering, 114, 122, 125

networks, family, 33, 37–47
newspapers. *See* press
New York: as imperial city, 2, 3, *4*, 90–91; and imperial wars, 5; as mercantile capital, 11–12, 161n5; nature of population, 6; as port, 5; privateering promoted by, 114; winter of 1740–41, 132–33, 137, 188n2
New-York Gazette: dancing school advertisement, 86; defense of balls, 87–90; on governor's ball, 95; on manners, 81–82, 87–90; on privateering, 111
New-York Mercury, satire on gentility, 101–2
New York Supreme Court: and conspiracy trials of 1741, 139, 141–43, 145; indictment of William Kempe, 79

New-York Weekly Journal: and James Alexander, 52, 171n67; and female dependence, 50–51; on opposition ball, 99; on privateering, 111; and satire, 84
Nivelon, François (*Rudiments of Genteel Behavior*), 93, *94*

Oglethorpe, James (governor of Georgia), warnings of Spanish plots, 104, 138, 143, 145, 147–48

pair dances. *See* court dances
paper money: counterfeiting of, 18–22; types of, 11–14
patriarchy, 37
pawning, 58, 65, 66, 73–75, 78, 133
peddlers: dancing masters as, 8, 82–87, 105; restrictions on, 70–71
Pennsylvania Gazette, on John Ury's execution, 146–47
personal interactions: and bills of exchange, 13–16, 22–25; and con artists, 22–23, 26, 28; and the "culture of credit," 14–16, 22–26, 28, 31
Philadelphia, 11, 161n5
Philipse, Frederick (justice), 135
Pinkethman, Charles (privateer), 106
plantation slavery vs. Atlantic slavery, 107–8, 123, 176n79
"The Polite Philosopher" (James Forester), 89
politics, factional: and balls, 89–90, 179n23; and gentility, 84
politics, imperial: and balls, 90, 95–100, 180n48; and dancing masters, 101, 103–5
Pope, Alexander, 35
popery. *See* anti-Catholicism
power of attorney, 14–16
press: anti-Catholicism of, 112–13; privateering in, 110–13; women's representation in, 50–51
Prince (slave), 133–34, 140
prisoners of war: accused of conspiracy, 137–39; black sailors as, 8, 107, 113, 123–31; and international law, 115–16, 123–24; and race, 116–17, 128
privateering: and imperial goals, 109–13; New York promotion of, 114; in press, 110–13; profitability of, 111–13; and vice-admiralty courts, 114–15
privateers: black sailors captured by, 8, 107,

111, 113, 117; and New York favored by, 114; racial distinctions made by, 116–17
Prize Act of 1708, 109
Prize Act of 1740, 109
prize cases: defined, 109; and slave status uncertainty, 118–20; and vice-admiralty courts, 114–15, 117–20, 125, 183n10. *See also* freedom suits
property crime. *See* theft
prostitution, 48, 64, 173n21
public celebrations, 96–100

Quack (slave), 137, 140–41
Queen Anne's War, 5, 12, 97, 104, 125

race: and conspiracy trials of 1741, 157; and informal market, 8, 61–65; and prisoners of war, 8, 116–17, 128
Rainey, Moses (con artist), 26–27
rank. *See* status
rape, 24–25, 60, 77–80, 132
"real money" vs. "imaginary money," 12, 161 n.9. *See also* bills of credit; bills of exchange
reputation: and bills of exchange, 13–16, 22–25; and the "culture of credit," 22–25, 31; and defamation suits, 48–50. *See also* credibility
retail trade: licensing regulations, 70–72; and slave code, 72–73
Rombouts, Helena (trader), 37–38
Romme, Elizabeth: and Hogg robbery, 133–34; implicated in conspiracy, 140
Romme, John: and Hogg robbery, 133–34; implicated in conspiracy, 140
Rudiments of Genteel Behavior (François Nivelon), 93, *94*

Sarly, Jacob (privateer), 137–38
satire: and dancing masters, 100–102; and *New-York Weekly Journal*, 84
Schuyler, Ann Elizabeth (trader), 39, 41–43, 45, 46, 74
Schuyler, Swantje Van Duyckhuysen (trader), 37, 50, 72
secondhand market: and formal economy, 66; in informal economy, 60, 66–70, 73–75; legal ambiguities in, 75, 77; and licensing regulations, 70–71; status undermined by, 8, 65–66, 81–82
servitude types, 115, 119–20, 122, 185n51

Seven Years' War. *See* French and Indian War

slander suits. *See* defamation suits

slave code, 72–73, 135, 157, 176n79

slavery: Atlantic vs. plantation, 107–8, 123, 176 n.79; and English law, 121–22, 130; through privateer capture, 113–14, 123; and skin color, 115–18, 130–31. *See also* servitude

slaves: black sailors considered as, 111, 113, 115–18; and conspiracy trials of 1741, 1, 3, 73, 135, 137, 140–42; as consumers, 66; and "disorderly house" charges, 64–65; in New York population, 6–7; and secondhand market, 75; and theft, 61; in trading networks, 5–6, 57–59, 61; uncertain status of, 118–22, 130–31, 185n51

Smith, William, Jr.: on Mary Alexander's death threat, 54; on conspiracy's beginning, 135

social fluidity: of commercial culture, 3, 6–9, 11, 24–25, 31, 83, 101; and conspiracy trials of 1741, 151, 154, 157–58. *See also* gentility

social hierarchy. *See* status

Spain: colonial governments of, 124–25, 128; and espionage, 103–5, 137–39, 143, 145, 147–48; as rival, 4–5

status: and balls, 89–92, 96; and commerce, 7, 9–11, 28, 31, 158; and conspiracy trials of 1741, 151, 154, 157–58; consumer goods as markers of, 8, 58–59, 65–66, 80, 81–82; and credibility, 10, 25–31, 83–84, 150–53, 156; fluidity of, 3, 6–9, 11, 24–25, 31, 83, 101; and informal economy, 8, 58–59, 65–66, 68–69, 80, 81–82, 136; manners as marker of, 8, 81–84. *See also* gentility

Stepney, Francis (dancing master), 85–86

Sylva, Juan de la (slave), 137–39

theft: and conspiracy trials of 1741, 133–35; and "disorderly house" charges, 64–65; and pawning, 75; and women, 60–62, 68, 171n7

trade, unregulated. *See* informal economy

trading networks: in informal economy, 5–6, 57–59, 61; personal and impersonal in, 14–16, 22–26, 28, 31

transience. *See* itinerancy

trust: and bills of credit, 12; and bills of exchange, 13–16, 22–25; and conspiracy trials of 1741, 152–56; and counterfeit money, 16–22; and power of attorney, 14–16

unregulated trade. *See* informal economy

Ury, John (schoolmaster), 143–49, 154, 157

Van Ranst, Cornelius, 115, 126, 130

Van Ranst, Peter, 113, 115

Van Ranst, Sarah, 113, 119, 122

Vernon, Thomas, 26

Vetch, Margaret (trader), 42–47

Vianey, Peter (dancing master), 102–3

vice-admiralty courts: and prize cases, 114–15, 117–19, 125, 183n10; records as historical source, 114–15; treatment of black sailors, 117–19, 125, 128–31

Walker, Garthine, 68

war: and commerce, 110–12, 114–15, 131; and enslavement, 113–14

War of Jenkins' Ear, 11, 108

Weeks, Miles Peartree (con artist), 23

white sailors, 116–17

widows: politicized in print, 50; as traders, 5–6, 46–47

Wilson, Christopher, 133–34, 136

women: and coin clipping, 16–17; in court records, 48–50; and coverture, 7, 32–38, 40–41, 51, 55–56, 136; and credit, 33, 47–51, 55; and dependence, 33, 35–36, 46–51, 53–54; and "disorderly house" charges, 63–65; and family networks, 45–47; in informal economy, 59–62, 70–75; in print, 50–51; and regulation of commercial activities, 70–73; and theft, 60–62, 68

women merchants. *See* female traders

Zenger, John Peter, 52, 84, 171n67

Acknowledgments

The networks that crisscrossed the British Empire are nothing compared to the networks of support I have had over the many years I have worked on imperial New York. My first and most grateful thanks go to Jan Lewis, who taught me so beautifully by both word and example how to be a historian and a teacher. I could not have dreamed of more extensive, generous, and engaged support than the help that Jan has given me over the years during which this book has slowly developed. Jan's dazzling integration of the political, the intellectual, and the personal continues to be an inspiration to me.

This book has its roots in the supportive and stimulating history department at Rutgers University–New Brunswick. I count myself especially fortunate to have been able to work with Paul Clemens, Jennifer Jones, and John Murrin while I was in New Jersey as well as after I left. In my first term at Rutgers, Tom Slaughter showed me why I should care about the eighteenth century. From my cohort at Rutgers, very special thanks to Dana Capell, who first helped me think through Daniel Horsmanden's narrative and then helped me enjoy fabulous food from New York to Seattle, all the while offering carefully nuanced readings of my drafts. Other friends from that program—Jennifer Brier, Finis Dunaway, Dina Lowy, Karen Balcom, Melissa Klapper, Becca Gershenson, and especially my early American cohort, Sara Gronim and Lucia McMahon—made the process of becoming a historian an awful lot of fun. Even before I started drafting, Jennifer Ritterhouse, Kirsten Wood, Alison Sneider, and Jason McGill let me join their writing group in Philadelphia, where I learned several invaluable lessons about writing. Harold and Hilary Meltzer let me stay in their wonderful New York City apartment for months on end while they shared with me their love for their city. Julia Markham generously shared her home around the corner from the New-York Historical Society during the sobering autumn of 2001.

In Nashville, the stars aligned (with some help from Beth Rose) to introduce me to Kate Haulman, my wonderful co-conspirator in early American history. Kate read countless versions of many chapters, talked shop by the hour, and has cheered me on through the thickets of academia. Her thoughtful insights into the eighteenth century have informed every part of this book.

Also in Nashville, Guy Nelson, Meaghan Duff, and Joyce Chaplin pushed me to explain many an inchoate idea. The members of the Vanderbilt history community generously welcomed me into their midst. And I must thank our neighbor who introduced me to Nashville's informal economy when he recovered my stolen computer—with its hard drive full of recent research—from a local pawn shop.

When I started this project, a few skeptics thought it unlikely that I could find enough material to write on eighteenth-century New York. The capacious memories and cheerful willingness of many of New York's archivists turned up far more material than I could put into this book. Without Megan Hahn, Melissa Haley, and Richard Fraser at the New-York Historical Society, Joseph Van Nostrand and Bruce Abrams of the Division of Old Records of the New York County Clerk's Office, and Kenneth Cobb of the Municipal Archives, this project would never have gotten off the ground.

From its inception, this study has been made possible by the generous institutional support of many entities. Fellowships from the Immigration and Ethnic History Society, the Woodrow Wilson Foundation, the New-York Historical Society, the New Jersey chapter of the Daughters of the American Revolution, the American Association of University Women, and the Gilder-Lehrman Foundation all provided financial aid as well as much-appreciated affirmation of interest.

No institution has done more to support my work on this book than Carleton College. I deeply appreciate the fellowship that first brought me to Carleton as a Mellon Postdoctoral Fellow. Later, I was the grateful recipient of a Carleton College Wallin Research Fellowship that allowed me a full year of research leave. Then-Associate Dean Scott Bierman helped me find a way take the leave when I needed it most.

The people at the University of Pennsylvania Press believed in this project from the beginning. Dan Richter gave me permission to take as long as I needed to write the best book I could, and gave me meticulous, thoughtful, and careful feedback that was always leavened with a bit of humor. I am deeply appreciative that Bob Lockhart, too, gave his time and red pencil in abundance; his unfailing tact, encouragement, and decisiveness were all essential to bringing this book to fruition. Andrew Burstein and an anonymous reader offered close and creative readings of a draft that made this book immeasurably better. Erica Ginsburg and others gave it a painstaking reading, responded instantly to email queries, and shepherded it assiduously through production. All errors, of course, are my own.

The Early American seminar at the University of Minnesota welcomed me warmly and gave me helpful feedback on many of these chapters; particular thanks go to Sarah Chambers, Kirsten Fischer, John Howe, Rus Menard, Jeani O'Brien, and most of all, Lisa Norling. Generous audiences at the Program in Early American Economy and Society at the Library Company, particularly Cathy Matson and Jeanne Boydston, and the Newberry Library helped me refine my thinking.

At Carleton College, my writing group—Shahzad Bashir, Andrew Fisher, Jessica Leiman, Lance McCready, Lori Pearson, and Parna Sengupta—provided support and set a high bar. My colleagues in the history department have created a wonderful intellectual community. Special thanks to my eighteenth-century Atlantic cohort, Andrew Fisher, Susannah Ottaway, and most especially to Parna Sengupta, friend and colleague extraordinaire. Nikki Lamberty was an immense help, particularly in making available to me several of the department's excellent student workers, including Mike Austin, Ted Falk, Peter Grassman, and Lauren Nakamura.

Other friends in Northfield, especially Lori Pearson and Brian Murphy, Nancy Hill and Shahzad Bashir, Bill North and Victoria Morse, and George Shuffleton and Michelle Martin, have helped me enjoy the competing demands of my life. Meanwhile, my family has done its best to help me finish this book. My in-laws welcomed us to Minnesota, fed us, watched our children, and asked politely about the progress of my work. My own brothers somewhat less politely wondered if I would ever finish; their love of history and impressive intellects reminded me of the audiences I try to reach.

My parents have supported this book intellectually, materially, and lovingly since its inception. Their fierce engagement in the world and passionate love both of thinking and of their family has been a model to me throughout my life. Thank you.

Sue Moyles's love and care for my children and me has made it possible for me to write for the last four and a half years. Writing and child rearing do not always fit together seamlessly. My son Julian alarmed me by demonstrating his newfound literacy as he read drafts over my shoulder, and Leo and Sebastian arrived before I had finished revising the full manuscript. But the joy that they all bring to my life is immeasurable.

It is not an exaggeration to say that I would never have completed this book without the unstinting help and support of Chris Brunelle. I suspect that even he does not know how many drafts he has read over the years, how many misplaced commas he has tidied up, or how many infelicities he has quietly corrected. As privileged as I feel that Chris turned his brilliant mind to this book, that is nothing to how fortunate I am to share with him joy's bonfire.